THE FRANKFURT SCHOOL

THE FRANKFURT SCHOOL

THE CRITICAL THEORIES OF MAX HORKHEIMER AND THEODOR W. ADORNO

ZOLTÁN TAR
The City College of CUNY
New York, New York

Foreword by
Michael Landmann

A WILEY-INTERSCIENCE PUBLICATION

JOHN WILEY & SONS
New York · London · Sydney · Toronto

Library of Congress Cataloging in Publication Data:

Tar, Zoltán.
  The Frankfurt School.
  "A Wiley-Interscience publication."
  Bibliography: p.
  Includes index.
  1. Frankfurt school of sociology. 2. Horkheimer,
Max, 1895–1973. 3. Adorno, Theodor W., 1903–1969.
I. Title.

HM24.T27   301'.01   77–2353

ISBN 0–471–84536–1

Printed in the United States of America

10 9 8 7 6 5 4 3 2 1

To the memory of my parents

They forget. . . that they are in no way combating the real existing world when they are merely combating the phrases of this world.

Where speculation ends. . .
there real, positive science begins. . .

Marx–Engels: *The German Ideology*

FOREWORD

By the end of the fourth century B.C. the great metaphysical impulse of the pre-Socratic and Platonic-Aristotelian philosophy had run its course. By then two philosophical schools of thought emerged, the Stoics and the Epicureans, both of which dominated the Hellenic and Imperial periods that followed. Both philosophies were no longer interested primarily in Nature and Being but in man. Both represented philosophical schools of ethics. They wanted to help man take up a dignified defense against the storms of passions and fate.

An analogous change has taken place in our century in the shift from the ontological to the subjective realms, from the purely theoretical sphere to "concern." And again, there were two philosophical schools in which this quasi-Hellenistic shift manifested itself: existentialist philosophy and Critical Theory. Existential philosophy turns immediately to the individual, thus continuing along the classic line. For Critical Theory, both self-fulfillment and the happiness of the individual depend on the conditions of the whole societal environment. The individual can only achieve self-fulfillment in a society that is liberated from wants and from the oppression of man by man, that is, in a society in which conditions for a dignified human existence are established.

For both orientations, however, it is the world of the humans that matters. They remind us furthermore of the Stoics and the Epicureans in that they do not strive for self-contented, contemplative knowledge; they intend to be *medicina mentis*, that is, therapy. Unity of ascertainment of facts (*Feststellung*) and valuation, or what is even more, unity of theory and (revolutionary) praxis is now the aim. By exposing decay and letting essence shine through, existential philosophy shows us the path to essence. By rejecting the existing bad society and keeping alive the image of the better, more humane society (early) Critical Theory wished to help change society.

The slogan of the intended transformation of society, meaning its radical transformation and not its gradual reformation in order to help it function better, gives Critical Theory a place in the intellectual history of Marxism. Indeed, early Critical Theory was almost a nom de guerre for an intellectualized Marxism. The Frankfurt School then stands in line with a tradition initiated by Georg Lukács (History and Class Consciousness) and Karl Korsch (Marxism and Philosophy). Both are precursors of Critical Theory without really being connected with it. Thus a variation on Marxism without a Communist Party connection emerges; it opposes the regimentation of the intellect and the ensuing sterility within the communist parties. Still, the Frankfurt School transmitted species of "neo-Marxism" to the student rebels of the "New Left."

The Frankfurt School intensified its hopes for Marxism in the early 1930s when the Nazi rise to power became imminent. Marxism as a weapon against fascism takes on a new form. The studies of the Institute dealing with problems of authoritarianism (Autorität und Familie, 1936) must be viewed in this context. The first phase of the German student movement still called itself the "anti-authoritarian movement."

More specific elements of the Marxist doctrine—historical and dialectical materialism, base and superstructure, economic determinism, a critique of capitalism and class struggle—did not become dominant component parts of Critical Theory. If they were used at all, it was in a modified and very general way. Friedrich Pollock was the only scholar in the Zeitschrift für Sozialforschung who labored in the political economy tradition. At first sight only a "neo-Marxism," Critical Theory makes the latent bourgeois Enlightenment content of Marxism topical. Indeed, it is a "new Enlightenment."

As is the case with all enlightenments, knowledge of Critical Theory is then guided by engagement, by concern. It constitutes thereby a component part of future-oriented praxis. Concern, as Horkheimer states explicitly, is not an addition to enlightened cognition, but something that arises out of its very essence. Initially this concern has a negative direction. Critical Theory turns against affirmative traditional theories. Movements of enlightenment are always movements of opposition. Critical Theory intends to remind us of unreconciled sufferings; it wants to denounce prevailing injustice, strengthen resistance to it, and thereby contribute to its abolition (*Aufhebung*).

The struggle against authoritarianism has already been mentioned. Critical Theory turns against "enslaving conditions" with all its accompaniments—metaphysics and ideologies. The struggle cannot be limited to the "real sphere" (*Realebene*); it must be extended to the changing of consciousness. This is the prevalent notion of Herbert Marcuse's rejection of the consumer society; that external coercion is internalized; it leads to the shortchanging of the individual through immediate erotic gratification, thereby preventing his real personality from unfolding. "Total administration" absorbs the administrator himself. Critical Theory stands up positively for emancipation, for "man's coming of age," for a free society of autonomous individuals, for a "rational society," for the "good life." To be sure, this positive side of Critical Theory remains intentionally unspecified. "The Absolute" cannot be depicted, only yearned for, as Horkheimer writes in his obituary on Adorno. It is "The Other" from which the verdict on present society is being spoken out.

The Frankfurt School distinguishes between two types of reason. The one is enlightening and emancipating. It measures human conditions based on the ideas of the French Revolution—justice, peace, and happiness (*Glück*). The other, its opposite, is "instrumental reason." It merely provides, without reflection, effective means for any accepted purpose. This conceptualization corresponds to Max Weber's *Zweckrationalität* (instrumental rationality), which characterizes the modern age. Today such technocratic thinking is dominant in industry and administration. It merely reproduces existing structural conditions and serves domination, not emancipation. This kind of thought perverts the impulse of enlightenment.

The social thought of the Frankfurt School confronts empirical sociology in the above context. The latter is accused of accepting social facts as quasi-neutral facts, analogous to the natural sciences. For the Frankfurt School "the fetishism of facts" is a "glorification of whatever exists," and therefore is anti-Enlightenment. Sociology must not completely sever its ties with its philosophical roots in the Enlightenment, as positivism does. By isolating individual social facts, the facts can be more exactly determined and quantified, but at the same time they will be "reified," to use the expression of Lukács. By contrast, according to the Frankfurt School, social facts must be looked on in the context of "societal totality," again a concept that was first introduced by Lukács. One must investigate the reciprocal interconnections of social phenomena and see them in a connection with the historical laws of the movement of society. In contrast to "facade" sociology one must find the "structural interconnections" (*Verstrickungszusammenhang*), as Horkheimer said.

Second, the positivistic sociology confuses social facts with the material objects of the natural sciences in that it is ready to accept the former in a value-free manner. This kind of scientism overlooks the fact that, without exception, propositions about social phenomena are based on normative prejudgments. One must "suit the thing to its concept" (Adorno), not the concept to the thing. If these two prerequisites of social science are ignored, social science is bound to become an integral part of the existing society instead of being a means of critique and a ferment of renewal. Social science itself becomes one of the forces of production contributing to the reproduction of existing power relations. Scientific progress will thus contribute to societal regression. In sum, social science is no less guilty than the natural sciences, which help industrial enterprises flourish by their domination of nature.

The so-called "Positivism debate," that is, the dispute over methodology (*Methodenstreit*), is generally regarded as representing the closing phase of Critical Theory. Chronologically this is correct, since the debates took place in the late 1950s and early

1960s. But it is only partly correct in regard to the substance of the debates, because the critique of empirical sociology lay at the roots of the Frankfurt School. The *Methodenstreit* only set forth what was originally a constituent part of Critical Theory. One could say, in fact, that something like a reconstruction of the original doctrine took place in the final "second phase" of the school, but on a different plane.

The 1930s witnessed the Moscow trials in which the opposition was totally destroyed; this in turn seriously weakened the chances for the effectiveness of a nonpartisan Marxism. In 1939, the Hitler–Stalin pact came into existence. In the years that followed, East and West stood helplessly by watching Hitler's annihilation of European Jewry. Horkheimer and Adorno were strongly—but not exclusively—motivated by these events to conduct a deeper and more thorough search for the evils of our world. The outcome of their search culminated in the following insights: what matters now is more than to overcome fascism, and it will not be Marxism alone that can bring salvation. The arch malady (*Urgebrechen*) is not the exploitation and the oppressive domination of man. Rather it is domination itself. Usually viewed positively and celebrated as the basis of the technological easing of life, domination of nature and its concomitant constraints are thus regarded as unjustified, indeed, as a manifestation of nonreconciliation between man and nature. Nature, too, is exploited by technology. The question is : is there a possibility for another kind of technology, a nonexploitive kind? "Reconciliation with nature" becomes the new goal, and the dissolution of tension between subject and object is desired. The Frankfurt School, less metaphysically inclined, unexpectedly shares this notion with Ernst Bloch's *Naturphilosophie*, in which a "resurrection of the natural subject" à la Schelling is anticipated.

Even the subsuming of the specimen to the species and the single object to the general concept is in itself domination. The individual has, therefore, to be defended against this so that it can retain its uniqueness, its particularity and otherness. The much touted autonomous subject, that is, the rational ego, has its drawback: violence. Violence manifests itself in the domination of nature, of fellow human beings, indeed, in the constraint of oneself. The ego has patriarchal tendencies. Violence becomes man's second nature; it carries man to triumphs that are based on inhumanity. As a result, domination does not make man happy; indeed, it takes revenge in the form of alienation.

In the end this means that a noneconomic domination exists too. Capitalism is only one form of domination. In fact, domination began early. It can be traced back to mythical times. Nothing else is meant by the first chapter of Genesis which says that man is to be the master of nature. Domination will presumably survive capitalism and the bourgeoisie.

Critical Theory goes beyond its starting point in this respect: domination, denounced and condemned to elimination by Marxism, is now seen as part of a more general injustice.

In its later phase, the Frankfurt School displayed tendencies analogous to those of Heidegger in its depreciation of technology, of Aristotelian logic, and of the Cartesian subject. Consciously, however, the Frankfurt School would not want to have anything in common with this romantic-conservative thinker.

The later Critical Theory developed an imaginary position called "mimesis" that opposed the rational, goal- and power-oriented attitude. This position has thus all the characteristics of a primordial condition of mankind in which image and dancing ruled instead of formula and machinery. A return to mimesis would thus constitute a regressive development; anyway, after the development of powerful reason, the return might prove to be an impossible task indeed. Hence mimesis is not a utopia in the way that Ernst Bloch understood it to be, but rather a yearning for "Paradise Lost" and for a romantic "prehistory."

Critical Theory claimed at one point to be the new Enlightenment. Now, however, Enlightenment itself is being condemned. Not only has Enlightenment degenerated into Positivism, we are told, but it is, indeed, a poisoned well. Knowledge is power, as Bacon said. The confirmation of truth lies in the "know-how." In reason itself lie buried the germs of its eclipse, its operativeness, and its reduction to a mere instrument of universal manipulation. Enslaving reason happens to be just as genuine as liberating reason: "Dialectic of Enlightenment." Enlightenment destroys itself—it ends up in barbarism. Thus barbarism is not the effect of outside forces; it is not brought along by the enemies of civilization.

Critical Theory brings together in a rather unhistorical manner the Enlightenment of the 18th century with its antichurch and antifeudalism attitude, with its fight against the meanness of the powerful and the stupidity of the masses on the one hand, and the ethos of the mechanical natural sciences with their technical consequences on the other, the latter marking the beginnings of modern times. For Adorno and Horkheimer, totalitarianism is not the effect of irrational tendencies; it is engendered by the Enlightenment. Totalitarianism only drew the final consequences.

In the same way that the Enlightenment breaks nature up into objects and atoms and makes it function for the sake of manipulative-formal rationality, totalitarianism manipulates the human world: the individual is quantified first and subsequently subjugated to a total administration. These accusations, addressed to the Enlightenment, should properly be directed against technology. In the end, this historically undifferentiated interpretation results in the vague theories that concern the present.

Originally, Critical Theory was of the opinion that, since instrumental reason rendered itself too independent, it should be brought back in line with enlightened, emancipatory reason and be forthwith guided by it. In this way, things still might work out all right. Now, however, it is believed that the scientific and technological process evolves its own aim. Technocracy is totally autonomous. It cannot be penetrated from the outside through the imposition of goals catering to human needs. Thus the self-liquidation of reason is completed. In these circumstances, the single individual is confronted with seemingly irrational and irrevocable powers that were once engendered by reason but now have become autonomous. The later Frankfurt School thus finds itself in agreement with the revisionists

of the socialist countries who also regard technocracy and
bureaucracy as enemy number one. As a result, some degree
of attraction exists between those revisionists and the Frankfurt theorists.

For Ernst Bloch there is *hope* even in the material world
itself. Man represents only the highest, most developed manifestation of this metaphysical features of the world. Unlike Ernst
Bloch, the later Frankfurt School is unable to look forward to a
brighter future. One can see a similarity in this respect with Max
Weber, who saw clearly the ever enlarging power of *Zweckrationalität* (instrumental rationality), which has both positive
and negative sides. But Weber saw no hope for the reversal of
this process. There are many who talk about the later or "second
phase" of the Frankfurt School as coming close to being a kind of
"Lebensphilosophie," a conservative kind of "Kulturkritik" and
a critique of modern times. They say it is a neo-Romanticism
disguised as neo-Enlightenment. This assessment is correct
insofar as the school extends its critique of the economic, social,
and political aspects to the culture, as a more encompassing
notion.

A conservative thinker always believes that the past was
better and condemns the indaequate present. He dreams of a
revival, of a renaissance. The later Frankfurt School offers a
more ominous view: the misfortune of mankind is not the result
of certain historical developments; it is something inherent in
man's being. It would thus not disappear after the overthrow of
fascism or capitalism. The friction only seems to be the result of
a historical development that could be changed. In reality, it lies
in the "essence." This interpretation presented by the later
Frankfurt School illustrates a basically anthropological-
metaphysically pessimistic position. (It is not accidental that
Horkheimer now returns to his early philosophical roots, to
Schopenhauer.) It means the radical negation of the existing
coupled with despair; in short, nihilism. In the early 1920s,
Walter Benjamin characterized the irrational-eccentric position
of some of his contemporaries as being "to the left of everything
possible," and coined the phrase "Melancholy Left" (*linke*

Melancholie). Horkheimer and Adorno finally arrived at this position of "linke Melancholie."

At its beginning, Critical Theory professed to be an instance of enlightened revolutionary praxis. Now, however, its resignation set in, resulting in political abstinence. The theory developed proves to be so radical as to be irreconcilable with praxis. If injustice is inherent in man's relationship to nature, that is, in man's given right of mastery over nature, where is the revolutionary subject that would put an end to injustice supposed to come from? The historical moment has passed when the realization of philosophy that Marx envisioned could have taken place. There is no way to make up for this lost opportunity, says Adorno. The role of philosophy can now be only a theoretical one: it has to bring to consciousness the fact that the world did not change. From now on, philosophy's only duty will be to voice its protest, to unmask unreason, and to articulate man's suffering. In spite of its powerlessness and hopelessness, philosophy has one remaining function: to accuse, to call things by their names. Through its relentless opposition to a very bad reality, philosophy constitutes an island of resistance.

Precisely because of its severed relationship to praxis, the Frankfurt School was characterized by some critics as representing "the end of the bourgeois Marxist intelligentsia, . . . the end of the purely theoretical individual enterprise."* So there came a complete break between the student activists and later Critical Theory. The students adopted its revolutionary impulse, but then they had to proceed beyond it. Adorno's death in 1969 has been attributed in part to his deeply felt shock when student demonstrators attacked him personally.

In 1933 the general secretary of the Comintern, Georgi Dimitrov, made the following statement at the Comintern's Seventh Congress: "Fascism is the terroristic dictatorship of the most reactionary, chauvinistic and imperialistic elements of finance capitalism." This theory of a dogmatic Marxism that tries to explain everything economically, and attributes all the ills of

*Gerhard, Zwerenz, *Kopf und Bauch.* Frankfurt am Main, S. Fischer, 1973, p. 125.

the world to the machinations of the capitalist class is inadequate. German National Socialism (which was what was primarily meant by "fascism") has its roots in the political and social
development of Germany as well as in its history of religion and
ideas. The same or similar economic conditions that characterized pre-Hitler Germany also existed at times in other countries that did not turn fascist. The fascist mentality and style
seem to have to do more with the transitional period when
mankind reaches the age of the technological mass culture than
with a certain economic order. To couple fascism with the
capitalist system indicates a prejudice or interest in such an
association. A universal world-explanatory scheme is now
being applied to the phenomenon of fascism.

It does not honor Critical Theory's critical instincts, of
which it is so proud, to simply take over a party doctrine as
advanced by Dimitrov. "Those who do not want to speak of
Capitalism," said Horkheimer, "should be silent in the face of
fascism." Both he and Marcuse viewed fascism as the natural
outcome and the highest stage of capitalism; the capitalists
cannot hold on to their power without the destruction of
bourgeois-liberal democracy.

This interpretation defends not only the false theory about
the genesis of fascism but it also throws a misleading light on its
whole development since the beginnnings of modern times. The
Frankfurt School always had a tendency to overrate the her-
meneutic function of the present. In his aesthetics, for example,
Adorno treats expressionism as a modern art form that can help
to interpret even the art forms of earliest times. In the same way,
Auschwitz discloses the secret meaning of the whole course of
history and society. Because of the Holocaust, history has to
mean a "progress toward hell."

The establishment of the Frankfurt School coincides with
the emergence of National Socialism as a real threat. Capitalism
is blamed entirely by the Frankfurt theorists for this fateful
development. From beginning to end, the Frankfurt School
retained this "primary fixation." In its later phase it despised
communism and remained silent about it. It equated brown with

Foreword xvii

red totalitarianism. In Horkheimer's case, it finally came to an open attack against the Soviet Union.

In sum, one can say that the later Frankfurt School persisted in a political attitude that might have been plausible in the 1930s but failed to take into consideration worldwide historical developments since then. The School was unable to disassociate itself from its early interpretations and to carry out a radical reassessment of its views. By overlooking the new realities, the Frankfurt theorists committed an unforgivable act for philosophers, and thus confused more than they clarified.

It was with great pleasure that I complied with the wishes of the author and the publisher by writing the introduction to the critical analysis of the Frankfurt theorists by my good friend, Professor Zoltán Tar. The theoretical problems that I could only touch on in my introduction are admirably discussed and minutely analyzed in his book. I am deeply convinced that his book will greatly contribute to a better understanding of Critical Theory in the United States.

DR. MICHAEL LANDMANN

Free University, Berlin
and University of Haifa
February 1976

ACKNOWLEDGMENTS

It is my pleasure to give my special thanks to a number of scholars and colleagues who were kind enough to give their advice and to offer many valuable suggestions during the preparation of this study. It greatly benefited from their penetrating comments relating to substance and style.

My deepest gratitude goes to Professor Alexander Vucinich of the University of Texas at Austin for his intellectual guidance and generous help from the very inception of this study. His detailed and patient evaluation of the original manuscript, his wisdom as a scholar and his experience as a writer helped to make this book what it is.

I am very grateful to my colleagues and friends who gave most generously of their time to read and discuss the entire manuscript: Professors Joseph Bensman, Robert Lilienfeld, and Betty Yorburg of the City College of CUNY, Arthur J. Vidich of the New School for Social Research, Peter C. Ludz of the University of Munich, Michael Landmann of the Free University in Berlin, Iring Fetscher of the Johann Wolfgang Goethe University of Frankfurt am Main, Rita J. Simon, Robert A. Jones, and Norbert Wiley of the University of Illinois at Champaign-Urbana, Klaus Peter of the University of Massachusetts at Amherst, Emil Oestereicher of Richmond College, and Mr. G. L. Ulmen of New York.

Thanks are due to Mr. Gyula Puskás and Miss Marianne Fischer of Zurich, Switzerland, for their willing assistance in securing material from libraries in Europe. My thanks go to Mrs. Hope McAloon for her technical assistance.

Mr. Peter W. Peirce's editorial advice has been of great help in seeing the book through to completion.

To my wife, Dr. Judith Marcus, for her encouragement, her critical judgment on matters of organization and substance, and her patience I owe a special debt. She also rendered invaluable assistance in the translation of German texts and in the preparation of the bibliography.

For errors of fact and interpretation, I am, of course, alone responsible.

ZOLTÁN TAR

New York, New York
February 1977

CONTENTS

THE FRANKFURT SCHOOL

INTRODUCTION

A specter is haunting the sociological enterprise—the specter of the Frankfurt School. But a certain cloud of myth, ambiguity and confusion surrounding the Frankfurt School of sociology and philosophy must be dispelled at the outset of this study. The notion that the school represents a Marxist orientation in sociology rests only on a superficial acquaintance with the work of Max Horkheimer, Theodor W. Adorno, and other thinkers of the Frankfurt School.[1] There are two principal reasons for this sad state of affairs. First, the unavailability, until recently, of English translations of the major writings of the Frankfurt School kept most American sociologists ignorant of them. Second, the demand and search among a large segment of younger sociologists for a "relevant" science of society, one that would provide an alternative to mainstream academic sociology, which they feel is preoccupied with research into irrelevant minute details of a repressive social order, further that ignorance. These sociologists believe that an alternative social science might unmask the contradictions of the existing social structure, and instead of merely describing what *is*, might show what *ought* to be. Hopefully, the increasing number of translations will gradually alleviate this unfortunate situation and result in a more realistic appraisal of the Frankfurt School in the English-speaking world.

SOURCES OF MISUNDERSTANDING

The impact of the Frankfurt School on the American academic community and intellectual circles during its sojourn in the United States was minimal, mainly because of the language barrier consciously maintained on both sides. There have been three kinds of response to the Frankfurt School among American scholars: First, a criticism of their work on methodological grounds. Second, a rejection of the school for political reasons—the meddling of left-wing, high-brow intellectuals into the affairs of the natives. One representative of this group writes:

> Nothing shows more clearly the inherent contradiction in the
> position of the left-wing intellectuals fighting a losing battle
> within the confines of an ideologically hostile sociology than
> the way in which the proponents of left-wing democracy and
> humanism have dug themselves in along the last ditch of an
> elitist defense of high culture.[2]

Third, an uncritical praise without real acquaintance with the
work of the Frankfurt School. As early as 1954, C. Wright Mills,
in his critique of American sociology, pleaded for a return to
"the classical sociological endeavor" by pointing to the example
of the Frankfurt School. He wrote:

> I know of no better way to become acquainted with this
> endeavor in a high form of modern expression than to read the
> periodical, *Studies in Philosophy and Social Sciences*, pub-
> lished by The Institute of Social Research. Unfortunately, it is
> available only in the morgues of university libraries, and to the
> great loss of American social studies, several of the Institute's
> leading members, among them Max Horkheimer and Theodor
> Adorno, have returned to Germany.[3]

Yet, this declaration aside, it would be difficult to ascertain any
impact of Horkheimer or Adorno in the substantive writings of
Mills.

To assess the influence of Frankfurt School ideas, in recent
years popularized and disseminated through the writings of
Herbert Marcuse, would be equally problematic. Professor Paul
Breines, a former Marcuse student, comments on Marcuse's
impact:

> *One Dimensional Man* and the essay, *The Repressive Toler-
> ance*, let alone his earlier works, remain unread by large por-
> tions of the Left; only a very small percentage has, or cares to
> have, more than the vaguest comprehension of the
> philosophical tradition in which Marcuse stands; and, as his
> work is well outside the Anglo-American framework of social
> thought, he is often misunderstood by sympathetic as well as
> unsympathetic readers.[4]

Young radical students of sociology in the late 1960s, influenced by a variety of critical sociologies (from Marx to Marcuse), are in a process of transition; they are gradually joining the junior ranks of "the establishment." How much they might retain of their youthful orientation, enthusiasm, and radicalism remains to be seen. The possible lasting impact can only be guessed on the basis of historical analogies with earlier radical student movements in the United States. Many Trotskyite graduate students of the 1930s and Trotskyites and Stalinists of the 1940s became staunch pillars of the academic establishment of the 1950s and 1960s, respectively.[5] Thus it is safe to guess that radicals of the late 1960s are likely to follow this historical pattern and are candidates for the establishment of the 1970s. Two observers, Joseph Bensman and Arthur Vidich, express the obvious sociological reasons:

> A college youth who is organizationally successful in revolutionary campus politics is likely to become a college president, a dean, or, at least, a best selling journalist. . . revolutionary training is perhaps the best training a youth can get for a career in the establishment.[6]

The recent publication of Martin Jay's book, *The Dialectical Imagination*, has clarified many hitherto unknown details of the history of the Frankfurt School, but it deals only with the first half of the school's 50-year history.[7] The uninitiated usually erroneously equate the Frankfurt School of philosophy and sociology with the Institute for Social Research, which Jay does not. His book, significantly, has the subtitle: *A History of the Frankfurt School and the Institute of Social Research, 1923–1950*. Although Jay's title indicates that it is "A History of the Frankfurt School, . . . 1923–1950," yet the term *Frankfurt School* was never used by anyone during the period under discussion. It was invented by outsiders, mostly by critics after 1950, and grudgingly accepted but seldom used by Horkheimer and Adorno. The *and* of the subtitle, it should be kept in mind, refers to the two related but not identical entities under discussion here. Thus Jay's subtitle legitimates the inclusion of the work of all scholars who were affiliated at various times and in various ways with the institute, and who represented considerable variations of political commitment and scholarly orientation. However, Jay never explicitly states this distinction, but merely implies it, when he distinguishes between the "inner circle" of the institute and the rest of its membership and acknowledges that the work of the latter has never been integrated into Critical Theory proper.[8] There is even less justification for including the work of Walter Benjamin as one of "the major aestheticians of the Frankfurt School." Benjamin never really became a member of the institute; as Horkheimer and Adorno never ceased to emphasize, his theoretical and political orientation was alien to mainstream Frankfurt thought. They criticized his "crude" Marxist approach and censored the writings he submitted for publication to the journal of the institute. Some recent scholarship even asserts that Horkheimer and Adorno falsified the posthumous edition of Benjamin's writings.[9]

Martin Jay's study was intended to be a historical account of the Frankfurt School, and as such it completely succeeds. Its impact and importance were heightened by the fact that it was the first serious attempt to record the origins and development of this intellectual movement for an American audience. At times it reads like a "court history" of the institute; this might be explained by the fact that it was written in close cooperation with the leading members of the institute, most notably Max Horkheimer, its long-time director, and Theodor W. Adorno, who made private material available. It is to be regretted that the study breaks off in the middle of the story, in 1950.

Jay's study has given us part of the history of the institute and the school, meticulously researched. What is long overdue is a sociological analysis and scrutiny of the thought and shifting interests of this remarkable group of intellects of the Weimar Republic. (Interestingly enough, *The Dialectical Imagination* has not one entry on sociology in its index.) An analysis of the existential determination of their work is still needed. In Jay's study, for example, the Jewish background of Horkheimer and Adorno is either dismissed or considered marginal or irrelevant.[10] It is our contention that the Judaic influence was active in Frankfurt thought throughout its history and even became dominant in its final phase, as suggested by Horkheimer's "yearning for God" and Adorno's "negative dialectic."

For all its merits, *The Dialectical Imagination* is not and cannot be the definitive study of the Frankfurt School. A truly definitive study cannot be undertaken until the critical edition of the collected works of Horkheimer and Adorno is published. The publication of the *Collected Works* of Adorno, expected to be in 22 volumes, has just begun.

The only other study on the subject presently available in English (a translation from the German) is Albrecht Wellmer's *Critical Theory of Society*, which consists of three loosely connected articles: the first and third attempt to develop further some key ideas of Horkheimer and Habermas; the central piece, "The Latent Positivism of Marx's Philosophy of History," is an attack on Marx's alleged positivistic inclinations and deviations.[11] Chapters 1 and 3, altogether some seventy pages, could hardly be considered an exhaustive treatment of or a definitive statement on Critical Theory despite the implied claim of the title.

EUROPEAN RESPONSES TO CRITICAL THEORY

Turning to the European scene, we encounter conflicting reactions to Critical Theory. René König, a leading exponent of modern German empirical sociology, asserts that one must distinguish between sociological theory and the "Theory of Society" of the Frankfurt School. He writes: "Sociological theory has been developed independently of the general Theory of Society, which makes pronouncements about the totality of society in the manner of a social philosophy and philosophy of history.[12] König uses the designation "sociological theory" for empirically oriented sociology and refers to the Frankfurt School of sociology as the "Theory of Society." Rejecting pluralism in sociological theorizing, he excludes it from sociology.

Karl Popper, the philosophical mentor of German "positivist" sociology, describes the influence of the Frankfurt School in such harsh terms as "irrational and intelligence-destroying."[13] Hans Albert, an outstanding representative of the same positivism, calls the sociology of the Frankfurt theorists "Marxist dialectical theology."[14]*

There remains a third view in German sociology that views the ideas set forth by the Frankfurt School as a basis for some future work. Helmut Schelsky is the best known proponent of this view. Writing on the "transcendental theory of society," he asserts that this theory has not yet come to fruition. "However, a demand for it has been represented in the last decade by *Max Horkheimer* and *Theodor W. Adorno*. Yet it is only a desideratum."[15]

In the light of the grand tradition of German historical scholarship, it remains an intellectual puzzle that no comprehensive study of the Frankfurt School or of the institute has been published, although numerous articles and a few monographs deal with specific aspects of the work of Horkheimer and Adorno.[16]

The most ambitious undertakings have been one full-scale study and two smaller monographs in the Italian language, unfortunately inaccessible to a larger audience because of the language barrier.[17]

The definition of the Frankfurt School here agrees with the existing Italian language monographs and takes the position that the term "Frankfurt School" or Frankfurt School of

---

*Neither Popper nor Albert would accept the label "positivism" for their philosophies or sociologies, respectively; they prefer the term "critical rationalism." To make clear distinctions we use the term *Critical Theory* for the social theories of Horkheimer and Adorno up to 1950, a term coined by Horkheimer and most frequently used for this period. The theories of Horkheimer and Adorno after 1950 are called *Theory of Society*, a term most frequently used by them after 1950.

philosophy and sociology is identical with the work of Horkheimer and Adorno, that is, identical with their writings in
sociology, social philosophy, and general philosophy by virtue
of continuity, institutional position, and publication records.
Continuity refers to Horkheimer's 40-year and Adorno's 30-year
institutional affiliation. All other members were affiliated with
the institute for considerably shorter periods. Horkheimer was
the institute's director from 1931 until his retirement in 1958,
and Adorno was his codirector from 1955 until he became director in 1958. No other member of the institute ever stated the
theoretical position and the methodological and political commitment of the institute. Marcuse's contribution in this respect
is only touched on; no comprehensive treatment of his work, the
subject of many monographs, is attempted here.

Jürgen Habermas, the most prominent of the second generation Frankfurt theorists who deviates significantly from the
basic tenets of the original Frankfurt School orientation, left the
institute in 1972, in the middle of his career. These factors
justify excluding a discussion of his work.

OUR APPROACH TO THE FRANKFURT SCHOOL

This book, then, is a study of the Frankfurt School of philosophy
and sociology as developed first by Max Horkheimer in the
1930s and continued and modified by him in collaboration with
Theodor W. Adorno since 1940. (The scrutiny of the voluminous
writings of Adorno on problems of art, music, and literature lies
outside the objectives of this study.)

The unity of Horkheimer's and Adorno's thoughts is
emphasized time and again in all their publications after 1940.
They coauthored several volumes and insisted on the single
identity of their ideas and theories. Thus we read in Horkheimer's *Eclipse of Reason* (1947):

> These lectures were designed to epitomize some aspects of a
> comprehensive philosophical theory developed by the writer

during the last few years in association with Theodor W. Adorno. It would be difficult to say which of the ideas originated in his mind and which in my own; *our philosophy is one* (italics mine).[18]

Adorno writes in his *Minima Moralia* (1951) of a "mutual philosophy from the point of view of subjective experience." He asserts the "there is no one single motif in it which does not belong to Horkheimer as well as it does to the writer who had found the time to formulate it."[19] Last, in *Sociologica II* (1962), coauthored by Horkheimer and Adorno, we are told that the work's "unity consists of the common experience and intention of the authors."[20]

This repeated assertion of Horkheimer and Adorno about the identity of their thought can be accepted for the 1940s, but not for their life work. One major difference in the thinking of the two men should be mentioned at the outset: the dominant influence of Schopenhauer on Horkheimer and that of Hegel on Adorno, the wavering of the former between Schopenhauer and Marx and of Adorno between music and sociology.

The history of the Frankfurt School falls into three periods. The first term begins with Horkheimer's assumption of the directorship in 1931 and his subsequent elaboration of a Critical Theory. In the second period, from 1940 to 1950, Horkheimer and Adorno closely collaborated on several writings and projects. Finally, from 1950, after their return to Frankfurt, they continued to cooperate on the development of a Theory of Society, a modified version of the earlier Critical Theory.

The organization of this study follows the different periods of the history of the Frankfurt School. In Chapter 1, the years 1923–1931 of the institute, prior to Horkheimer's takeover, are sketched as a prelude. Then Horkheimer's theoretical contribution as an alleged Marxist social theory during the 1930s is assessed.

Chapter 2 deals with a variety of Horkheimer's and Adorno's attempted theoretical explanations and social philosophical reflections on fascism. The threat of fascism and the fear that advanced industrial societies might embrace some variety of the fascist system provided the greatest challenge to the Frankfurt School. Horkheimer proposed the thesis of fascism as "the highest stage of capitalism." While exiled in New York City and California, Horkheimer and Adorno developed a close cooperation that resulted in social philosophical reflections on Western civilization and the worldwide danger of fascism. And last, in an inter-disciplinary empirical study, The Authoritarian Personality, the human roots of fascism were investigated. Chapter 2, also deals with Horkheimer's critique of science and with his proposed new Naturphilosophie, which was to supplant it. Modern science, as a new form of legitimation for societal domination, and positivist philosophy of science as its theoretical justification, has been a concern of Horkheimer's theory from the very beginning.

After Horkheimer and Adorno returned to Frankfurt am Main in the 1950s, the institute was reconstructed and integrated into West German academic life. The reconstruction of Critical Theory under the new label, Theory of Society, the critique of positivist empiricist sociology, and the final phase in the development of Horkheimer to a quasi-religious position and of Adorno to nihilism are discussed in Chapter 3.

The examination of the work of Horkheimer and Adorno intends to be both expository and critical in regard to three points: (1) the original intention and actual accomplishment; (2) the examination of their reputation for being a continuation of the original critical theory of Marx, and (3) the validity of their theories in the light of generally accepted canons of the natural and social sciences. Thus this study aims to go beyond existing studies of the Frankfurt School by covering the entire period of its history and measuring it by comparison to both Marxism and scientific sociology.

The career of Critical Theory is a manifestation of the thinking of a group of German bourgeois intellectuals whose old social order in Central Europe was collapsing. Their tragic existence might best be characterized by the term "linke Melancholie" (left melancholy), a term Walter Benjamin coined in

1937 in an essay about two famous German leftist bourgeois writers, Kurt Tucholsky and Erich Kästner. Benjamin pinpointed their problematic radicalism as a position that

> stands not left of this or that orientation, but simply left of everything that is possible (*links nicht von dieser oder jener Richtung: sondern ganz einfach links vom Möglichen überhaupt*).

In Benjamin's harsh words, this *Weltanschauung* and attitude of pseudoradicalism "has only one aim from the start: to relish its negativistic peace (*Er hat ja von vornherein nichts anderes im Auge, als in negativistischer Ruhe sich selbst zu geniessen*)."[21] Benjamin's description of still another group of left-wing intellectuals of the Weimar Republic—and there were many groups—is certainly self-critical and also prophetic for Critical Theory.[22] The wish and will "to have their peace and enjoy themselves," albeit with a bad conscience, is an attitude that continued with the critical theorists; as late as 1944 Adorno reflected in his California exile: "Rien faire comme une bete, to lie on the water and to gaze into the sky, 'to be, nothing else, to be without any further determination and fulfilment,' could replace process, action and satisfaction. . . ."[23]

NOTES

1. One could take the Adorno obituary of the respected and usually well-informed *New York Times* as a symbolic expression of the confusion surrounding the work of Adorno in the U.S.A. The obituary tells at length of Adorno's reflection on "the sociological implications of jitterbug dancing" in one of his articles (*The New York Times*, Aug. 7, 1969, p. 35). The following few examples should suffice to illustrate our point about the confusion and misconceptions that surround the Frankfurt School. Devra Lee Davies, for example, recently stated that "a sometime member of the Frankfurt School, Ernst Bloch, formulated his magnum opus, *Das Prinzip Hoffnung* . . . in a self-consciously post-Auschwitz *Weltschmerz*. Although associated with the spirit of utopia,

Bloch's work reverberates with the negativism of an atheist." "Theodor W. Adorno: Theoretician Through Negations," in *Theory and Society*, Vol. 2, No. 3 (Fall 1975), pp. 389–400. Even the usually well-informed George Lichtheim wrote that "Lukacs was briefly associated with the Institute but so were heretics like Karl Korsch," and so on. See *From Marx to Hegel*, New York: The Seabury Press, 1974, p. 129.

2. J. P. Nettl, "Ideas, Intellectuals, and Structures of Dissent," in Philip Rieff (Ed.), *On Intellectuals*, New York, Doubleday, 1969, p. 110.

3. C. Wright Mills, *Power, Politics and People*, New York, 1963, p. 572.

4. Paul Breines, "Marcuse and the New Left in America," in Jürgen Habermas (Ed.), *Antworten auf Herbert Marcuse*, Frankfurt am Main, 1969, p. 137.

5. The intellectual-autobiographical writings of leading American philosophers and sociologists are revealing in this respect. Sidney Hook who called himself a "Communist without dogma" in the 1930s later became an anti-Communist crusader. Edward Shils, translator of the "bourgeois-Marxist" Karl Mannheim, endorsed Richard Nixon for President in 1972. Seymour Lipset tells about his socialist leanings as a student at The City College of New York in the 1940s in the *Sociological Self-Images*, edited by Irving Louis Horowitz, Beverly Hills, Calif., Sage Publications, 1969, p. 144. Peter M. Blau relates the story of how he posted the pictures of his intellectual heroes, Marx and Freud, on the wall of his room as a young graduate student at Columbia. Robert K. Merton's pioneering writings in the sociology of science were first published in the Marxist theoretical journal, *Science and Society*, as were the writings of Lewis S. Feuer in the 1950s. The list continues ad infinitum. Yet no lasting theoretical or political commitments remained from those youthful aberrations. It is safe to forecast a similar course of development for the graduate student Left of the 1960s.

6. Joseph Bensman and Arthur J. Vidich, *The New American Society*, Chicago, 1971, p. 256.

7. Martin Jay, *The Dialectical Imagination. A History of the Frankfurt School and the Institute of Social Research, 1923–1950*, Boston, 1973. The book is based on Jay's dissertation, *The Frankfurt School: An Intellectual History of the "Institute für Sozialforschung" 1923–1950*, Harvard University, 1971. For a more detailed discussion of Jay's study see my review, "The Career of 'Critical Theory'," in *The Nation*, Nov. 5, 1973, pp. 473–475.

8. *Ibid.*, p. 152.

9. Hildegard Brenner, "Theodor W. Adorno als Sachwalter des Benjaminschen Werkes," in Wilfried F. Schoeller (Ed.), *Die neue Linke nach Adorno*, München, 1969, pp. 158–175.

10. Martin Jay, *The Dialectical Imagination*, pp. 32–33.

11. Albrecht Wellmer, *Critical Theory of Society*, New York, 1971.

12. René König (Ed.), *Soziologie*, Frankfurt am Main, 1967, p. 305.

13. Karl Popper, "Reason or Revolution," *European Journal of Sociology*, XI (1970), p. 253.

14. There is a wide range of labels applied to the Frankfurt School or to Critical Theory. The term "Critical" carries reference to both Immanuel Kant and Karl Marx. The three main works of Kant are *Critique of Pure Reason, Critique of Practical Reason* and *Critique of Judgment*. A perusal of the works of Marx reveals an astonishingly frequent use of the noun "critique" and the adjective "critical": *Contribution to the Critique of Hegel's Philosophy of Right* (1844), *The Holy Family* or *Critique of Critical Critique* (1844), *Grundrisse, Foundations of the Critique of Political Economy* (1857), *A Contribution to the Critique of Political Economy* (1859), *Capital. A Critical Analysis of Capitalist Production* (1867), *Critique of the Gotha Programme* (1875).

15. Helmut Schelsky, *Ortsbestimmung der deutschen Soziologie*, Düsseldorf, 1959, p. 96.

16. Among the German language monographs, the following ones deal with some aspect of the Frankfurt School: Günter Rohrmoser, *Das Elend der kritischen Theorie*, Freiburg, 1970; Wilhelm Raimund Beyer, *Die Sünden der Frankfurter Schule*, Berlin (East), 1971; Michael Landmann, *Entfremdende Vernunft*, Stuttgart, 1975. On Horkheimer see: Werner Post, *Kritische Theorie und metaphysischer Pessimismus*, München, 1971; Alfred Schmidt, *Zur Idee der Kritischen Theorie als Geschichtsphilosophie*, München, 1974; Anselm Skuhra, *Max Horkheimer. Eine Einführung in sein Denken*, Stuttgart, 1975. On Adorno see: Friedemann Grenz, *Adornos Philosophie in Grundbegriffen*, Frankfurt am Main, 1974; Otwin Massing, *Adorno und die Folgen*, Neuwied und Berlin, 1970.

17. G. E. Rusconi, *La Teoria Critica della Societa* 2nd ed., Bologna, 1970; Alfred Schmidt and G. E. Rusconi, *La Scuola di Francoforte*, Bari, 1972; and Goeran Therborn, *Critica e Rivoluzione La Scuola die Francoforte*, Bari, 1972. A French monograph came to our attention after the completion of this study: Pierre V. Zima, *L'ecole de Francfort. Dialectique de la particularite*, Paris, 1974.

18. Max Horkheimer, *Eclipse of Reason*, New York, 1947, p. vii.

19. Theodor W. Adorno, *Minima Moralia. Reflexionen aus dem beschädigten Leben*, Frankfurt am Main, 1969, p. 12.

20. Max Horkheimer and Theodor W. Adorno, *Sociologica II*, Frankfurt am Main, 1962, p. 1.

21. Walter Benjamin, *Angelus Novus, Ausgewählte Schriften*, Vol. 2, Frankfurt am Main, 1966, p. 459. For sociological, philosophical, and psychological discussion of "melancholy" see, Wolf Lepenies, *Melancholie und Gesellschaft*, Frankfurt am Main, 1972; Michael Landmann, "Melancholien der Erfüllung," in *Anklage gegen die Vernunft*, Stuttgart, 1976, pp. 208–230; Sigmund Freud, "Mourning and melancholia," in *The Standard Edition of the Complete Psychological Works of Sigmund Freud*, Vol. 14, London, 1957, pp. 243–258.

22. For general history of the Weimar Republic see Arthur Rosenberg, *Entstehung und Geschichte der Weimarer Republik*, Frankfurt am Main, 1955; Erich Eyck, *A History of the Weimar Republic, From the Collapse of the Empire to Hindenburg's Election*, New York, 1970; on "Weimar culture" and intellectual history see, Istvan Deak, *Weimar Germany's Left-Wing Intellectuals: A Political History of the Weltbühne and its Circle*, Berkeley and Los Angeles, 1968; Peter Gay, *Weimar Culture: The Outsider as Insider*, New York, 1970; Walter Laqueur, *Weimar. A Cultural History 1918–33*, London, 1974; Hans-Helmuth Knütter, *Die Juden und die deutsche Linke in der Weimarer Republik 1918—33*, Düsseldorf, 1971; Jenö Kurucz, *Struktur und Funktion der Intelligenz während der Weimarer Republik*, Köln, 1967.

23. Theodor W. Adorno, *Minima Moralia*, p. 208.

ONE

THE CRITICAL THEORY
OF MAX HORKHEIMER

INSTITUTIONAL BACKGROUND

The beginnings of the institutional matrix of the Frankfurt School date back to 1923, when the Institute for Social Research (*Institut für Sozialforschung*), affiliated with the University of Frankfurt, was founded. Felix J. Weil first proposed the idea of an institute of social research along Marxist lines. His father, Hermann Weil, had previously left Germany for South America to become a wealthy Argentinian grain dealer and financially supported the socialist ambitions of his son. Felix J. Weil, born and raised in Argentina, went to Frankfurt and earned his Ph.D. in 1921.[1]

Carl Grünberg, professor of political economy in Vienna and editor of a journal devoted to the history of socialism and the labor movement (*Archiv für die Geschichte des Sozialismus und der Arbeiterbewegung* or *Grünberg Archiv*), became the first director of the institute and held that position until 1928. An economist of the historical school, he later became a Marxist and the first *Kathedermarxist* (academic Marxist) at a German university. Marxism as an economic and sociological system, until then a stepchild at German universities, was to have a home in the new institute.

The first years of the institute were shaped by the influence of Grünberg, who considered Marxism to be both a *Weltanschauung* and a research method. He was convinced that contemporary society was in a "transition from capitalism to socialism." His interpretation of Marxism was vehemently antiphilosophical:

> Philosophical and historical materialism have conceptually nothing to do with each other . . . . The problem of materialist, historical conceptualization is not to arrive at eternal categories by way of speculation, or to grasp the "thing-in-itself," or to investigate the relationship between mind and external reality.[2]

To Grünberg, historical materialism had no validity independent of space and time, but only a relative and historically conditioned meaning. Its task is the investigation of "the given concrete world in its becoming and change ('*die gegebene konkrete Welt in ihrem Werden und Wandel*')". He declared induction the correct scientific method. Grünberg's opening address emphasized the necessity of "the dictatorship of the director" of the institute: "A sharing of the direction of the institute with those who have a different *Weltanschauung* or methodological approaches is entirely inconceivable."[3]

Among the first members of the institute were such young intellectuals as Max Horkheimer, Friedrich Pollock, Henryk Grossman, Richard Sorge, and the Sinologist Karl Wittfogel. Later in the 1930s, Leo Löwenthal, Herbert Marcuse, Erich Fromm, Franz Neumann, Otto Kirchheimer, and Theodor Wiesengrund-Adorno joined their ranks. The research associates represented a truly interdisciplinary cross section of academia, ranging from philosophy and sociology to literary scholarship, political science, and economics. Most of them had a Jewish middle- or upper-middle-class background and were in some way active in left-wing politics. At least four of them were Communist Party members: Sorge, who later became a master spy for the Soviet Union and was executed in Japan, Wittfogel, a CP candidate for the *Reichstag*, Grossman, and Pollock.

In 1928 illness forced Grünberg to give up his directorship. After a short interim period under the directorship of Pollock, Horkheimer became the director, and a new era began for the annals of the institute.

THE BIOGRAPHICAL AND EXISTENTIAL MATRIX OF CRITICAL THEORY

A real understanding of Critical Theory would require a close scrutiny of the men, their works, and their socio-historical matrix in order to show the existential determination of the Frankfurt theorists, that is, to shed light on the correlation between biographical data and theoretical achievements. A definitive study along these lines must wait until all the information and manuscripts are available. Yet, in the light of the existing material, the significant factor of biographical information must not be ignored, and certain tentative propositions can be made. It is mandatory to look into the existential determination of the intellectual development of Horkheimer to demonstrate how his authoritarian, domineering father led to the young Horkheimer's defiance of this immediate authority, which symbolized for him the authoritarianism of the larger society of contemporary Wilhelminian Germany, prior to its collapse in 1918.

Protest against human suffering and social injustice coupled with "longing for another world" were permanent themes for Horheimer's thinking throughout his life. His Jewish *haute bourgeois* family background was the source of both his protest and his longing. Working in the family business as his father wished, and being next to him in the line of command, the 20-year-old Horkheimer reflected on the situation in his diary:

> I have a splendid position and an even more promising future in my father's business. I can afford all the pleasures of the world that attract me. I can immerse myself in my work or amuse myself and follow my hobbies—and yet. . . the burning flames of yearning consume me. . . . I do not seem to be able to control this longing, and so I will let myself be guided by it through all my life, regardless of where this mad journey might take me.[4]

Young Horkheimer, shocked and repelled by the working conditions in his father's factory, wrote to a friend:

> Who can complain about suffering, you and me? We, who are complaining that the flesh of the slaughtered gives us belly aches, are cannibals. . . . You enjoy your peace and property for whose sake others have to suffocate, to bleed to death. . . and to endure the most inhuman conditions.[5]

This motif of remonstrance never disappears; it develops into Horkheimer's later longing that "the murderer might not triumph over his innocent victim."[6] Vehement rejection of the existing social order and a metaphysical yearning for a more perfect world were the chief motives of Horkheimer's philosophy from the very beginning. Young Horkheimer stated his *Weltanschauung* in 1914.

> The positive, the existing is always bad, yet its constitution is the only point of reference from which we can proceed to divine its spiritual content that we cannot grasp but that constitutes its great beauty. Therein lies the reason why beautiful things can never quite satisfy us and a painful yearning remains. This is a yearning for perfection, which cannot be attained as long as we possess a body and perceive it through senses. . . . We wish salvation from the earth and yet we are attached to it with our whole heart.[7]

Horkheimer's conflict and his revolt against paternal authority was aggravated by additional problems. At the age of 21 he fell in love with his father's secretary, Rose Riekehr. She was the daughter of an Englishwoman and a bankrupt German in the hotel business. In addition, she was a gentile and eight years older than Horkheimer. His parents opposed their marriage vehemently.

A 10-year strained relationship and confrontation between father and son and a struggle for emancipation followed.[8]

In 1916 Horkheimer was drafted into the army, but he was never sent to the front. Under the impact of the senseless and murderous war, he turned pacifist. This marks the beginning of his political awakening. Half a century later he recalled those times:

> I had been in Paris and London and so could never believe that the people there were more for war than our "peace-loving" *Kaiser*; I could not see that they were worse human beings than I and that therefore now I have to shoot them. . . .My faith in the childhood teachings of the German Reich was shaken. I had the distinct feeling that something horrible had happened to Europe and mankind that could not be reversed.[9]

Indeed, his immediate reaction was the rejection of the criminal war that was destined to protect the property of a few under the guise of national interests. He wrote in 1914:

> I cannot believe that an act deemed to be criminal for the individual should be a noble one for a nation. . . . I hate the armies that are on the march to protect property. . . . Bestial motives guide their arms—motives that must be overcome in our drive for enlightment and have to be destroyed if we want to become human beings.[10]

The dominant ideas of the young Horkheimer were the rejection of nationalism coupled with the embracing of mankind; there was also a deep underlying pessimism of mankind's future prospects, as expressed in his early writings:

> Why can't I be a human being only. . . without belonging to any nation. . . .What you fight for is not my concern. Your order within nations and laws might be necessary for you because you are all predatory beasts (Raubtiere). . . .As long as the majority of mankind consists of blockheads and rowdies, their union, i.e., society, cannot be anything else but an inferior one whether it calls itself autocratic, socialistic or anarchistic; and I have to believe that this "as long" may seem eternity.[11]

The end of the war found Horkheimer in Munich, where he experienced the November 1918 revolution. He greeted the revolution enthusiastically and hailed it as a liberation from the authority of father and fatherland. The experience of the revolution moved young Horkheimer toward the problems of society and toward Marxism. In an autobiographical short story, entitled "Jochai," he wrote of his hero:

> Private Jochai could not force himself to shoot and chose to run. . . . The deep resentment compelled him, the Jew, not to kill but to vent his desperation, the desperation of all slaves, in a piercing scream that would reach the ears of the masters and destroy their contended indifference and help to demolish the consciousness-betraying facade of their world; in this way, he chose intellectual victory.[12]

Years of study at Frankfurt University with the neo-Kantian philosopher, Hans Cornelius, who was in addition a painter and a musician, was followed by further study with Husserl and Heidegger in Freiburg. Heidegger's impact is explicitly acknowledged by Horkheimer: "Today, I know that Heidegger is one of the most important personalities whom I ever came across in my life...."[13] Yet, on the whole, his encounter with academic philosophy ended in disappointment, and he summarized his Freiburg experience as follows:

> The more I am taken by philosophy, the further I grow from the academic understanding of philosophy as practiced at this university. What I mean is we have to look for matter-of-fact assertions [*materielle Aussagen*] about our life and its meaning and not search for formal laws of a theory of knowledge that are basically irrelevant.[14]

Yet, in view of the continuous opposition of his parents to his marriage, Horkheimer decided to pursue an academic career. He wrote in one of his fictional letters that he hated "the university and its pedantic ways" but regarded the university career as the "one and only acceptable profession" in which one can assist in the problems of society.[15] Horkheimer received his Ph.D. in 1922 and three years later handed in his *Habilitationsschrift*. Thus he started his academic career as a *Privatdozent* and married Rose Riekehr.

THE CURRENTS OF THE 1920s

At the time at which young Horkheimer entered the academic scene in the 1920s, a revival of Marxian theory took place in Central and Western Europe. This revival took on a multiplicity of forms, such as the Marxism of Georg Lukács in Vienna, that of Antonio Gramsci in Rome, that of Karl Korsch in Leipzig, and the "bourgeois" Marxism of Karl Mannheim in Frankfurt.

The Marxism of Lukács and Korsch was an immediate reaction to, and a theoretical reflection on, the post World War I
revolutionary situation in Europe. Waves of revolutionary
movements in Russia, Germany, and Hungary inspired both
Lukács and Korsch. A revolutionary messianism and optimism,
the expectation of a world revolution permeated the *Zeitgeist* of
the postwar period. Lenin wrote in his farewell address to the
Swiss workers that the Russian revolution is "a *prelude* to and a
step toward the world socialist revolution." He continued: "The
objective conditions of the imperialist war make it certain that
the revolution will not be limited to the *first stage* of the Russian
revolution, that the revolution will *not* be limited to Russia."[16] In
spite of the defeat of the 1919 Hungarian proletarian revolution,
Lukács still saw in 1923 the European working class as the agent
of world historical change, and as the subject and object of the
world historical process. At the same time, Lukács and Korsch
rediscovered the philosophical (Hegelian) and the humanist
dimensions of the Marxian theory. It might be noted that a
renewed interest in Hegel had commenced at the beginning of
the century with Dilthey's *Die Jugendgeschichte Hegels* (1906)
and Croce's *What is Alive and What is Dead in Hegel's
Philosophy* (1906). Marx's lifelong interest in man's alienation
in a capitalist society was uncovered by Lukács' and Korsch's
careful reading of *Das Kapital*, especially its "commodity
fetishism" chapter, a decade before the publication of the
Economic and Philosophic Manuscripts of 1844. Korsch's *Marxismus und Philosophie*, first published in 1923, was republished in the *Grünberg Archiv* in 1925. Lukác's *History and Class
Consciousness*, a collection of essays, some of them written
during the short-lived Hungarian Soviet Republic when Lukács
occupied the position of Commissar of Cultural Affairs, was also
published in 1923.[17] Because of the diversity of these essays,
they are sometimes considered somewhat contradictory, that is,
Lukács is celebrated as the founder of a modern humanist-
existentialist Marxism on the one hand, and he is condemned for
the glorification of the Communist Party's vanguard role, sup-
posedly outdoing Lenin, on the other. Yet creative Marxism is

the unifying theme of Lukács' book, and its main theses can be summed up under five major propositions. First, "orthodox Marxism" means a return to Marx's method, which emphasized the primacy of *totality*. Second, Marx's dialectics is a method to be applied to historical studies of society as opposed to Engels' *Dialectics of Nature*. Third, the phenomenon of "re-ification" is the essence of capitalist society. Lukács wrote:

> at this stage in the history of mankind there is no problem that does not ultimately lead back. . . to the riddle of commodity-structure. . . .Its basis is that a relation between people takes on the character of a thing and thus acquires a "phantom-objectivity," an autonomy that seems so strictly rational and all-embracing as to conceal every trace of its fundamental nature: the relation between people.

Reification is "the central, structural problem of capitalist society in all its aspects."[18] Fourth, Lukács' philosophy of history claims that the proletariat is the agent (subject–object) of an inevitable world-historical process. Fifth, the party is the "objectification of its [the proletariat's] own will [obscure though this may be to themselves]."[19]

The influence of the "Occidental Marxism" (Merleau-Ponty's term) of Lukács and Korsch on the Frankfurt theorists is undeniable, although the relationship is rather complex, and it is difficult to determine its exact nature. Early Critical Theory did not emphasize unequivocally the primacy of totality as expressed in Horkheimer's critical review of Mannheim (1930): "It is not the grasping of a 'totality' or of a total and absolute truth but the changing of certain societal conditions that was the intention of his [Marx's] science."[20] Yet at the same time Critical Theory aspired to be the comprehensive social philosophy of contemporary capitalist society. There is considerable agreement between the Frankfurt School theorists and Lukács in their anti-Engels and antiscience sentiments, both having their roots in German Idealism and romantic anticapitalist social thought. All the dichotomous formulations such as *Verstand* (intellect) versus *Vernunft* (reason), civilization versus culture,

Gesellschaft versus *Gemeinschaft*, and *Naturwissenschaft* versus *Geisteswissenschaft* are just different manifestations of the same issue. For the early Critical Theory of Horkheimer, "exchange" was a basic category: "Critical Theory of society begins with the idea of the simple exchange of commodities. . . ."[21] Adorno too relied on Lukács' theory of reification in his "On the Fetish Character in Music" (1938), and later the notion of society based on the "dominance of exchange value" became a central category for his Theory of Society: "The spread of the [exchange] principle imposes on the whole world an obligation to become identical, to become total."[22] The theories of both Lukács and the Frankfurt School took an all pervasive, but by no means identical, ethical stand. The main difference, due to changed historical circumstances and to differences in personalities, was concerned with the alleged "historical mission" of the proletariat, the vanguard role of the Communist parties and the use of violence—as is discussed later in this chapter.

In 1930 a chair for social philosophy was created for Horkheimer at the University of Frankfurt, and in 1931 he became the new director of the institute. In the 1930s the Frankfurt theorists faced a different social reality than Lukács and Korsch had faced a decade earlier. European societies were in deep economic and political crises. The powerlessness of bourgeois-liberal democracies had become evident. Only the communists and fascists seemed to offer alternative solutions. Horkheimer accused the communists of authoritarianism and of being addicted to the use of force. The rise of fascisms, and the emerging Stalinism, with its bureaucratic, authoritarian traits and consequent purges, and also the gradual integration of American labor into what C. Wright Mills called "the middle levels of power"—the outcome of all these historical events—left no working-class movement with which to be allied. The German working-class movement was split. In Horkheimer's opinion, the splitting of the working class on the basis of the economic process into one stratum of the unemployed, who were immediately interested in the revolution but lacked a theoretical orientation and class consciousness, and another stratum with clear theoretical consciousness but without immediate interest in revolution, was reflected in the existence of two working class parties and the fluctuation of great masses of the unemployed between the Communist and Nazi parties.[23]

Horkheimer, never having been committed to any organization, attempted to steer a middle course between official Party Marxisms and unaffiliated liberal left bourgeois intellectuals. He hoped to salvage the philosophical-theoretical heritage of a humanist Marxism combined with other elements of European bourgeois thought, in the hopes of being able to work out some theoretical guidelines for a possible future course of action that was destined to lead ultimately to a just society.

HORKHEIMER: DIRECTOR OF THE INSTITUTE

Horkheimer took over his new office as director of the institute in January 1931. His opening address (*Antrittsvorlesung*), entitled, "The Present Situation of Social Philosophy and the Tasks of an Institute for Social Research," indicated the shift in emphasis of the future course of the institute.[24]

Edward Shils, in contrasting the career of Max Horkheimer and Karl Mannheim (who was also a professor of sociology at Frankfurt University before going into exile in London in 1933), concluded that Horkheimer's position at the institute was a key factor in the subsequent success of his ideas, in spite of the fact that "Mannheim was the more original and many-sided of the two." Mannheim was not associated with any institution and truly became a "free-floating intellectual" in exile. In Shils' opinion,

> institutionalization. . . renders more probable the consolidation, elaboration and diffusion of a set of ideas. It serves to make ideas more available to potential recipients, it renders possible concentration effort on them, it fosters interaction about them, and it aids their communication.[25]

In my opinion, Shils' statement seems beside the point. Mannheim has indeed become, albeit somewhat marginally, a part of American sociology through his book *Ideology and Utopia*, whereas the name and theories of Horkheimer never entered the mainstream of American sociology. Adorno is remembered mainly as the first name on the list of coauthors of *The Authoritarian Personality*, and Marcuse's world wide success in the late 1960s was not a result of his one-time association with the Frankfurt Institute for Social Research some 20 years earlier.

HORKHEIMER'S INITIAL PROGRAM

In Horkheimer's opening address, he placed the essence of Marxian theory in the universal explanation of societal movements on the basis of class relations, as determined by economic developments. In his view, "the ultimate aim of social philosophy is the philosophical interpretation of man's fate as a member of a community."[26] Horkheimer outlined the main task of examining the interrelationship among three spheres: the economic substructure of society, the psychic development of the individual, and cultural phenomena. According to Horkheimer, the real order of the day was to establish a close and fruitful cooperation between philosophy and the specialized disciplines. Social philosophy was seen as a materialist theory of history combined with empirical research. Philosophy, in the Hegelian sense, aims at the grasping of the objective essence of appearances. It must be receptive to change and to the impact of empirical studies. The immediate task was to organize research based on philosophical formulations of problems, in which philosophers, sociologists, economists, historians, and psychologists unite in permanent research teams. The first research projects were to deal with problems of skilled laborers and white collar employees in Germany. Horkheimer called attention to the excellence of American research methods that were to be emulated and incorporated into the work of the institute, a branch of which was established in Geneva, Switzerland.

The *Grünberg Archiv*, the journal of the institute until 1930, ceased publication, and a new journal of the institute, the *Zeitschrift für Sozialforschung* [*Journal for Social Research*] was launched. Horkheimer's *Preface* to the first volume of the *Zeitschrift* states that social research (*Sozialforschung*) is research in special areas at different levels of abstraction intended to "promote the theory of contemporary society in its totality." Its aim was the grasping of the societal process in its totality and presumed the possibility of comprehending forces active underneath the chaotic surface of historical events. History may appear arbitrary, but its dynamics are dominated by laws. Therefore, its cognition is a science. The work of the *Zeitschrift* would be based on that assumption. Thus history is concerned with all the factors of economic, psychic, and societal nature that determine social life. The treatment of problems belonging to the realm of *Weltanschauung* and philosophy would be included if they bore on the "theory of society".

Social research and traditional academic sociology were not seen as identical: although both deal with societal phenomena, the former extends its research into "nonsociological areas". The problems of this social research concern the interrelationship of specific areas of culture and the laws governing their change. One of the major tasks for the solution of this problem would be "the creation of a historically oriented social psychology". The *Zeitschrift* was to deal with both general theoretical problems and specific investigations of concrete problems of contemporary society and economy.

Interestingly enough, a "value-free" social research was announced as the objective: "The obligation to scientific criteria separates social research also methodologically from politics. It must preserve the independence of its claim to cognition *vis-à-vis* positions of all *Weltanschauungen* and political stands".[27] Part 1 of Volume 1 of the *Zeitschrift* (1933) was still published in Germany; The second part of Volume 2 was put out in Paris by *Libraire Felix Alcan*. In the preface, Horkheimer thanked the publisher for making the "scholarly publication in the German language" possible and pledged the continuation of the effort of the institute "to promote the theory of society and its auxiliary sciences". Continuity with the German cultural heritage was always emphasized and stated again in the preface to the sixth volume: (1937) "The *Zeitschrift* and other publications of the institute today are among the few scholarly publications that continue the German *geisteswissenschaftliche* tradition in the German language abroad".[28] Only the third section of the 1939 volume and the last (1940/1941) volume were published under the title *Studies in Philosophy and Social Science* in New York, with all contributions in English.

The *Zeitschrift* was somewhat comparable in its aspirations to Durkheim's *Année Sociologique*. A perusal of its nine volumes reveals a broad interdisciplinary spectrum of an attempted grand program. Critical Theory has no *magnum opus*, no *Cours de philosophie positive*, no *Das Kapital*, no *Wirtschaft und Gesellschaft*, no systematic explication of its principles, concepts, methodology, and findings. Its dominant form of expression has been essays, articles, aphorisms, fragments, and monographs devoted to specific topics. Despite this fragmentary and multiple character, the volumes of the *Zeitschrift*, a torso in view of Horkheimer's program, are nevertheless a remarkable document of European intellectual history.

THE GENESIS OF CRITICAL THEORY

Horkheimer's Critical Theory was developed in about a dozen essays, most of them written in German while he was in exile in New York City and published in the *Zeitschrift* between 1933 and 1940. Critical Theory was meant to be a critique of the "bourgeois" (traditional) theory. It is an amalgamation of diverse influences on Horkheimer's thought, the German idealist philosophy of Kant and Schopenhauer the most notable among them. Judaic ethics (i.e., concern with social justice), Gestalt psychology, and certain selected elements of Marxian thought all played their parts in the crystallization of Critical Theory.

CRITICAL VERSUS TRADITIONAL THEORY

The term "Critical Theory" was coined by Horkheimer in a programmatic article to contrast with "traditional theory". Horkheimer identifies "traditional theory" with the influence of Descartes and Husserl. Descartes' scientific method asserts as one of its maxims,

> to conduct my thoughts in an orderly way, beginning with the simplest objects and the easiest to know, in order to climb gradually, as by degrees, as far as the knowledge of the most complex, and even supposing some order among these objects which do not precede each other naturally.[29]

Descartes asserts that

> everything which can be encompassed by man's knowledge is linked in the same way. . . and that one always keeps the right order for one thing to be deduced from that which precedes it; there can be nothing so distant that one does not reach it eventually, or so hidden that one cannot discover it.[30]

Thus traditional or hypothetical-deductive theory is a sum of propositions in a research area in which the propositions are interlocked so that some of them can be deduced from others. Husserl maintained that theory is "a systematically linked set of propositions in the form of a systematically unified deduction".[31] Validity depends on the congruence of propositions with empirical evidence. Theory is accumulated knowledge. Theoretical explanation means the establishment of a connection between pure perception of facts and the conceptual structure of knowledge. Traditional theory aims at establishing a mathematical sign system. Logical operations are rationalized to the extent that, in a great part of the natural sciences, theory construction has become identical with mathematical constructs. The same conceptualization is applied to living and nonliving nature. The unity of scientific method is a primary objective. The sciences of man and society are to follow the examples of the more successful and advanced natural sciences.

Representatives of dominant schools of "traditional theory," the philosophers of science, positivism, and pragmatism, designate prognosis and utility of results as the main task of science.

In Horkheimer's opinion:

> The fruitfulness of newly discovered factual connections for the renewal of existent knowledge, and the application of such knowledge to the facts, do not derive from purely logical or methodological sources but can rather be understood only in the context of real social processes.[32]

If theory is made an independent predicament, that is, if it is established ahistorically, as emanating from some inner essence of cognition, then it is transformed into a reified, ideological category. But the changes exhibited by scientific structures, both of all-embracing grand theories and minute everyday research operations, always depend on specific social situations. The influence of the subject matter on theory, as well as the application of theory on the subject, is not merely an intra-scientific but also a societal process. As Horkheimer argues: "Bringing hypotheses to bear on facts is an activity that goes on ultimately, not in the savant's head but in industry."[33] Regardless of the belief or nonbelief of the scientist in an independent, suprasocial knowledge, he and his science are integrated into the societal apparatus. They are moments of the self-preservation and continuous reproduction of existing socio-economic systems. Science is part of the forces of production that makes possible modern industrial systems. Diverse branches of production, in the division of labor of the capitalist mode of production, are not independent entities but historical specifications of the mode of society's confrontation with nature. This includes science, which only appears to be independent, just as there appears to be freedom of the economic subject in bourgeois society in that individuals seem to make decisions when in reality they are merely agents of concealed societal mechanisms.

Critical Theory is a critique of the "traditional theory" from an ethical standpoint. Horkheimer emphasizes continuity—the idea that there is no absolute break with past theoretical achievements, because Critical Theory "contains within it elements from traditional theories and from our declining culture generally."[34] Traditional and Critical Theory differ mainly in regard to the subject's, that is, the scientist-scholar's attitude toward his society. Critical Theory's opposition to the traditional concept of theory springs in general from the difference not so much of objects as of subjects. "For men of critical mind, the facts, as they emerge from the work of society, are not extrinsic to the same degree as they are for the savant or for members of other professions who all think like little savants."[35]

"Traditional theory" is bent on the preservation and gradual reformation of society to achieve a better functioning of the social structure as a whole or of any of its particular elements. Its intention is to eliminate the abuses and disturbing or dysfunctional elements. This attitude is based on the premise that

> the individual as a rule must simply accept the basic conditions of his existence as given and strive to fulfill them; he finds his satisfaction and praise in accomplishing as well as he can the tasks connected with his place in society and in courageously doing his duty despite all the sharp criticism he may choose to exercise in particular matters.[36]

Critical Theory considers the "abuses" or "dysfunctional aspects" of capitalist society "as necessarily connected with the way in which the social structure is organized." It does not intend to achieve a better functioning of class society by perfecting and promoting dominant social arrangements. Even the terms "better, useful, appropriate, productive, and valuable" are suspect. The sum total of blind interactions of individual activities in capitalist society, based on its division of labor and class structure, ultimately "originates in human action and therefore is a possible object of planful decision and rational determination of goals."

Critical Theory, concerned with a radical transformation of existing social arrangements, is proposed, in opposition to the system-maintaining "traditional theory." As Horkheimer argues:

> The self-knowledge of present-day man is not a mathematicized natural science, which claims to be the eternal Logos, but a critical theory of contemporary society, *a theory permeated at every turn by a concern* for reasonable conditions in life (italics mine).[37]

The term critical is to be understood "less in the sense it has in the critique of pure reason than in the sense it has in the dialectical critique of political economy."[38]

Consequently, the adherence to certain basic notions of the original Marxian conceptual framework, such as the theory of impoverishment (*Verelendung*) and the inevitability of the breakdown of capitalism, is asserted by Horkheimer:

> The categories of class, exploitation, surplus value, profit, pauperization, and breakdown are elements in a conceptual whole, and the meaning of this whole is to be sought not in the preservation of contemporary society but in its transformation into the right kind of society.[39]

Thus Critical Theory is permeated by the idea of a future society as a community of free men, which is possible through technical means already at hand. Today there is a duality of social totality: the economy and culture of the present era are products of conscious human activity with which representives of Critical Theory can identify themselves, but at the same time they state that certain phenomena of the same society (wars and oppression) seem to work like "nonhuman natural processes." Horkheimer argues: "That world is not theirs but the world of capital."[40] This duality is manifested in thought by their acceptance and at the same time their condemnation of societal categories such as work, value, and productivity. Today men act "as members of an organism which lacks reason." Organism as a naturally developing and declining unity, Horkheimer contends, cannot be a sort of model for society, but only a form of deadened existence from which society must emancipate itself.[41] A critical theoretical work must serve this aim of emancipation and must be permeated by it. Therefore, it must reject the "separation of value and research, knowledge and action" of traditional theory. A major part of this research might be devoted to the social determination of ideas and theories, as the sociology of knowledge does. But whereas the latter contents itself with establishing a relationship between thought and its societal conditioning, Critical Theory must go beyond that stand to "look towards a new kind of organization of work." Its aim is to "transcend the tension and to abolish the opposition between the individual's purposefulness, spontaneity, and rationality, and those work-process relationships on which society is built."[42] The issue is the rational individual versus the irrational society; Horkheimer's firm belief in the former is emphasized again and again. He maintains that "the thrust towards a rational society. . . is really *innate in every man* (italics mine).[43] A more elaborate discussion of the term rationality and its modification under different stages of bourgeois society came about when the era of the "eclipse of reason" began.

Critical Theory aims at the coordination of thought and action. For the critical theorist,

> the subject is no mathematical point like the ego of bourgeois philosophy; his activity is the construction of the social present. . . . [Today] in reflection on man, subject and object are sundered; their identity lies in the future.[44]

The path to this projected identity is not only a logical process of clarification for Critical Theory but also a concrete socio-historic process, in the course of which the entire social structure changes, as does the relationship of the theorist to society. The role of historical experience in reorganizing society on the basis of reason is crucial for Critical Theory. Today production does not serve the interest of the majority but the profit interests of a minority, a state of affairs that is ultimately rooted in existing property relations.

THE SEARCH FOR AN AGENT OF CHANGE

Horkheimer's search for the societal agent of the necessary historical transformation of an unjust capitalist socioeconomic order into a "just society" leads him to an analysis of the revolutionary potential of the capitalist social structure, which in turn ends in pessimism, even though at times he wavers between optimism and pessimism.

Marx and Engels saw the proletariat as the class that "experiences the connection between work that puts even more powerful instruments into men's hands in their struggle with nature, and the continuous renewal of an outmoded social organization."[45] In view of the decline of the European proletarian revolutionary movement in the late 1930s, Critical Theory is sceptical of this insight and subsequently of the role of the proletariat. In Horkheimer's words: "Even the situation of the proletariat is, in this society, no guarantee of correct knowledge."[46] False consciousness dominates proletarian insight and Weltanschauung. Critical Theory cannot belong exclusively to the proletariat, or, for that matter, to any social class. As Horkheimer expresses it: "Nor is there a social class by whose acceptance of the theory one could be guided." A clear rejection of the historical role of the proletariat as primary agent of revolutionary change, a role rooted in its objective socioeconomic situation is reiterated: "It is possible for the consciousness of every social stratum today to be limited and corrupted by ideology, however much, for its circumstances, it may be bent on truth."[47]

It is clear that the bureaucratization of German working class parties served as a major source of Horkheimer's fear of any organized movements. In Horkheimer's words: "Where the unity of discipline and freedom has disappeared, the movement becomes a matter of interest only to its own bureaucracy, a play that already belongs to the repertory of modern history."[48]

Furthermore, Horkheimer stated that if Critical Theory consisted of the formulation of the specific sentiments and ideas of a class, it would not differ from other special disciplines. Systematizing the consciousness of the proletariat would not produce the real picture of its existence and interests. It would be another traditional theory with a specific problem setting and not the intellectual side of the historic process of the emancipation of the proletariat. This would be so even if one limits oneself to pronouncing not the ideas of the proletariat in general but those of its most advanced segment or part of its leadership. The process of thought and of theory construction would remain one thing and its object, the proletariat, another.

THE ROLE OF THE INTELLECTUALS

As for the intellectuals, they waver between positions of exaggerated optimism, emanating from a feeling of power because of their alliance with the immense forces of defeat. This description of the attitude and sentiments of intellectuals in general was certainly characteristic of the critical theorists. Expressing a firm and militant optimism, Horkheimer wrote: "Today. . . in the transition from the present form of society to a future one, mankind will for the first time be a conscious subject and actively determine its own way of life."[49] On the other hand, under the impact of the Nazi onslaught on the German and European labor movement, Horkheimer wrote pessimistically that

> under the conditions of late capitalism and the impotence of the workers before the authoritarian state's apparatus of oppression, truth has sought refuge among *small groups of admirable men*. But these have been decimated by terrorism and have little time for refining the theory (italics mine).[50]

Consequently, Horkheimer advocates withdrawal as the only possible attitude because "the kind of thinking which is the most topical, which has the deepest grasp of the historical situation and is most pregnant with the future, must at certain times isolate its subject and throw him back upon himself."[51]

Horkheimer's position on the role of the critical theorist is somewhat ambivalent. On one hand, he believes that the proper role of theory must be conceived in the dynamic sense of Marx, who asserted that "theory itself becomes a material force when it has seized the masses." Therefore, if the critical

> theoretician and his specific object are seen as forming a dynamic unity with the oppressed class, so that his presentation of societal contradictions is not merely an expression of the concrete historical situation but also a *force within it to stimulate change*, then his real function emerges (italics mine).

The course of confrontation between the vanguard of the class and the individuals who pronounce the truth about it, and the confrontation of this most advanced group and its theorist with the rest of the class are to be understood as a socio-historic process, a reciprocal interaction, in which the liberating consciousness unfolds itself along with the driving and disciplining power. The image of the future arises out of a thorough understanding of the present, but it takes imagination as well. It is the theorist among the most advanced groups who most have this "obstinacy of imagination [*Eigensinn der Phantasie*]."

Yet, on the other hand, Horkheimer advocated a demarcation between the orthodox Marxism of working class organizations and Mannheim's *freischwebende Intelligenz*. "Critical Theory," Horkheimer contends, "is neither 'deeply rooted' like totalitarian propaganda nor 'detached' like the liberal intelligentsia."[53] The critique of the theorist aims at both conscious apologists of existing conditions and at the diverting, conformist, or utopian tendencies in his own camp. The critical theorist must maintain a certain independent status, because "the theoretician whose business is to accelerate developments which will lead to a society without injustice can find himself in opposition to views prevailing even among the proletariat."[54]

A deliberate antiorganizational stand is expressed by Horkheimer; Critical Theory's "transmission will not take place via solidly established practice and fixed ways of acting but *via*

concern [*Interesse*] for social transformation" (italics mine).[55]
"Concern" refers to a small circle of intellectuals bound together
by their shared theoretical knowledge of capitalist society and
their longing for a society with no exploitation and oppression.
"The circle of transmitters of this tradition. . . is constituted and
maintained not by biological or testamentary inheritance, but *by
a knowledge* which brings its own obligations with it" (italics
mine).[56]

As Horkheimer repeats again and again:

> In the general historical upheaval the truth may reside with
> numerically small groups of men. History teaches us that such
> groups, hardly noticed even by those opposed to the status
> quo, outlawed but imperturbable, may at the decisive moment
> become the leaders because of their deeper insight.[57]

THEORY OF KNOWLEDGE AND SOCIAL CHANGE

In regard to questions of epistemology, Horkheimer asserts that
materialism has in common with positivism that it acknowledges as real only what is given in sense experience. The
materialist theory of knowledge considers sense experience a
starting point for all thought, but it does not absolutize sensation. Critical Theory opposes the reduction of all knowledge to
sensation. Theory is always more than sensibility alone and
cannot be totally reduced to sensations. Relying heavily on the
work of Kurt Koffka and Max Wertheimer of Gestalt psychology,
Horkheimer asserts, that far from being the elementary building
blocks of the world or even of psychic life, sensations are deriva-
tives arising through a complicated process of abstraction
involving the destruction of formations that the psyche had
shaped. He approvingly quotes Koffka: "Sensations, which for
so long were the basis of psychology are. . . not the starting
points but the end points of a development."[58] Sensations are
also historicized; like the relation of the subject to data, they are
conditioned and changeable. The historically changing and

active aspect of both subject and object and the active role of the former are emphasized. This theory of knowledge is dialectical, which means that subject and object interact. Horkheimer writes:

> The world which is given to the individual and which he must accept and take into account is, in its present and continuing form, a product of the activity of society as a whole. The objects we perceive in our surroundings—cities, villages, fields, and woods—bear the mark of having been worked on by man.[59]

Horkheimer goes on to explain the dialectical and historical character of sense perception:

> Even the way men see and hear is inseparable from the social life-process as it has evolved over the millennia. The facts which our senses present to us are socially performed in two ways: through the historical character of the object perceived and through the historical character of the perceiving organ. Both are not simply natural; they are shaped by human activity.[60]

In Critical Theory, materialism does not mean the ontological primacy of matter over consciousness. "Materialism is not tied down to a set conception of matter," Horkheimer argues. "No authority has a say on what matter is except natural science as it moves forward."[61]

Any treatment of materialism, then, Horkheimer argues, is misguided, for it is interested primarily in metaphysical questions. For the age of the rising bourgeoisie, materialism was a weapon for mastering nature and man. Problems of epistemology and of natural science dominated the materialism of that time. The practical requirements of concrete problems affect both the content and the form of materialist theory. Theory is only a tool, the essence of which arises from the tasks that, at any given historical period, are to be mastered with the help of the theory. In our age, we are told, the knowledge of movements and tendencies affecting society as a whole is immensely important for materialist theory. Thus, whereas idealism attempts to answer the same perennial questions, the same eternal riddle, problems of materialist philosophy are essentially determined by the tasks to be mastered at the moment.

It seems that the difference between materialism and idealism in Critical Theory is reduced to the question of the historical versus ahistorical character of problems and categories. Furthermore, "materialism" in Critical Theory means a predominance of imminent societal problems of the age wedded to the instrumentalism of the theory. "Materialism is not interested in a world view or in the souls of men. It is concerned with changing the concrete conditions under which men suffer and in which, of course, their souls must become stunted."[62]

Horkheimer repeatedly asserted the primacy of ethics over epistemological and ontological issues. In his words:

> The principle that the materialist doctrine designates as reality is not fit to furnish a norm. . . . Matter in itself is meaningless: its qualities cannot provide the maxims for the shaping of life either in regard to the commandments or to the ideal. . . . Knowledge. . .yields no models, maxims or advice for an authentic life.[63]

The relegation of epistemological and ontological issues to a secondary position was, of course, determined by the socio-historical situation and possibly motivated by Judaic thought. As is known, Judaic philosophy consists predominantly of ethics and has no ontology.

CRITICAL THEORY AND MARXISM

In concluding this discussion of Critical Theory, one must consider Horkheimer's convergence with Marxism or his divergence from it, since the reputation of Critical Theory as having a Marxist orientation is based primarily on his formulation of Critical Theory in the 1930s.

Before examining whether or not Horkheimer's Critical
Theory represents a neo-Marxist orientation, a short discourse
about Marxism is necessary. Marxism, as a convergence of German philosophy, British political economy, and French
socialism, represents the unity of theory and practice (praxis).
Marxian social theory is an empirical, positive, and verifiable
social science. In other words, it is a sociological orientation,
usually called historical materialism, that is, the use of a conceptual apparatus and the adherence to a materialist epistemological and ontological position. Thus Marxism, in a comprehensive
sense, means the grasping of the relationship between economics
and politics and the praxis derived from that understanding.

There is an additional problem in discussing Marxian social
theory. Its interpreters usually contrast the "young-humanist-
philosopher" Marx with the "mature-scientist-economist"
Marx.[64] In my opinion, it is more appropriate to speak of the
unity of Marx's work and a gradual widening of the Marxian
framework and approach, Marx's theoretical life work constitutes a continuous Aufhebung—the suppression and preservation of a previous stage on a higher level. Marxian theory is then
what one would now call an interdisciplinary approach of
philosophy, history, and political economy with an underlying
"value-commitment." Marx's successive incorporation of the
disciplines can easily be traced. Until about 1844, philosophy
dominated Marx's approach.[65] Around 1845 the emphasis
shifted to history. In a passage of The German Ideology, not
usually translated in the English editions, Marx and Engels
state: "We know only of one science, the science of history."[66]
An increasing awareness of the ills of capitalist society and the
search for their root causes had already gradually shifted Marx's
attention to the study of political enomomy in the mid 1840s.
The Paris Manuscripts of 1844 are economic and philosophic
manuscripts. Marx later gave an account of his intellectual
development:

> I was led by my studies to the conclusion that legal relations as
> well as forms of State could neither be understood by them-

selves, nor explained by the so-called general progress of the human mind, but that they are rooted in the material conditions of life... and that *the anatomy of civil society is to be sought in political economy* (italics mine).

Marx's shifting emphasis did not mean a drifting from discipline to discipline, but rather a synthesis of the various perspectives.[68]

MARXISM AND ACADEMIC SOCIOLOGY

In nineteenth century Western European societies, two sociological orientations emerged independently of each other as theoretical responses to the socio-historic developments after the French Revolution. They were Comte's positivist sociology and the social theory of Marx and Engels. The line of development of the former orientation can be followed up to Talcott Parsons and contemporary Western academic sociology, and the latter from Marx and Engels to modern Marxist social sciences both in the East and the West.[69] Within both orientations further differentiations took place, most notably the emergence of the German historical–sociological school of Dilthey, Rickert, Weber and Simmel.[70]

Both lines of development contain continuities and discontinuities, and scientific and ideological elements. The two orientations started out with an ignorance and a contempt for each other.[71] A mutual distrust and ignorance was present much of the time in the relationship of academic sociology and Marxian social sciences from the days of Comte and Marx. Yet in the work of the leading articulators of both orientations a fruitful cross fertilization took place. Weber had a lifelong debate with the "ghost" of Karl Marx, whose work he considered "a work of scholarship of the highest order,"[72] as did Ferdinand Tönnies, Georg Simmel, Thorstein Veblen, Vilfredo Pareto, Karl Mannheim, Joseph Schumpeter, and C. Wright Mills. In the Marxist camp, Max Adler, Georg Lukács, Karl Korsch, and others engaged in a scholarly dialogue with "bourgeois" sociology.

After the mutual debunking and denouncing period of the Cold War era in the 1950s, the issue of their relationship was reopened in both camps. With the revival of Marxist sociology as an academic discipline within the larger framework of Marxism in the Soviet Union and Eastern European countries in the 1960s the dialogue between Marxist and "bourgeois" sociology began anew.[73]

Marxian sociology, then, has five basic characteristics. First, it is *historical*, in opposition to ahistorical, formalistic sociologies. Second, it is *materialistic*, in opposition to idealistic social theories.[74] Third, it is *empirical* as opposed to speculative theorizing.[75] Fourth, its subject matter is the research of societal relations that result from the relation of production, which determine the objective *structure* of historically concrete societies and the law-governed conditions of its development.[76] Fifth, Marxian sociology makes use of the category of *totality*, including the analysis of socioeconomic base and that of political, cultural, and ideological superstructure, in its reciprocal interrelationship.[77] Sixth, it is value committed, that is, committed to the optimistic idea that society can become perfect and just.

CRITICAL THEORY AND MARXIAN SOCIAL THEORY

In sum, early Critical Theory adhered to certain basic tenets of Marxian social theory, such as the historical approach and the notion of societal developments founded on societal laws, and recognized the importance of empirical research. However, Critical Theory also deviates from the basic tenets of classic Marxist epistemology and ontology: these tenets can be summarized as follows:

1 Objective external reality exists independently of our consciousness and perception.
2 There is no limit to what science can explain in regard to the laws of nature and society. Consequently, the difference

between phenomenon and the unknowable *Ding an sich* is rejected. (Here a point of agreement with positivism should be noted.)

3 The image of objective reality is given to us by our senses (theory of reflection or copy theory).

4 Practice serves as the verification of the correctness or falseness of the images of external reality.

5 The ontological assumption of the primacy of matter is the basis for the idea of the unity of the sciences.[78]

Although Critical Theory never took a systematic stand on questions of Marxian epistemology and ontology and never presented its own position in a systematic way, one can detect the points of disagreement between the two. In Critical Theory, the question of objective reality was brushed aside as a question of secondary importance. Critical Theory never subscribed to the theory of reflection (the copy theory), considering it a nineteenth century relic. Although Critical Theory lamented the positivist separation of theory and praxis, it abstained from praxis, for a variety of reasons, throughout its career, as discussed later. The idea of the unity of sciences was explicitly rejected by Critical Theory. Dilthey's doctrine of the dichotomy of the natural sciences and the cultural–social sciences was the most important single influence in this respect. The Marxian optimistic belief in progress was shaken by political events in Europe and by the impact of Schopenhauer's philosophy. Critical Theory cannot qualify as Marxist because it deviates from the basic tenets of Marxist social theory, on one hand, and because it never represented a synthesis of theory and praxis, on the other. The many complex reasons for this lack of synthesis require a brief discussion.

THEORY-PRAXIS: DEBATES OVER VIOLENCE

At decisive historic times, the theory–praxis issue often boils down to the problem of justifying the use of force. Many great political thinkers of our age, Weber, Sorel and Lukács among others, wrestled with this question and have come up with different answers. Three "ideal-type" answers given by intellectuals of post World War I Europe can be identified: first, the *Realpolitik* (middle-of-the-road) solution of Weber; second, the unconditional endorsement of violence as a historical necessity by Lukács; and third, the pacifist–humanist attitude of Horkheimer.[79]

As a *Realpolitiker*, Max Weber was fully aware of the sociological fact that legitimate violence is part of the political process at certain stages in the historical development of every society. He summed up:

> Violent social action is obviously something absolutely primordial. Every group, from the household to the political party, has always resorted to physical violence when it had to protect the interests of its members and was capable of doing so. However, the monopolization of legitimate violence by the political–territorial association (the state) and its rational consociation (*Vergesellschaftung*) into an institutional order is nothing primordial, but a product of evolution.[80]

Weber also approvingly quoted Trotsky's dictum that "Every state is founded on force." However, everyday politics and salvation are different spheres for Weber. He emphatically stated: "He who seeks the salvation of the soul, of his own and of others, should not seek it along the avenue of politics, for the quite different tasks of politics can only be solved by violence."[81] Violence and politics even work against the salvation of the soul: "Everything that is striven for through political action operating with violent means. . . *endangers the 'salvation of the soul'*" (italics mine).[82] Two ethics are then in conflict here: the ethic of responsibility (*Verantwortungsethik*) and the ethic of absolute ends (*Gesinnungsethik*). At one point Weber declares that "One cannot prescribe to anyone whether he should follow an ethic of absolute ends or an ethic of responsibility, or when the one and when the other."[83]

Nevertheless, in his conclusion Weber pleads for some kind

of compromise and declares that "an ethic of absolute ends and an ethic of responsibility are not absolute contrasts but rather supplements, which only in unison constitute a genuine man—a man who *can* have the 'calling for politics.'"[84]

Weber's opposition to revolutionary violence rested on his experience with Central European revolutions. He believed that those immature attempts had only discredited the cause of socialism. He wrote to Lukács in 1920: "My dear friend, we are naturally separated by our political views. I am absolutely convinced that these experiments will only have one effect: to discredit socialism for the coming 100 years."[85] He also had considerable misgivings about Jewish overrepresentation in the Central European (especially German and Hungarian) post World War I revolutions. In spite of his understanding of and sympathy for the complexities of the Jewish predicament in Europe, he feared that the overrepresentation would result in a strengthening of anti-Semitism—a fear that was certainly vindicated by subsequent tragic historical events. Marianna Weber reports:

> Weber despised anti-Semitism, but he regretted the fact that in those days there were so many Jews among the revolutionary leaders. . . . He said that on the basis of the historical situation of the Jews it was understandable that they in particular produced these revolutionary natures. But given the prevailing ways of thinking, it was practically imprudent for Jews to be admitted to leadership and for them to appear as leaders.[86]

Weber's essay "Politics as a Vocation" summarizes the long debates of the so-called Weber-*Kreis* that took place in Heidelberg during the war years and engaged such participants as Georg Lukács, Ernst Bloch, Karl Jaspers, and scores of young revolutionary intellectuals from Tsarist Russia.[87]

The Weber lecture was delivered in Munich in 1919 as the German revolution was being played out in the background. Young Horkheimer attended one of Weber's lectures and recorded his disappointment 40-odd years later:

Max Weber lectured on the Soviet system. The auditorium was crowded to its doors, but great disappointment followed. Instead of theoretical reflection and analysis, which would have led to a reasoned structuring of the future, not only in posing the problem but in every single step of thinking, we listened for two or three hours to finely balanced definitions of the Russian system, shrewdly formulated ideal types, by which it was possible to define the Soviet order. It was all so precise, so scientifically exact, so value-free that we all went sadly home.[88]

The same year that Weber delivered his speech in Munich, his one-time student and friend, Georg Lukács, in Budapest in the midst of revolutionary turmoil, faced the same dilemma about the use of force. A bourgeois-democratic revolution took place in Hungary in October 1918. Masses of former prisoners of war, many of whom participated in the Bolshevik revolution, returned from Russia and pushed events in Hungary toward the repetition of the Russian historical course, that is toward a transition from the bourgeois to the Bolshevik phase of the dual revolution. Lukács and his circle, all of them progressive bourgeois intellectuals, were caught up in a moral and political dilemma.

As related earlier, Horkheimer and Lukács had in common the predominance of the ethical element in their thought. However, whereas Horkheimer's ethical stance was pacifist, passive–pessimistic–messianic, we can characterize Lukács' position as militant, active–progressive–messianic. Much of the Lukács literature points to a break—sometimes called radical—in Lukács' intellectual career and appears to be vexed by the sudden and unexpected conversion of the formerly bourgeois esthete to Marxism. Recent scholarship, however, rightly emphasizes the basic continuity and unity in the Lukácsian life and work in general and in its strong ethical bent in particular.[89] It has been demonstrated that embracing Marxism and joining the Communist Party was a culmination of his development, that is, a logical step partly due to his personality development, his gradual disenchantment with decaying European bourgeois-capitalist civilization, and partly to the thrust of historical events, the revolutionary wave of post World War I Europe.

A tracing of Lukács' career, sketchy and incomplete as it unavoidably must be, shows young Lukács, the critic, to be always "longing for value and form, for measure and order."[90] Writing in 1910, Lukács, the essayist, longing for harmony, could not see any room for solution any other than "the formation and salvation" of the individual soul. He proclaimed that a "new type of esthete is in the process of being born."[91] Young Lukács' messianism was clearly expressed in language reminiscent of the prophets of the Old Testament. He wrote: "The critic has been sent into the world. . . to proclaim . . . to judge."[92] The intellectual tool of the critic (Lukács) is the essay, and "the essay is a judgment."[93] Lukács believed in the redeeming power of the form, proclaiming that "esthetic culture is the formation of the soul."[94] Aesthetics and ethics were thus brought together: Form is the highest judge of life. "Form-giving is a judging force, an ethic; there is a value judgment in everything that has been given form. Every kind of form-giving, every literary form, is a step in the hierarchy of life-possibilities. . . ."(italics mine).[95] This was a radical view of the form, and the concept of violence found its place in it:

> The essence of art is the creation of form, the conquering of resistance and of hostile forces, the creation of unity out of discord. . . .Form is the last judgment over things. It is a last judgment that means the salvation of everything possible, a judgment that *forces salvation on everything by a holy terror* (italics mine).[96]

Young Marx too, it should be recalled, advocated a universal liberation and salvation. Marx approvingly quoted Thomas Münzer, the German revolutionary theologue, who declared it intolerable "that every creature should be transformed into property—the fishes of the water, the birds of the air, the plants of the earth: the creature too should become free."[97]

The uncertainties of a disintegrating bourgeois order drove young Lukács toward a "longing for certainty, for measure and dogma." Marx's doctrine seemed to provide the solution to that uncertainty. After the 1917 Russian Revolution and the first (bourgeois) Hungarian revolution of October 1918, Lukács moved from his romantic anticapitalist stance to a quasi-social-democratic position. His theory was summarized in the December 1918 article, "Bolshevism as a Moral Problem."[98] Lukács' article discusses the alternatives: either the gradual creation of a new world order through peaceful and democratic means or the adoption of the position of the dictatorship of the proletariat through terror and an even more ruthless class domination than the existing one, in hopes of ultimately abolishing all class conflicts.

A few weeks later, after meeting Béla Kun, the charismatic leader of the 1919 Hungarian proletarian revolution,[99] Lukács joined the Communist Party and fought both with gun and pen for the cause of proletarian internationalism. The theoretical basis for his conversion was summarized in a second political essay "Tactics and Ethics." The concluding sentence of the essay reads as follows:

> Only he who acknowledges unflinchingly and without any reservations that murder is under no circumstances to be sanctioned can commit the murderous deed that is truly—and tragically—moral. To express this sense of the most profound human tragedy in the incomparably beautiful words of Hebbel's Judith: 'Even if God had placed sin between me and the deed enjoined upon me—who am I to be able to escape it?'[100]

Indeed, Lukács firmly believed in the historical necessity of violence: "Violence is now put to the service of man and it serves his unfolding as a man."[101]

Another contemporary German thinker, Ernst Bloch, a friend of Lukács and a member of the Weber circle, called this attitude "the categorical imperative with a revolver in the hand." "Now and then," Bloch wrote in 1918, "evil can be conquered in order to destroy the bad that exists." Otherwise, Bloch warns, "the soul might take upon itself an even greater guilt by retreating into the idyllic state of mind, and by accepting a seemingly harmless tolerance of injustice."[102] It might be noted parenthetically that Lukács and Bloch agreed with Marx, who assigned a specific role to violence. Marx wrote that "revolution is necessary. . . . not only because the *ruling* class cannot be overthrown in any other way, but also because the class *overthrowing* it can only in a revolution succeed in ridding itself of all the muck of ages and become fitted to found society anew."[103]

As for Lukács, many influences combined to shape his ethical attitude and personality, most notably of Dostoyevski, Sorel, and the Russian anarchist Savinkov.[104] The personality of Lukács, the revolutionary thinker, had been masterfully portrayed by Thomas Mann in the figure of Leo Naphta of his monumental *Magic Mountain*. Lukács met Mann in 1922 in Vienna, where Lukács was living in exile after the defeat of the Hungarian proletarian revolution, and made a great impact on Thomas Mann.[105]

The combination of many factors, most notably, the differences in intellectual and psychological temperament and sociohistorical circumstances, accounts for the divergence between Lukács and the critical theorists (here primarily Horkheimer) regarding their views on the use and justification of violence. Horkheimer's reluctance to condone and accept violence under any circumstances can be traced more specifically to his adherence to a bourgeois life style, his interpretation of the Judaic ethic, and the early impact of the pessimistic *Weltanschauung* of Schopenhauer.

Some of the autobiographical and semiautobiographical writings of Horkheimer are most revealing in this respect. Although Horkheimer was disappointed with Weber's "value-free" political analysis of the 1919 events, he could never bring himself to make an unequivocal decision about the moral dilemma over violence. Therefore, the search for a solution, "the yearning for something entirely different," was a permanent theme of his entire life. In the late 1920s he reflected on the use of violence, on pacifism and harmony:

It is definitely more innocuous to reject violence in every form than to try to eliminate violence by the use of violence. A pacifist is always sure of himself; should he become the object of violence, he will choose not to take up the challenge. His life is thus more harmonious than that of the revolutionary. In situations of extreme misery he must appear to the revolutionary as an angel in the realm of hell. Just imagine the scene: the man of violence lies unconscious on the floor, conquered by his enemies and victimized by the opposing forces just as the masses he led experienced before him. Then he is assisted by an angel who is in the position to help him because the man never approved the practice of violence and was therefore spared of it! But then the thought keeps coming back: would not humanity have sunk deeper into barbarism without those in the course of history who set out to liberate it by the use of force? Is it possible that humanity needs such violence? Is it conceivable that we have to pay for our "harmony" with the renunciation of all practical help? These questions are enough to destroy one's peace of mind.[106]

Having lived up to his confession, as stated in this quotation, Horkheimer all his life remained a pacifist with a somewhat uneasy conscience.

The problem of alternative lifestyles, that is, the choice between a revolutionary path always threatened by misery, persecution, and jail or a comfortable academic career admired by students and honored by the authorities, was carefully weighed by Horkheimer, He wrote:

The development of the proletarian elite does not take place in an academic setting. Rather, it is brought about by battles in the factories and unions, by disciplinary punishments and some very dirty altercations (schmutzige Auseinandersetzung) within the parties and outside of them, by jail sentences and illegality. Students do not flock in large numbers there as they do to the lecture halls and laboratories of the bourgeoisie. The career of a revolutionary does not consist of banquets and honorary titles, of interesting research projects and professional salaries; more likely, it will acquaint him with misery, dishonor and jail and, at the end, uncertainty. These conditions are made bearable only by a super-human faith. Understandably, this way of life will not be the choice of those who are nothing more than clever.[107]

Horkheimer could never call up "the super-human faith" required for a revolutionary career under those circumstances. The later Horkheimer states explicitly his interpretation of Judaism as consisting of two basic themes: suffering (Leid) and the refusal to accept violence. In 1960 he categorically declared:

> No people has suffered more than the Jews. . . . The refusal to accept violence as a proof of the truth is a perennial trait in Jewish history, and Judaism has turned the suffering it endured in consequence in its own unity and permanence. . . . Suffering and hope have become inseparable in Judaism.[108]

In light of this summarized statement of Horkheimer, it is easy to trace this Judaic theme throughout the earlier phases of Critical Theory. It was definitely there in 1933: "Past injustice will never be made up; the suffering of past generations receives no compensation."[109] It is reiterated in a reformulated version four years later: "And even after the new society shall have come into existence, the happiness of its members will not make up for the wretchedness of those who are being destroyed in our contemporary society."[110] After Auschwitz, the culmination of the theme in the following declaration is understandable: "The real individuals of our time are the martyrs who have gone through infernos of suffering and degredation. . . . The anonymous martyrs of the concentration camps are the symbols of humanity that is striving to be born. The task of philosophy is to translate what they have done into language that will be heard. . . ."[111] In the same vein, the cofounder of the Frankfurt School, Adorno, wrote: "The need to lend a voice to suffering is a condition of all truth. For suffering is objectivity that weighs upon the subject; its most subjective experience, its expression, is objectively conveyed."[112]

SCHOPENHAUER'S INFLUENCE

The pessimism of Critical Theory rested on Horkheimer's inability to find an agent of socio-historical transformation, and his lifelong preoccupation with Schopenhauer.

Schopenhauer was the first real "bourgeois" of German philosophy. His career differed from those of all other earlier German philosophers. Throughout his life he was free of financial problems, travelled all over Europe, and felt no pressure to pursue an academic career; he was independently wealthy— a capitalist "rentier." (The close biographical agreement between Horkheimer and Schopenhauer might be noted: both were from an upper bourgeois social background that gave them lifelong, financial independence, and they both turned to philosophy after a short apprenticeship in business.)

In terms of philosophy, Schopenhauer has usually been considered the first representative of philosophical irrationalism. Although his main work, *The World as Will and Idea*, was published in 1818, his real impact commenced only after the defeat of the 1848 German bourgeois-democratic revolution. The basic sociological fact of German development after 1848 was the bourgeoisie's renunciation of any claim to political power in exchange for free capitalist development.[113]

Schopenhauer's philosophy, an "indirect apologetics of capitalism," (Lukács) explains all the negative aspects of capitalist society as eternal features of the general human condition. Consequently, the fight against the evils of capitalism is declared to be a senseless and hopeless endeavor. This tenet leads to the kernel of Schopenhauer's philosophy, his *pessimism*, which is a justification of the senselessness of all political activity. Instead of activism, contemplation is suggested. This is the basic social function of his philosophy of "indirect apologetics."[114]

Horkheimer acknowledges his debt to Schopenhauer and comments on the primacy and dominant influence of Schopenhauer's philosophy on him: "My first acquaintance with philosophy was with the work of Schopenhauer. My relationship to the teachings of Hegel and Marx. . . could not obliterate my encounter with his [Schopenhauer's] philosophy."[115] Horkheimer's relation to Schopenhauer is most clearly manifested in his pessimism about the society of the future. Horkheimer claims that perfect justice can never be realized in history, because, even if a better society replaces the present disorder, the past misery is not undone. Consequently, Critical Theory has always contained an element of sadness. Even after the new society is realized, the happiness of its members cannot compensate for the misery of those who are presently being destroyed in contemporary society. (Later Adorno called his science "sad science" [*traurige Wissenschaft*] as opposed to Nietzsche's "gay science" [*fröhliche Wissenschaft*].)[116]

Horkheimer always had a high esteem for Schopenhauer, "the clairvoyant pessimist" who anticipated the "dialectic of enlightenment," the historic process that was to become the main theme of Horkheimer and Adorno's philosophy of history in the middle period (1940s) of Critical Theory. It was Schopenhauer who

> saw things too clearly to exclude the possibility of historical improvement. The end of almost all manual labor, especially of hard physical labor, is something he foresaw more precisely than most of the economists of his day. But he also suspected the result of such a change. He took technical, economic and social improvements into account; but from the very beginning he perceived other consequences: the blind devotion to success and a setback for a peaceful course of events. In sum, he saw the dialectic of enlightenment.[117]

Schopenhauer measured the world in terms of its professed ideals and found it wanting. A conservative theorist can be just as critical as a revolutionary Marxist, argued the later Horkheimer, pointing out that Marx's protest was made when the aims of the bourgeois revolution—*liberté, égalité, fraternité*—had been realized only for a minority in a capitalist society. Although in the 1930s Horkheimer could still envision a proletarian revolution in Germany as an alternative to National Socialism, his vision of a successful revolution was marred by serious doubts. The later Horkheimer reflects: 'I was already sceptical at that time that a Marxian proletarian solidarity would ultimately lead to the right society.'[118]

The underlying pessimism of Critical Theory echoes

Schopenhauer's scepticism, which holds that a radical change in the world faces almost insurmountable difficulties. Horkheimer writes:

> It might seem a wonderful objective that future generations will live a happier and more intelligent life on earth than today's generation does under the present bloody and stupefying conditions. But ultimately even those future generations will disappear and the world will continue in its orbit as if nothing happened.[119]

It should be emphasized that this point is not marginal to Critical Theory. Horkheimer is convinced that even "future generations. . .will irrevocably pass away (*vergänglich*) and at the end nothingness triumphs over happiness (*Freude*)."[120]

Because the Schopenhauerian notion is that all satisfaction has a negative character and consequently only pain and suffering have a positive character, the idea of love for humanity is characterized by an all-pervading pessimism. Thus there cannot be a joyous coactivity between human beings. Love for humanity is manifested solely as *Mitleid* (universal solidarity and compassion). *Mitleid* is the only ethical motivation. Hence, Schopenhauerian ethics—and Horkheimerian ethics, too—have a passive, sorrowful bent. The notion of *Mitleid* is mainly attributed to the animal world, and Schopenhauer sees it almost as a metaphysical duty; he states that cruelty to animals is never a mark of a good man. He considers the moral teachings of Christianity to be deficient in their neglect of the animal world.

Horkheimer shares with Schopenhauer this theme of *Mitleid* with all suffering creatures, human and nonhuman. He writes in 1933, the year fascism triumphed in Germany: "Men might. . . overcome pain and illness. . . but in nature the reign of suffering and death will continue (*in der Natur aber herrscht weiter das Leiden und der Tod*)."[121] This theme might have come both from Schopenhauer and from Judaism, but its pessimistic tone suggests that its source is more likely the former, since in the Old Testament, the prophet Isaiah foresees a world of perfect reconciliation in which "the wolf shall dwell with the lamb, and the leopard shall lie down with the kid. . . and the lion shall eat straw like the ox."[122] Whatever the origin of Horkheimer's *Mitleid* with the sufferings of animals and nature, the theme remained a permanent one for Horkheimer and Adorno.

JUDAIC INFLUENCES ON HORKHEIMER

It was not until the last phase of Horkheimer's lifework (and Adorno's as well) that explicit references to Judaism were made and indebtedness to Judaic thought was in any way indicated. However, if we accept Marx's dictum that "the tradition of all past generations weighs like a mountain on the minds of the living," then this factor of existential determination cannot be ignored, even if it is only latent in the Critical Theory of the 1930s.

Selma Stern's summary describes the post-Enlightenment situation best when "the Jew achieved some sort of synthesis between Judaism and European culture." At the end of the eighteenth century it was possible to achieve this synthesis because

> his [the Jew's] demand for civil, social and economic equality were in harmony with the literary, pedagogic and philosophical concepts of his age. The ideas of Reason and Enlightenment, of Deism and Humanism, the doctrines of Tolerance and Humanity were not foreign to the spirit of Judaism. It was not difficult to reconcile and harmonize the moral doctrines of Kant with the moral doctrines of the Talmud, the fervor of Schiller with the fervor of the prophets. . . .[123]

As a result of this synthesis between "Judaism and the *Zeitgeist*," it was possible to try to understand one's own existence or "to penetrate the surrounding world and come to an understanding with its spiritual forces."[124]

Habermas tried to clarify the close and fruitful relationship between German idealism and Jewish philosophers in an essay in which he established a sort of "elective affinity" (*Wahlver-*

wandtschaft). He remarks that certain central motives of the basically Protestant German idealist philosophy are made more accessible through the experience of Jewish tradition. This is so because German idealist philosophy incorporated in itself a cabbalistic heritage; thus, the idealist philosophy in turn becomes more luminous when reflected in a mind that, even though it may not be aware of the fact, contains a shot of Jewish mysticism.[125]

Franz Rosenzweig in his work, *Der Stern der Erlösung* (1921), undertook a new interpretation of German idealism from the standpoint of Jewish mysticism.[126] When Rosenzweig writes that true philosophy is that which cannot "ignore the scream of despairing humanity," we are reminded of the young Horkheimer's fictional hero Jochai: "The intellectual victory of Private Jochai would bring salvation for his fellow man, for the 'desperate slaves.'"[127] Redemption is one of the central categories of Judaic thought. In rejecting the war, Horkheimer went one step beyond pacifism in saying that he did not want to belong to any nation, that being a human being is enough for him. True enough, he did not identify the cause and source of his feelings. However, Franz Rosenzweig wrote a letter from the front, at the very same time that Horkheimer wrote of Jochai, that identified the reason for his own feelings:

> Because the Jews stand already beyond the antitheses of world history and particularly homeland and belief, heaven and earth, antitheses that govern the actions of nations, they do not need wars any more.[128]

Horkheimer's early realization of what he expected of philosophy and a university career were directed toward the problems of society and humanity. Habermas very convincingly argues the why of Horkheimer's interest:

> The Jews have experienced society as a limiting and threatening force more keenly than anybody else, and it followed that their life-experience served as a sociological training. . . . And so it happened that Jews dominated German sociology since the days of Ludwig Gumplowicz.[129]

If Horkheimer perceives no possibility of praxis, he can still cling to the yearning for justice and truth. Herein lies the direct link between Horkheimer and Hermann Cohen, one of the greatest German-Jewish philosophers at the turn of the century. It might be added parenthetically that both Horkheimer and Adorno were students of another neo-Kantian thinker, Hans Cornelius, under whom they wrote their dissertations.

Neo-Kantianism was the dominant philosophical school in Germany around the turn of the century. Its basic slogan was "back to Kant," and its aim was to make philosophy scientific. Helmholtz, an eminent physicist and physiologist, restated the epistemological question of space and spatial perceptions; and in the work of Hermann Cohen "neo-Kantianism reached its climax" (Cassirer). The two branches of neo-Kantianism are the Marburg school and the Baden school. In the latter, Windelband and Rickert, building on the work of Dilthey, restated the notion of a sharp distinction between natural and cultural-social sciences; they attempted to work out a systematic epistemological foundation for the latter.

Hermann Cohen (1842–1918) was the founder of the Marburg or natural scientific branch of neo-Kantianism, and Paul Natorp and Ernst Cassirer became its other most outstanding representatives. Cohen not only conducted an in-depth analysis of Kantian philosophy and transformed it in the process, but, toward the end of his career, he introduced his own philosophical system in the work of *Logik der reinen Erkenntnis* (1902). Relatively less known is Cohen's interest in the significance of Judaism for the religious progress of mankind, a topic that he discussed in many essays during his life and that culminated in his posthumous *Religion der Vernunft aus den Quellen des Judentums* (*Religion of Reason from the Sources of Judaism*).

Cohen's numerous treatises on Kant and his expositions of Kantian philosophy were based on his view of philosophy as a science, based on the laws of logic. He was more consistent and therefore more successful than Kant in applying the transcendental critical method in ethics. Cohen's critical methodology made the logical science of jurisprudence the basis for ethics. Judaism proved to be as strong a philosophical influence on Cohen as Kantian philosophy, and he strove to prove an intimate relationship between these two, especially in regard to ethical teachings. One of the main similarities lies in the primacy of reason.

Furthermore, both Judaism and Kant base their ethics on voluntarism (although supplemented by "commandments," that is, ethical legislation). However, their origins of ethical legislation differ: whereas Kant designates creative reason as the source, Judaism derives the law from God.

Cohen wrote many essays relating Kant and Judaism, the most important one entitled "Innere Bezeihungen der Kantischen Philosophie zum Judentum" (Intimate Relationships between Kantian Philosophy and Judaism). All these essays are collected in the book *Jüdische Schriften (Judaic Writings)*.[130] Here Cohen states among others that Kant's categorical imperative is "in the blood of the Jew" because it too affirms the dignity of human beings without exploitation that is explicitly stated in the social legislation of Judaism:

> The prophets would indeed not have been the originators of true political ethics had they not taught the self-purpose of man in so aggressive a manner, and had they not given their blood for it. Their accomplishment is the social legislation of the Pentateuch, the greatest creation of social-ethical idealism, which has not remained a mere utopia.[131]

Cohen points out that Judaism couples social justice with peace to form the basic ingredients of messianic era. Social justice and peace, as we have seen, were the two main concerns of Horkheimer's early writings.

> Yearning for God means yearning for salvation, for deliverance from the constricting burden of feelings of guilt. This yearning stems from anxiety, which might compel man to flee himself, to lose his way. Thus, yearning for God is equal to man's natural impulse not to fall into despair but to cling to the anchorage of his self-confidence so that he can save himself

from desperation and self-condemnation. This is to say, yearning is nothing less than the hope for rescue in a threatening
death-struggle.

However, Horkheimer's yearning for social justice became increasingly tempered by pessimism. He wrote in 1933 that "past
injustice will never be made up; the suffering of past generations
receives no compensation." In the same vein, he restated the idea
in 1937: "And even after the new society shall have come into
existence, the happiness of its members will not make up for the
wretchedness of those who are being destroyed in our contemporary society."[132]
    As we have seen, the language of Critical Theory even in the
1930s is saturated with biblical terminology such as true, truth,
false, salvation (*Erlösung*), suffering (*Leid*), compassion (*Mitleid*), and reconciliation (*Versöhnung*). These remarks lead to
another aspect of Horkheimer's Judaism, which is of immediate
relevance, the problem of language. George Steiner remarks that
the European Jew came late to secular literature. Since languages are the codifications of immemorial reflexes and communal experiences, the Jew, even if he passed from the Hebrew
into any of the European languages via Yiddish, "had to slip into
the garb and glove" of his oppressors.[133] Jewish writers tried to
weld their legacy, that is the uniqueness of their social and
historical condition and their collective experience, to a borrowed idiom. The most obvious example is Franz Kafka, the Jew
living in Prague, a Czech city of the Austrian-Hungarian Empire,
who wrote in German. He was conscious of this specific form of
alienation and was tormented by it. In 1911 he wrote in his diary:

> Yesterday it occurred to me that I did not always love my
> mother as she deserved and as only I could have loved
> her because the German language prevented it. The Jewish
> mother is not "*Mutter*", to call her "*Mutter*" makes her a little
> comic. . . . For the Jew, "*Mutter*" is specifically German, it un-
> consciously connotes Christian splendor together with Chris-
> tian coldness; also, the Jewish woman who is called "*Mutter*"
> therefore becomes not only comic but strange. . . . I believe

that it is solely the memories of the Ghetto that preserve the
Jewish family, for the word "Vater" does not approximate the
Jewish father either.[134]

Horkheimer and Adorno, also well aware of the problem of
language, were concerned with it throughout their lives. Independent of Kafka, Horkheimer expressed the very same ideas in
almost identical terms at the same time in *My Political Confession*:

> Had I just arrived from my homeland of Palestine, and in an
> amazingly short time mastered the rudiments of writing in
> German, this essay could not have been more difficult to write.
> The style here does not bear the mark of a facile genius. I tried
> to communicate with the help of what I read and heard, sub-
> consciously assembling fragments of a language that springs
> from a strange mentality. What else can a stranger do? But my
> strong will prevailed because my message deserves to be said
> regardless of its stylistic shortcomings.[135]

There is obviously more to this Horkheimer statement than the
worry that he would lack the power and poignancy to express
perfectly what he wished to say. The existential character of the
passage is evident. Horkheimer shares with Walter Benjamin,
Kurt Tucholsky, Karl Kraus—not to speak of Kafka—the preoccupation with language[136] and the feeling of either homelessness or estrangement. Again it was Kafka who summarized the
problem best in one of his letters to Max Brod, written in 1921.
Kafka spoke about the relationship of the young Jews of his time
to their Jewishness, and about "the terrible inner situation of this
generation." They want to become German writers (or intellectuals) and wish to get away from Judaism but "with their hind
legs they remained stuck with the Jewishness of their fathers,
while their front legs were unable to find new ground. The
despair about this was their inspiration. . . ."[137] (Problems of
language specifically relating to Adorno are discussed in
Chapter 3.)

The Critical Theory of Max Horkheimer

NOTES

The following abbreviations are used throughout the book:

ZfS: *Zeitschrift für Sozialforschung*
SPSS: *Studies in Philosophy and Social Sciences*
KZfSS: *Kölner Zeitschrift für Soziologie und Sozialpsychologie*

1. The playwright Bertolt Brecht, who was acquainted with members of the Frankfurt School and participated in several discussions in their California exile, wrote in his diary on May 12, 1942: "Lunch with Eisler at Horkheimer. Afterwards Eisler suggests the story of the Frankfurt Institute of sociology as topic for *The Tui Novel.*" Brecht had been engaged in the writing of a satirical portrayal of intellectuals in the Weimer Republic, with the working title, *The Tui Novel. Tui* was defined by him as "the intellectual of this era of markets and commodities." Brecht continued: "A rich old man, the grain speculator Weil dies, disturbed by the miseries on earth. In his will he leaves a large sum for the establishment of an institute to investigate the sources of that misery, which is, of course, he himself." Brecht's novel was never completed. (Bertolt Brecht, *Arbeitsjournal 1938–1942,* Werner Hecht (Ed.) vol. I, Frankfurt am Main, 1973, p. 443).
2. Carl Grünberg, "Festrede, gehalten zur Einweihung des Instituts für Sozialforschung an der Universität Frankfurt a.M. am 22. Juni 1924," *Frankfurter Universitätsreden,* 1924, p. 10.
3. *Ibid.,* p. 7.
4. Unpublished, Horkheimer Archives, quoted in Helmut Gumnior and Rudolf Ringguth, *Max Horkheimer in Selbstzeugnissen und Bilddokumenten,* Reinbek bei Hamburg, 1973, p. 17.
5. *Ibid.,* p. 7.
6. Max Horkheimer, *Die Sehnsucht nach dem ganz Anderen,* Hamburg, 1970, p. 62.
7. Max Horkheimer, *Aus der Pubertät. Novellen und Tagebuchblätter,* München, 1974, p. 22.
8. Gumnior-Ringguth, pp. 18–27.
9. Max Horkheimer, "Nachwort," in *Porträts deutsch-jüdischer Geistesgeschichte,* Thilo Koch (Ed.) Köln, 1961, pp. 256–7.
10. Horkheimer, *Aus der Pubertät,* p. 14.
11. *Ibid.,* pp. 19–20.
12. *Ibid.,* p. 257.

13. Quoted in *Gumnior-Ringguth*, p. 24. Hans Cornelius is remembered in the history of philosophy as the philosopher who was denounced by Lenin as "this police sergeant in a professorial chair." See, V.I. Lenin, *Materialism and Empirio-Criticism*, Moscow, 1952, pp. 223–224.

14. *Ibid.*, p. 23.

15. Horkheimer, *Aus der Pubertät*, p. 20.

16. V. I. Lenin, *Selected Works*, Vol. VI, New York, 1929, p. 17.

17. Karl Korsch, *Marxismus und Philosophie*, Leipzig, 1923; and Georg Lukács, *Geschichte und Klassenbewusstsein*, Berlin, 1923. See also, István Mészaros, *Lukács' Concept of Dialectic*, London, 1972, and G. H. R. Parkinson (Ed.), *Georg Lukács, The Man, His Work and His Ideas*, London, 1970, and Paul Breines, *Lukács and Korsch 1910–1932. A Study in the Genesis and Impact of Geschichte und Klassenbewusstsein and Marxismus und Philosophie*, unpub. diss. The University of Wisconsin, 1972, and Mihály Vajda, "Karl Korsch's 'Marxism and Philosophy'" in Dick Howard and Karl E. Klare (Eds.), *The Unknown Dimension. European Marxism since Lenin*, New York, 1972, pp. 131–146.

18. Georg Lukács, *Geschichte. . .*, p. 94.

19. *Ibid.*, p. 54. For a modern assessment of this work see István Mészáros (Ed.), *Aspects of History and Class Consciousness*, London, 1971.

20. Max Horkheimer, "Ein neuer Ideologiebegriff?," *Grünberg Archiv*, Vol. 15, 1930, p. 33.

21. Max Horkheimer, "Traditionelle und kritische Theorie," *ZfS*, VI, 2 (1937), p. 278.

22. Theodor W. Adorno, *Negative Dialektik*, Frankfurt am Main, Suhrkamp Verlag, 1966, p. 147.

23. Heinrich Regius (Horkheimer's pseudonym), *Dämmerung. Notizen in Deutschland*, Zürich, 1934, pp. 122–130.

24. Max Horkheimer, "Die gegenwärtige Lage der Sozialphilosophie und die Aufgaben eines Instituts für Sozialforschung," *Frankfurter Universitätsreden*, 1931, pp. 3–16.

25. Edward Shils, "Tradition, Ecology, and Institution in the History of Sociology," *Daedalus*, 99 (Fall, 1970), p. 777.

26. Horkheimer, "Die gegenwärtige Lage," p. 3. For a brief summary of the state of German sociology during the Weimar Republic see Karl Mannheim, "German Sociology (1918–1933)," in *Essays on*

The Critical Theory of Max Horkheimer 63

Sociology and Social Psychology, Paul Kecskemeti (Ed.) London, 1953, pp. 209–228.

27. Max Horkheimer, "Vorwort," *ZfS*, I (1932), p. III.
28. *ZfS*, VI, 1 (1937), p. 1.
29. Rene Descartes, *Discourse on Method and Other Writings*, Baltimore, 1968, p. 41.
30. *Ibid.*, p. 41.
31. Max Horkheimer, "Traditionelle . . .," *ZfS*, VI, 2 (1937), p. 247.
32. *Ibid.*, p. 251.
33. *Ibid.*, p. 252.
34. *Ibid.*, p. 292.
35. *Ibid.*, p. 264.
36. *Ibid.*, p. 262.
37. *Ibid.*, p. 254.
38. *Ibid.*, p. 261/n. 1.
39. *Ibid.*, p. 271.
40. *Ibid.*, p. 262.
41. The organistic model of society has haunted sociology throughout its history from Saint Simon via Spencer to Talcott Parsons. To Saint Simon, the study of society is general physiology that "addresses itself to considerations of a higher order. It towers above individuals, looking on them merely as organs of the social body, whose organic functions it must examine, just as specialized physiology studies those of individuals." Emile Durkheim, *Socialism*, New York, 1962, p. 126. Parsons maintains that "developments in biological theory and in the social sciences have created firm grounds for accepting the fundamental continuity of society and culture as part of a more general theory of the evolution of living systems." Talcott Parsons, *The System of Modern Societies*, Englewood Cliffs, N.J. 1971, p. 2.
42. Horkheimer, "Traditionelle. . .," p. 264.
43. Max Horkheimer, "Philosophie und kritische Theorie," *ZfS*, VI, 3, p. 630.
44. Horkheimer, "Traditionelle. . .," p. 265.
45. *Ibid.*, p. 267
46. *Ibid.*, p. 267.
47. *Ibid.*, p. 291.
48. *Ibid.*, p. 271.

49. *Ibid.*, p. 284.
50. *Ibid.*, p. 288.
51. *Ibid.*, p. 268.
52. *Ibid.*, p. 269.
53. *Ibid.*, p. 276.
54. *Ibid.*, p. 274.
55. *Ibid.*, pp. 290–291.
56. *Ibid.*, p. 291.
57. *Ibid.*, p. 291.
58. Max Horkheimer, "Materialismus und Metaphysik," *ZfS II*, 1 (1933), p. 31n.
59. Horkheimer, "Traditionelle. . .," p. 255.
60. *Ibid.*, p. 255.
61. Horkheimer, "Materialismus. . .," p. 24.
62. Marcuse was more outspoken on that issue; change must be brought about by a structural transformation of society, as he expressed it in the *Zeitschrift* in 1936. He wrote that change must come "not through an act of education or of the moral renewal of man but through an economic and political process encompassing the disposal over the means of production by the community, the reorientation of the productive process towards the needs and wants of the whole society. . . the active participation of the individuals in the administration of the whole. When all present subjective and objective potentialities of development have been unbound, the needs and wants themselves will change." Cf. Herbert Marcuse, "Zur Kritik des Hedonismus," *ZfS*, VI, 1937, pp. 55–89. Later, at the height of the worldwide student protest movement of the late 1960s, Marcuse reversed the order of the change and advocated the possibility, even the necessity, of changing consciousness first. Cf. Herbert Marcuse, *An Essay on Liberation*, Boston, 1963.
63. Horkheimer, "Materialismus. . .," p. 9.
64. There are two main reasons for the fad of contrasting the young Marx with the mature one. First, the post World War II years favored a more humanistic Marxism in the West as opposed to the dogmatic and unimaginative Stalinist Marxism. It was also easier to combine a humanistic Marxism with other philosophies, such as existentialism, as Sartre had attempted to do. Second, the centerpiece, the connecting element of the Marxian theoretical edifice, the *Grundrisse*, was not made available to the larger public until its 1953 East German publication. The

translator of the 1973 English language edition says that only three copies of the original 1939 Moscow publication reached the West. The *Grundrisse* continues to discuss the problem of alienation and thus reaches back to *The Economic and Philosophic Manuscripts of 1884* of the young Marx. Yet it also presents the first systematic analysis of capitalist society in terms of political economy and thereby represents the link to the mature Marx's *Das Kapital*. As the late Georg Lichtheim argued correctly, the discovery of the *Grundrisse* makes it impossible to dichotomize Marx into a young Hegelian existentialist philosopher and a mature Ricardian economist, because the *Grundrisse* marks the point at which the Hegelian and the Ricardian in Marx interpenetrate.

65. See Karl Marx, *Contribution to the Critique of Hegel's Philosophy of Right*, Karl Marx and Frederick Engels, *The Holy Family* or *Critique of Critical Critique*, Moscow, 1956, and Karl Marx, *The Economic and Philosophic Manuscripts of 1844*, New York, 1964.

66. Karl Marx and Friedrich Engels, *Werke*, Vol. 3, Berlin (East), 1962, p. 18.

67. Karl Marx, *A Contribution to the Critique of Political Economy*, New York, 1970, p. 20.

68. Noone could deny the philosophical interest of the mature Marx when reading the chapter on "The Fetishism of Commodities. . ." in *Das Kapital*. Neither could one overlook the moral indignation of Marx, again in *Das Kapital*, when discussing the enclosure movement and the role of slave trade in "The So-called Primitive Accumulation" chapter. His closing sentence reads: "If money, according to Augier, 'comes into the world with a congenital blood-stain on one cheek', capital comes dripping from head to foot, from every pore, with blood and dirt." (Karl Marx, *Capital*, Vol. 1, New York, p. 760). Thus the massive volumes of *Das Kapital* represent the history, sociology, and political economy of capitalist society.

69. See Alvin W. Gouldner, *The Coming Crisis of Western Sociology*, New York, 1970, pp. 11ff.

70. Rejecting the scientism of the positivists and insisting on the uniqueness of the cultural and historical sciences and their differences from the physical sciences, they also rejected the Marxian ideas of a goal towards which history is moving. At the same time Weber responded positively to influences from both these traditions, while seeking to establish a third orientation.

71. In 1866 Marx wrote to Engels in a letter: "I am now reading Comte, because the British and French make so much fuss over that guy (*Kerl*). What they are taken by is the encyclopaedic *la synthese*. But it is a miserable one compared to Hegel, though Comte is superior to him as a professional mathematician and physicist, that is, he is superior in details, yet Hegel is greater overall. And this shit-positivism (*Scheisspositivismus*) was published in 1832!" *Marx-Engels Gesamtausgabe (MEGA)*, Part 3, Berlin Vol. 3, 1931–1932, p. 345.

72. Max Weber, *Gesammelte Aufsätze zur Soziologie und Sozialpolitik*, Tübingen, Verlag von J. C. B. Mohr (Paul Siebeck), 1924, pp. 504–505.

73. For recent statements see Peter Berger (Ed.), *Marxism and Sociology. Views from Eastern Europe*, New York, 1969; Peter Bollhagen, *Soziologie und Geschichte*, Berlin, 1966; Gabor Kiss, *Marxismus als Soziologie*, Reinbek bei Hamburg, 1971; Georges Gurvitch, *La Sociologie de Karl Marx*, Paris, 1959; and Henri Lefebvre, *The Sociology of Marx*, New York, 1969. Alexander Vucinich, "Marx and Parsons in Soviet Sociology," *The Russian Review*, *33*, 1. (Jan. 1974), pp. 1–19.

74. Lenin and Bukharin used historical materialism and Marxist sociology as identical terms. See Nikolai Bukharin, *Historical Materialism. A System of Sociology*, Ann Arbor, Mich., 1969.

75. Marx and Engels insisted on this characteristic of their science: "The premises from which we begin are not arbitrary ones, not dogmas, but real premises from which abstraction can only be made in the imagination. They are the real individuals, their activity and the material conditions under which they live, both these which they find already existing and those produced by their activity. These premises can thus be verified in a purely empirical way." And again Marx and Engels assert that "Where speculation ends. . .there real, positive science begins." Karl Marx and Frederick Engels, *The German Ideology*, New York, 1970, pp. 42 and 48.

76. The interpretation of the Marxian emphasis on objective lawfulness versus human action led later to two divergent post-Marxian orientations: the mechanistic and the activistic. Kautsky, Plekhanov, and Bukharin of the first school overemphasized the objective, lawful determination of socio-historical movements. The other camp, the activists—Lenin, Rosa Luxemburg, and Antonio Gramsci—stressed the role of conscious human activity in the determination of historical events.

77. Marx and Engels summed up: "This conception of history depends on our ability to expound the real process of production, starting out from the material production of life itself, and to comprehend the form of intercourse connected with this and created by this mode of production (i.e., civil society in its various stages) as the basis of all history; and to show it in its action as State, to explain all the different theoretical products and forms of consciousness, religion, philosophy, ethics, etc., and then trace their origins and growth from that basis; by which means, of course, *the whole thing can be depicted in its totality* (and therefore, too, the reciprocal action of these various sides on one another) (italics mine).[11] Karl Marx and Frederick Engels, *The German Ideology*, New York, 1970, p. 58.

78. See particularly Frederick Engels, *Anti-Dühring*, Moscow, 1962; Frederick Engels, *Ludwig Feuerbach and the Outcome of Classical German Philosophy*, New York, 1967; and V. I. Lenin, *Materialism and Empiriocriticism*, Moscow, 1952. For modern assessments see, *Épistémologie et Marxisme*, Paris, 1972 and *Marxistische Erkenntnistheorie. Texte zu ihrem Forschungsstand in den sozialistischen Ländern*, Hans Jörg Sandkühler (Ed.) Stuttgart, 1973.

79. For definition of "ideal-type" see Max Weber, *The Methodology of the Social Sciences*, E. A. Shils and H. A. Finch (Trans. and Ed.) New York, 1949, pp. 90, 93, 103.

80. Max Weber, *Economy and Society*, Guenther Roth and Claus Wittich (Eds.) Vol. 2, New York, 1968, pp. 904–905.

81. H. H. Gerth and C. Wright Mills (Transls. and Eds.) *From Max Weber; Essays in Sociology*, New York, 1958, p. 126.

82. *Ibid.*, p. 126.

83. *Ibid.*, p. 127.

84. *Ibid.*, p. 127.

85. See Footn. 99 in Wolfgang J. Mommsen, *Max Weber und die deutsche Politik 1890–1920*, 2nd ed., Tübingen, 1974, p. 332.

86. See Marianne Weber, *Max Weber. A Biography*, Harry Zohn (Transl. and Ed.) New York, 1975, p. 648.

87. *Ibid.*, pp. 465–466. See also Paul Honigsheim, *On Max Weber*, New York, 1968, pp. 24–28; Karl Jaspers, "Heidelberger Erinnerungen," in *Heidelberger Jahrbücher*, V, 1961, pp. 1–10.

88. In Otto Stammer (Ed.) *Max Weber und die Soziologie heute*, Tübingen, 1965, pp. 65–66.

89. See Judith Marcus Tar, *Thomas Mann und Georg Lukács*, unpub-

lished dissertation for the German Dept. of the University of Kansas, 1976.

90. Georg Lukács, *Soul and Form*, Anna Bostock (Transl.) Cambridge, Mass., 1974, p. 17.

91. György Lukács, *Esztétikai Kultura*, Budapest, 1913, p. 26.

92. Lukács, *Soul and Form*, p. 16.

93. *Ibid.*, p. 18.

94. *Idem, Esztétikai Kultura*, p. 28.

95. *Ibid.*, p. 27.

96. *Ibid.*, p. 27.

97. Karl Marx, *Early Writings*, T. B. Bottomore (Transl. and Ed.), New York, 1964, p. 37.

98. György Lukács, "A bolsevizmus mint erkölcsi probléma," in *Szabadgondolat*, (December 1918), pp. 228–232.

99. I am indebted to Mr. Tibor Gergely, painter and illustrator, New York, for sharing with me his recollections of those times with the "Lukács-circle."

100. Georg Lukács, "Tactics and Ethics," in *Political Writings 1919–1929*, translated from the German version by Michael McColgan, London, 1972, p. 11.

101. *Idem., Geschichte und Klassenbewusstsein*, Studien über marxistische Dialektik, Neuwied-Berlin, 1968, p. 397.

102. Ernst Bloch, *Geist der Utopie*, München, 1918, pp. 405–406.

103. Karl Marx and Frederick Engels, *The German Ideology*, C. J. Arthur (Ed.), New York, 1970, pp. 94–95.

104. See Judith Marcus Tar, *Thomas Mann und Georg Lukács*, cf., Footn. 89; further see *Paul Ernst und Georg Lukács. Dokumente einer Freundschaft*, Karl August Kutzbach (Ed.), Emsdetten/Westf., 1974.

105. See Chapter 2 "Zauberberg als Zeitroman," in Judith Marcus Tar, *Thomas Mann und Georg Lukács*, cf., notes 89 and 104.

106. Heinrich Regius (Horkheimer's pseudonym), *Dämmerung. Notizen in Deutschland*, p. 22.

107. *Ibid.*, pp. 74–5.

108. Max Horkheimer, *Critique of Instrumental Reason*, Lectures and Essays since the end of World War II, Matthew J. O'Connell et al., (Transl.) New York, 1974, p. 122.

109. *Idem., Critical Theory*, Matthew J. O'Connell et al., (Transl.) New York, 1972, p. 26.

110. *Ibid.*, p. 251.

111. *Idem.*, *Eclipse of Reason*, New York, 1947, p. 161.

112. Theodor W. Adorno, *Negative Dialektik*, p. 27. For sociological and philosophical discussions of violence, see Christian von Ferber, *Die Gewalt in der Politik*, Stuttgart, 1970; Walter Benjamin, *Zur Kritik der Gewalt und andere Aufsätze*, Frankfurt am Main, 1965; and Hannah Arendt, "On Violence," in *Crises of the Republic*, New York, 1972.

113. See Frederick Engels, *The Peasant War in Germany*, New York, 1973, pp. 23–25. For a recent sociological treatment, see Barrington Moore, *Social Origins of Dictatorship and Democracy*, Boston, 1966.

114. See Georg Lukács, *Die Zerstörung der Vernunft*, Berlin (East), 1954, pp. 156–197 and Franz Mehring, *Gesammelte Schriften und Aufsätze*, Vol. 6, *Zur Geschichte der Philosophie*, Berlin, 1929–33.

115. Max Horkheimer, *Kritische Theorie*, Vol. 1, Frankfurt am Main, 1968, p. XII.

116. Theodor W. Adorno, *Minima Moralia*, Frankfurt am Main, 1969, p. 7.

117. Max Horkheimer and Theodor W. Adorno, *Sociologica II*, Frankfurt am Main, 1962, p. 126.

118. Max Horkheimer, *Die Sehnsucht* . . ., p. 55.

119. *Idem.*, "Bemerkungen zur philosophischen Anthropologie," *ZfS*, *IV*, 1 (1935), p. 8.

120. *Ibid.*, p. 8.

121. *Idem.*, "Materialismus und Moral," ZFS II, 2 (1933), p. 184.

122. *The Holy Bible. King James Version*, New York, n.d., p. 559. Friedrich Nietzsche, who greatly influenced Horkheimer's and Adorno's thinking, also dealt with the theme of *Mitleid* in his *The Genealogy of Morals*, New York, 1956, pp. 154 ff.

123. Selma Stern, *The Court Jew*, A Contribution to the History of the Period of Absolutism in Central Europe, Ralph Weiman (Transl.) Philadelphia, 1950, p. 241.

124. *Ibid.*, p. 242.

125. Jürgen Habermas, "Der deutsche Idealismus der jüdischen Philosophen, " in *Philosophisch-politische Profile*, Frankfurt am Main, 1971, pp. 37–66.

126. Franz Rosenzweig, *The Star of Redemption*, Boston, 1972.

127. Max Horkheimer, *Aus der Pubertät* . . ., p. 257.

70The Frankfurt School

128.Quoted in J. Habermas, "Der deutsche Idealismus . . .," pp. 41–42.

129. *Ibid.*, p. 58. See also Georg Simmel, "The Stranger," in *The Sociology of Georg Simmel*, Kurt H. Wolff (Ed.) New York, 1950, pp. 402–408; and Thorstein Veblen, "The Intellectual Pre-eminence of Jews in Modern Europe," in *Thorstein Veblen. Selections from his Work*, Bernard Rosenberg (Ed.) New York, 1963, pp. 91–100.

130. Hermann Cohen, *Jüdische Schriften*, 3 vols., Berlin, 1924.

131. *Ibid.*, Vol. 1, pp. 300–301.

132. Max Horkheimer, *Aus der Pubertät* . . ., p. 22. *Idem.*, "Materialismus und Metaphysik," *ZfS II*, 1 (1933), p. 16; and "Philosophie und kritische Theorie," *ZfS, VI*, 3 (1937), p. 630. I am thankful to Professor Michael Landmann who called my attention to the connection of Horkheimer's ideas with Talmudic thought.

133. Georg Steiner, *Language and Silence*, New York, 1972, p. 125.

134. Franz Kafka, *Tagebücher 1910–1923*, New York, 1949, pp. 115–116.

135. Max Horkheimer, *Aus der Pubertät*. . ., p. 265. Franz Rosenzweig writes on the problem: "While every other people is one with its own language, while that language withers in its mouth the moment it ceases to be a people, the Jewish people never quite grows one with the languages it speaks. Even when it speaks the language of its host, a special vocabulary, or, at least a special selection from the general vocabulary, a special word order, its own feeling for what is beautiful or ugly in the language, betray that it is not its own." Franz Rosenzweig, *The Star of Redemption*, p. 301.

136. Walter Benjamin wrote to his friend, Gershom Scholem, in January 1930, that he gave up all hope for being able to learn Hebrew while in Germany. "From now on, his ambition will be directed toward becoming the most noted critic of German litera-ture." Quoted in Gershom Scholem, *Walter Benjamin, die Geschichte einer Freundschaft*, Frankfurt am Main, 1975, p. 200. cf. Klaus Peter Schulz, *Kurt Tucholsky in Selbstzeugnissen und Bilddokumenten*, Reinbek bei Hamburg, 1959. Shortly before his suicide, Tucholsky wrote in one of his letters: "I will never be able to write in another language—almost without exception it is an impossibility. . . . It is due to more than merely political developments. The world as we knew it and toiled for, is . . .

dead. One has to draw the appropriate conclusion. . . . (p. 165)."

137. See Franz Kafka, *Briefe 1902–1924*, New York, 1958, p. 337. Later in his letter, Kafka speaks mournfully of "those young Jews" who had entered the German literary language "boisterously or secretively or even masochistically appropriating foreign capital that they had not earned but, having hurriedly seized it, stolen."

TWO

THE MIDDLE PERIOD
OF CRITICAL THEORY:
THE CONFRONTATION
WITH FASCISM AND THE
CRITIQUE OF DOMINATION

This chapter describes the middle period of Critical Theory (1940–1950), its theoretical confrontation with fascism and its various attempts to explain its rise and its nature. The discussion begins with an examination of Horkheimer's account, in socioeconomic terms, of the rise of Nazism in Germany; then the discussion turns to the idea of the "dialectic of enlightenment" and Horkheimer's critique of modern science and its philosophy. The third part of the chapter provides a brief summary of The Authoritarian Personality.

THE THEORETICAL CONFRONTATION WITH FASCISM

The practical and theoretical confrontation with fascism—the most imminent phenomenon of the age, which constituted the greatest threat to the very existence and survival of the institute, its members, and all of Western civilization—gradually became the central issue for Critical Theory.* Interestingly enough, it paid no attention to the first variant, Italian fascism, which it perhaps considered marginal with regard to the mainstream of development of European societies. The theoretical confrontation with fascism had its stages and diversity of approaches. In the early 1930s, Critical Theory attempted to locate the roots of Nazism in the specific authoritarian features of German society in general and in its family structure in particular. The outcome of this endeavor was the Studien über Autorität und Familie (1936).[1] Many of its ideas were incorporated later in The Authoritarian Personality, which constitutes the third phase of Critical Theory's theory of fascism. In the first stage up to 1940, the theoretical position of the institute was close to that of orthodox Marxism as accepted by the 1935 Seventh Congress of the Comintern and based on the formulation of its secretary general, Georgi Dimitrov. In Dimitrov's definition, "fascism in

* In the following chapter, the terms Nazism and fascism are used interchangeably. In spite of its specific Italian origin, fascism became the general term.

74

power is the open terrorist dictatorship of the most reactionary, most chauvinistic and most imperialistic elements of finance capital."[2] Both Horkheimer and Marcuse expressed the idea that fascism is the natural outgrowth of bourgeois-liberal democracy. In the second stage, the phenomenon of fascism became part of an all embracing philosophy of history or despair closely related to Horkheimerian *Naturphilosophie*. In the third phase, the emphasis shifted to the individual, to his receptivity to fascism, to the "authoritarian personality." Now, a combination of Freudian psychoanalytic theory with empirical social research techniques was to give the answer.

FASCISM "THE HIGHEST STAGE OF CAPITALISM"

By 1939, it was clear to Horkheimer that the possibility of changing capitalist society to a socialist one had been unmasked as an illusion. The heirs of the free enterprise system could maintain their domination only by the abolition of the freedom of bourgeois-liberal democracy. Fascism was the natural and logical outcome of a capitalist society in its stage of permanent crisis: "He who will not speak of capitalism should keep silent of fascism too."[3] The new totalitarian order differs from its predecessor only in the fact that it has lost its inhibitions. Earlier, the economic process of capitalist society was seen as the reproduction of relations of domination meditated by "free contracts"—a relationship that was enforced through the inequality of property relationships. "The mediation has been removed now. . . Fascism is the truth of modern society which [Critical] Theory had in mind from the beginning."[4]

To identify fascism, there is, Horkheimer argued, no need for any revision of Marxian theory. Only the forms of domination have undergone certain modifications. Instead of scattered command positions in individual plants, there emerges the totalitarian domination of particular interests over the whole society. The situation is parallel to that of early capitalism: free

masses of people are available. In early capitalism they were
forced into the emerging manufacturing system, and today the
"fascist agitator organizes them against democratic systems." If
it turns out to be a success, it will be repeated on an international
scale. Horkheimer writes:

> The task in late capitalism is to remodel the population into a
> collectivity ready for any civilian and military purpose, so that
> it functions in the hands of the newly restructured ruling
> class.[5]

The term late capitalism (Spätkapitalismus), originally coined
by Werner Sombart 40 years earlier, later popularized by Marcuse, is used for the first time in Critical Theory. The composition of the ruling class has changed too. The most important
aspect of this change is the enlarged bureaucracy, which ac-
quired a certain degree of autonomy. Horkheimer thus points
to an important phenomenon which was presented more systematically two years later by James Burnham as "managerial
revolution," and reiterated and discussed by many authors ever
since.[6]

    The growth of size and differentiation of industrial enter-
prise has led to the rise of a new industrial bureaucracy whose
top echelons can pursue their own purpose with the capital of
the stockholders and even against them. Horkheimer sums up:
Liberalism cannot be reinstated. It left a demoralized proletariat
abandoned by its leaders. It left a situation in which the unemployed constitute a kind of amorphous class that invites organization from above, and it left a peasantry whose consciousness
and methods of production are backward when measured
against the level of technological developments. It also left cap-
tains of industry and generals of the army and administration
who came to a mutual understanding to take the new order into
their own hands.

    According to Horkheimer, the German workers, who pos-
sessed all the qualifications to create a new social order, were
defeated. After their leaders had been killed, they were betrayed
by their own bureaucratic party machinery. In purely economic

terms, the long-term chances for the survival of the new totalitarian system are good. That the dependence of the people on authority is a condition of stability was recognized earlier by thinkers such as Mandeville, de Sade, and de Bonald. Even the older Kant came close to these thinkers, who are usually considered antihumanists. Kant wrote:

> The origin of the highest authority is for the people from a practical viewpoint impenetrable, i.e., the subject should not reason about it . . . ("*Der Ursprung der obersten Gewalt ist für das Volk, das unter derselben steht, in praktischer Absicht unerforschlich: d.i. der Unterthan soll nicht über diesen Ursprung. . . werkthätig vernünfteln . . .*")[7]

The concentration of the means of production continues. Behind the facade of unity and harmony is anarchy. "The stability of fascism is based upon the alliances against revolution."[8] Nationalism and the idea of *Volksgemeinschaft* represent a continuity of the historical mood of 1914 and have been permitted to flourish as surrogates for revolution. Fascism goes beyond the socioeconomic conditions prior to its rise in a negative as well as in a positive sense: centralization of administration and a formal abolition of estates are fulfillments of bourgeois demands, accomplished long ago elsewhere.

Fascism is a worldwide phenomenon. "The confrontation between liberalism and the totalitarian state no longer runs along national boundaries. Fascism triumphs from within and from without."[9] For the first time in history, the whole world is moving politically in the same direction. Even in that part of Europe in which fascism is not dominant, there are societal forces that tend to move the administrative, judicial, and political apparatus in the authoritarian direction. "Fascism saved the right of disposal over the means of production for the minority which emerged from the competitive struggle as the most determined force."[10] That is the Horkheimerian expression of Dimitrov's definition of fascism as "the open terrorist dictatorship of the most reactionary, most chauvinistic and most imperialist elements of finance capital." Anticipating the thesis

of the *Dialektik der Aufklärung*, Horkheimer sees the French
Revolution as a system that contained its negation from the very
beginning.

> The French Revolution which signalled the political victory of
> the bourgeois economic order and gave the Jews emancipa-
> tion, was more ambivalent than one would think today. . . .The
> plans of Robespierre and Saint Just provided for elements of
> etatism, a strengthening of the bureaucratic apparatus, which
> came close to those of the authoritarian systems of the present
> era. The order which began in 1789 as progressive, contained
> from its very beginning the tendency toward national
> socialism.[11]

The emancipation of the Jews had its purely utilitarian aspect
because of the role of the Jews as the agents of money circulation.
Not ideas, but practical interests, determined the bourgeois.
Because of the structural changes of capitalism, this utilitarian
aspect does not exist any longer. The market has been replaced
by planning. The function of monetary manipulation is taken
over by the state, a situation that makes the function of the Jews
in capitalism superfluous. Horkheimer here seems to accept
Marx's thesis on the Jewish question.[12] Consequently, the state
manipulation of money turns into a brutal manipulation of those
who represent it. The Jews who now must flee into exile are
received and looked on with suspicion and/or resentment in
their hostland as were the *Ostjuden* (Eastern Jews) in Germany
with their accent and strange customs. The newcomers are not
welcomed. In spite of the good will of enlightened minds, they
encounter cold competition and a deep and aimless hatred of the
masses. The future is hopeless. "The hopes of the Jews connected with the outcome of WWII are not very promising. No
matter how the war ends, the uninterrupted militarization leads
the world into authoritarian and collectivistic life-forms."[13]
Horkheimer has no illusions about the antifascist Western
democracies and is deeply pessimistic about the future. "A great
part of the masses, which are led against the totalitarian states,

are basically susceptible to fascism. [*Ein grosser Teil der Massen, die man gegen die totalitären Staaten führt, fürchtet den Faschismus im Grunde nicht.*][14] If, after a long war, the old economic conditions are reinstated, the development is bound to repeat itself. Fascism has emerged not by accident.

Horkheimer's theory of fascism of the second phase ends in absolute despair. He concludes:

> There is nothing to be hoped from the alliance of the great powers. One cannot hope for the collapse of the totalitarian economy. . . . It is completely naive to persuade from abroad the German workers to overthrow the system. . . . The confusion has become general to an extent that truth acquires the greater practical dignity the less it is concerned with alleged praxis. . . .[15]

Horkheimer's essay on fascism as the natural outcome of bourgeois-liberal democracy was omitted when Alfred Schmidt collected and reprinted two volumes of articles from the *Zeitschrift* in 1968. Horkheimer never referred to it in any of his later writings. The major shortcoming of this theory of fascism seems to be that Horkheimer is extrapolating the German historical case, motivated by the fear that all capitalist societies might turn into fascist systems. The theory does not account for the variety of fascist regimes in Europe, ranging from highly industrialized Germany to "underdeveloped" Spain and "half-developed" Italy or Hungary.

DIALECTIC OF ENLIGHTENMENT

The next stage of the fascism theory of the Frankfurt theorists represents a definite turn from a militant though somewhat ambivalent *Critical Theory* to a social philosophy of despair. In the early 1940s, a double shift took place in Critical Theory: the militant *Weltanschauung* was replaced by a despairing philosophy of history, and the grand program for the comprehensive analysis of the socioeconomic structure of capitalist society gave way to the analysis of the individual member of that society, with regard to his susceptibility to fascism.

In their writings of the 1940s, Horkheimer and Adorno increasingly replaced the Marxian conceptualization of class conflict by the concept of the conflict of man versus nature, as part of a theory of universal domination.[16] The term "class" vanishes from the terminology of Critical Theory. A combination of sociological and psychological factors, such as the withering away of every revolutionary working class movement, the zenith of fascist conquest, the diminishing hope in the possibility of genuine socialism in the Soviet Union, and the authors' isolation in America, accounts for this shift. Adorno's posthumously published "Reflexionen zur Klassentheorie" (1942) is the only writing of the middle period using the concepts of class and class conflict.[17]

The works of Horkheimer and Adorno at this time are supplementary and complementary in more than one way. Horkheimer explicitly states the identity of their thought in his introduction to the *Eclipse of Reason*:

These lectures were designed to present in epitome some aspects of a comprehensive philosophical theory developed by the writer during the last few years in association with Theodor W. Adorno. It would be difficult to say which of the ideas originated in his mind and which in my own; our philosophy is one.[18]

The *Dialektik der Aufklärung*, written during the years 1942–1944, is the product of Horkheimer's and Adorno's combined reflections. In 1937 the critical theorist's main job was still to accelerate social change toward a just society, but after having gained a more thorough acquaintance with American late-capitalist society and with the commencement of the final solution of "the Jewish question" in Hitler's Germany, the theorists' earlier slight hope for change "towards a rational society" gave way to utter despair. Western civilization was looked on by Horkheimer and Adorno as in the process of decay and collapse; accordingly, the world was conceived of as "the decay of one's own existence." They set out to answer the question "why mankind, instead of entering into a truly human condition, is sinking into a new kind of barbarism."[19] This reminds one of Spengler's *The Decline of the West.* Horkheimer and Adorno, too, reflected on the commencing "collapse of bourgeois civilization." The all permeating pessimism of the *Dialektik* was a reaction to their encounter with America and to the heyday of Nazi conquest in Europe.

Dialektik was intended to be a metatheoretical treatise on sociology, psychology, and epistemology. At one point the authors call it a "dialectical anthropology." Dialectic of enlightenment means the self-destruction of the Enlightenment, the metamorphosis of the once critical philosophy of Enlightenment into the affirmation of the existing state of affairs, by dominant positivist and pragmatist philosophies. The dialectical process here is not that of Hegel or Marx but that of the Enlightenment, the movement that comprises roughly all the historical development of Western civilization. The process is determined by two underlying propositions: myth is already enlightenment, and the enlightenment reverts to myth. In the words of the authors: "The course of irresistible progress is irresistible regression."[20] Although freedom in society has inseparably been linked with enlightened thought, the concept as well as its institutional embodiment has contained the kernel of its opposite, that is regression, which today is taking place everywhere. The regression of the Enlightenment into mythology is to be sought "in the Enlightenment itself when paralyzed by fear of the truth."[21] Here is a selective illustration: Odysseus, "the archetype of the bourgeois individual," cunningly circumvents the power of the mythical monsters that represent "ossified covenants, legal claims from pre-history."[22]

The program of the Enlightenment, the disenchantment of the world by means of knowledge, was outlined by Bacon, a precursor of the movement, who asserted that the "sovereignty of men lieth hid in knowledge." For him, the "true end, scope, or office of knowledge" consisted "in effecting and working, and in discovery of particulars not revealed before, for the better endowment and help of man's life."[23] Technique is the essence of this knowledge, aimed not at notions and insight, but at method. Formula was substituted for concept, rule and probability for cause. Concepts such as substance and quality, activity and suffering (*Leiden*), being and existence had been declared metaphysical and banned from science. For the Enlightenment, whatever does not conform to the rule of computation and utility is suspect. The unity of science was made possible by formal logic, and Bacon's *una scientia universalis* was its precursor. The Enlightenment acknowledges as being and occurrence (*Geschehen*) only that which can be grasped and expressed by unity. Its ideal is the system. Number becomes the canon of the Enlightenment. Whatever cannot be reduced to number is considered fiction.

Horkheimer and Adorno proclaimed as *petitio principii* that freedom in society is inseparable from enlightening thought and pondered on "the puzzling readiness of the masses of technological age to fall under the sway of any despotism," a notion reminiscent of Ortega's contempt for the masses. Under these circumstances, not only scientific work but even the meaning of science must be questioned. Thought has become a commodity and language merely an instrument for its advertisement. External and internal mechanisms of censorship prevent any attempted resistance against this course of events. Even the honest reformer, by conforming to the rules of the game, is only strengthening the power of the existing order which he intends to break. The same theme was repeated by Marcuse some twenty years later, when he asserted that

> within a repressive society, even progressive movements threaten to turn into their opposite to the degree to which they accept the rules of the game . . . the exercise of political rights (such as voting, letterwriting to the press, to Senators, etc. . . .) in a society of total administration serves to strengthen this administration by testifying to the existence of democratic liberties which, in reality, have changed their content and lost their effectiveness.[24]

The growth of economic productivity, which constitutes the material preconditions for a better society, supplies the techniques of repression for those who have them at their disposal. The individual is reduced to nothingness in the face of immense economic powers. Technology became the medium of total reification in capitalist society, and the Nazis' diabolic use of it made the Frankfurt theorists conclude that "terror and civilization are inseparable, . . . It is impossible to abolish the terror and retain civilization."[25] The order of the day is not the conservation of the past but "the redemption of the hopes of the past."

The next excursus is into the realm in which the fully rationalized modern consciousness, with dialectical necessity as the final result of civilization, means a "return to the terrors of nature." Here Marquis de Sade and Nietzsche are singled out as examples. With the former, the unfettered drive for power spills over into tyranny. De Sade's *Justine and Juliette*, forerunners of twentieth century mass culture, are "the Homeric epic with its last mythological covering removed."[26] Equivalent to mass culture and mass media, the "culture industry" is presented by Horkheimer and Adorno as the stage when the dialectic of enlightenment enters the phase of mass deception. Relying on the basic Marxian premise that "the class which has the means of material production at its disposal, has control at the same time over the means of mental production," Horkheimer and Adorno discuss the pacifying and stupefying role of the media more on a reflective than an analytical level. Considering the fact that their discussion preceded the TV age, one must acknowledge the insight and foresight of the authors. The fusion of culture and entertainment at the expense of the former has been accomplished by mechanical production and reproduction in the centralized and commercial media.

The last fragment on "elements of anti-Semitism" proposes that the enlightenment paranoia culminates in anti-Semitism. The concluding aphorisms add up to an extremely pessimistic philosophy of history. A philosophy of history "would have to show how the rational domination of nature comes increasingly to win the day. . . Forms of economy, rule and culture would also be derived from this position."[27] The conclusion is a warning and resignation:

> In Germany, Fascism won the day with a crassly xenophobic, collectivistic ideology which was hostile to culture. Now that it is laying the whole world waste, the nations must fight against it; there is no other way out. But when all is over there is nothing to prove that the spirit of freedom will spread across Europe; its nations may become just as xenophobic, pseudocollectivistic, and hostile to culture as Fascism once was when they had to fight against it. The downfall of Fascism will not necessarily lead to a movement of the avalanche.[28]

ECLIPSE OF REASON: SUBJECTIVE AND OBJECTIVE REASON

The "eclipse of reason" signifies the Zeitgeist of 1946 for Horkheimer and Adorno, that is, a universal feeling of fear and disillusionment, due to the diminishing hope that the individual will be able to resist the all-powerful apparatus of an increasing universal manipulation. Horkheimer fears that developments might "lead to a victorious re-emergence of the neo-barbarism recently defeated on the battlefields."[29] This is an age of the eclipse of "objective" reason. A differentiation is made between subjective and objective reason. The former has its emphasis on means, or rather on the probabilistic coordination of means with ends that are not questioned. All neo-positivists and pragmatists are designated by Horkheimer as representatives of subjective reason. For them, "reason has come to. . . be regarded as an intellectual faculty of co-ordination, the efficiency of which can be increased by methodical use and by the removal of any non-intellectual factors, such as conscious or unconscious emotions."[30] Subjective reason is instrumental reason; its worth is determined by the operational value for the domination of men and nature. According to the canons of formalized-subjective reason, an activity is reasonable only if it serves another purpose: business, health, relaxation, and so on. With regard to works of art, the subjectivization and formalization of reason is manifested as reification, which results in the transformation of all products of human activity into commodities. The mechanism for achieving that transformation is the anonymous economic apparatus.

In the philosophy of pragmatism (the ideal type of subjective reason), truth is measured by success. For this philosophy, "an idea, a concept, or a theory is nothing but a scheme or plan of action, and therefore truth is nothing but the successfulness of the idea."[31] Probability and calculability are the key notions. The logic of probability is subjected for that of truth. Verification and prediction are other essential elements of pragmatic thought. It is the philosophy of "a society that has no time to remember and to meditate." Following Wilhelm Ostwald, pragmatists assert that "all realities influence our practice, and that influence is their meaning for us." Instrumentalism versus contemplation is the key dilemma, the dividing issue for Horkheimer. He pleads for 'stationary contemplation' which was once the highest aspiration of man."[32] This stance, of course, runs counter to traditional Marxism. Unlike Marx, who criticizes Feuerbach for conceiving reality "only in the form of contemplation, but not as sensuous human activity, practice," Horkheimer takes an extremely speculative and contemplative stand.

As opposed to "subjective reason," objective reason emphasizes ends and harmony as a principle inherent in reality. "The degree of reasonableness of man's life could be determined according to its harmony with . . . totality"; the latter term designating "a comprehensive system, or hierarchy, of all beings, including man and his aims."[33] The great philosophical systems of Western civilization from Plato and Aristotle to German idealism were based on the objective theory of reason. The two distinct types of reason have not always been mutually exclusive, and the predominance of the former over the latter was achieved in the course of a long historical process. Reason has become subjectivized and formalized. The terms subjectivization and formalization are used interchangeably. (Horkheimer's "objective" reason, with its emphasis on ends, neces-

sarily includes *subjective* value judgments; therefore, his terminology is unfortunate and confusing.)

Objective reason has its structure inherently in reality and is
accessible to the individual "who takes upon himself the effort
of dialectical thinking, or, identically, who is capable of *eros*."[34]
It was Parmenides, the founder of ontology, who first distinguished between two worlds—the world of truth and the world of
appearances—as well as between two modes of cognition—one
based on mere sense perception resulting in the perception of
appearances [*doxa*] and another superior method, which is
reserved for the mind or spirit [*nous*] perceiving beings or
entities [*onta*]. Things [*pragmata*] have attributes, such as color,
shape, size, and so on, but their common predicate is that they
are. Horkheimer seems to combine the key ontological idea of
Parmenides with dialectics as the correct method of *nous* for
grasping *onta*. Already Plato's dialectic asserts that

> the summit of the intelligible world is reached in philosophic
> discussion by one who aspires, through the discourse of
> reason . . . to make his way . . . to the essential reality and
> perseveres until he has grasped by pure intelligence the very
> nature of Goodness itself.[35]

Horkheimer's distinction between subjective and objective
reason is roughly equivalent to Weber's formal and substantive
rationality. To Weber, formal rationality meant calculability,
efficiency, and impersonality, that is, the reduction of rationality to its formal instrumental side. He defined it with regard to
economic action: "A system of economic activity will be called
'formally' rational according to the degree in which the provi-
sion for needs . . . is capable of being expressed in numerical,
calculable terms, and is so expressed."[36] On the other hand, the
equivalent to Horkheimer's objective reason is Weber's "substantive rationality," a "concept that has many meanings." It is
like all substantive analyses in one respect: it is not satisfied
with the purely formal fact that the measurement of action is
based on rational calculation with the "technically most
appropriate means," but involves other criteria of ultimate ends
such as ethical, political and so on.[37]

According to Horkheimer, fascism is the culmination of the technical rationality of bourgeois-capitalist society, in which enlightenment is reversed into barbarism by a dialectical twist. Fascism encourages the revolt of the nature of the individual and suppresses that revolt at the same time. A qualitatively new perfection of instrumentation and formalization of reason had been achieved in fascism. Horkheimer puts forward the proposition that fascism is the satanic synthesis of instrumental reason and nature. He states that

> In modern fascism, rationality has reached a point at which it is no longer satisfied with simply repressing nature; rationality now exploits nature by incorporating into its own system the rebellious potentialities of nature. The Nazis manipulated the suppressed desires of the German people.[38]

In this connection Horkheimer does not refer to his former teacher, Heidegger, by name, but he certainly must have had him in mind, albeit in a negative sense. At Freiburg University, Heidegger in his 1935 lectures, "Introduction to Metaphysics," called the National Socialist movement "the encounter between global technology and modern man" and welcomed this encounter as the affirmation of "the inner truth and greatness of this movement."[39]

A CRITIQUE OF DOMINATION

Bourgeois-capitalist civilization is characterized by domination in a threefold sense: first, domination of physical nature; second, domination of man by man; and third, the subjugation of human nature. All three processes are historically and intrinsically intertwined. The domination of nature involves domination of man. "The history of man's effort to subjugate nature is also the history of man's subjugation by man."[40] Indeed, the thesis of Freud's *Civilization and its Discontents*, that civilization rests on the restrictions and suppression of the demands of human instincts, is linked up here with the socio-historic process of bourgeois society that aims at the domination of nature. According to Horkheimer, "each subject not only has to take part in the subjugation of external nature, human and nonhuman, but in order to do so must subjugate nature in himself."[41]

Both the idea of progress and "the disenchantment of the world" thesis of the Enlightenment are questioned: "Since the subjugation of nature, in and outside of man, goes on without a meaningful motive, nature is not really transcended or reconciled but merely repressed."[42] The process is not a smooth one; it is not without violent reaction on the part of nature, both physical and human. Resistance and revulsion arising from this repression of nature have beset civilization from its beginnings, in the form of social rebellions . . . as well as in the form of individual crime and mental derangement."[43] Today, by a dialectical twist, the revolt is used, or rather misused, by the very same forces against which it was directed originally—the forces bent on the domination of nature and man. "Typical of our present era is the manipulation of this revolt by the prevailing forces of civilization itself, the use of the revolt as a means of perpetuating the very conditions by which it is stirred up and against which it is directed."[44] Fascism is referred to as an extreme case in point.

The revolt of nature is being integrated into the mechanism of the perpetuation of civilization. Darwinism "pointed the way with inescapable logic to the cultural situation of the present day."[45] Survival, or rather success, of the individual vis-à-vis the pressure of society means, first of all, adaptability. It has been historically the fate of mankind, and today it has become deliberate and total. Every aspect of societal life processes is subjected to rationalization and planning, including man's most private domains. Free and anonymous market forces of society at large are being replaced by conscious decisions of small and large bodies of planning authorities, as are deliberate individual decisions of adjustment. In the words of Dewey, one must devote all his energies to being "in and of the movement of things."[46]

The individual's self-preservation presupposes his adjustment to the requirements for the preservation of the system. Horkheimer's problem was expressed some fifty years earlier in

Durkheim's "fatalistic" sociology, which asserted that "the individual finds himself in the presence of a force which is superior to him and before which he bows."[47] Durkheim welcomed and approved of the situation, since for him the superiority of society over the individual "is not simply physical but intellectual and moral."[48]

The necessity for adjustment has always existed, but what is qualitatively new today is its tempo and all pervasiveness. Tempo means the speed of reflexes. For the individual of modern society, self-preservation has become dependent on the speed of his reflexes. The totality is expressed in uniformity: "Pamphlets on how to improve one's speech, how to be saved, are written in the same style as those extolling the advantages of laxatives."[49]

The principle of domination has become the idol to which everything is sacrificed. The historical change has been the transition from domination based on brute force to domination of a more subtle kind. It is accomplished by the internalization of the commands of masters as the socio-psychologic process. Durkheim proposed that the hierarchical arrangement of primitive general concepts reflected the tribal organization and mirrored social relations.[50] For Durkheim, the "insatiability" of human nature was ultimately of biological origin and so were Freud's innate drives. Society, a godlike and mythical entity, undifferentiated in terms of economic and political power, must set limits for that insatiability. Although for Horkheimer, "man's boundless imperialism is never satisfied," it has a sociological dimension; it is linked with certain socioeconomic formations of the historical process. "Indeed, man's activity to extend his power in two infinities, the microcosmos and the universe, does not arise directly from his own nature, but from the structure of society."[51]

According to Horkheimer's and Adorno's *Naturphilosophie*, man must pay for the increase of his domination over nature by his increasing alienation from it.[52] This is a sociohistoric process that was accelerated in capitalist society during the reign of the bourgeoisie. The corresponding equivalent phenomenon to the socio-economic process has been the rise of modern science and its philosophical expression, the movement called Enlightenment, in the realm of superstructure. The culmination of man–nature antagonism commenced with the rise of fascism, which, in dialectical terms, is interpreted by Horkheimer and Adorno as the revenge of nature. The Enlightenment was directed at the destruction of myth, the "disenchantment of the world," but, since the domination of nature by man has had its corresponding societal part, that is, the domination of man by man, now by dialectical turn the Enlightenment has become another myth, the worship of the existing. As they argued: "The more the machinery of thought subjects existence to itself, the more blind its resignation in reproducing existence. Hence, enlightenment returns to mythology."[53]

The principle of the domination of nature opposes the idea of man's reconciliation with nature. In a covert allusion to Marx's dictum, quoted earlier, Horkheimer establishes Marx's connection with Enlightenment philosophy. "In actual fact," he writes, "every philosophy that ends in an assertion of the unity of nature and spirit allegedly as an ultimate datum, that is to say, every kind of philosophical monism, serves to entrench the idea of man's domination of nature."[54]

Yet no duality, Cartesian or other, is advocated. "The assumption of an ultimate duality is inadmissible," Horkheimer declares bluntly. He continues: 'The two poles cannot be reduced to a monistic principle, yet their duality too must be largely understood as a [historical] product."[55] The search for a third-road solution between monism and dualism becomes the keynote for Horkheimer's philosophy: 'The real difficulty in the problem of the relation between spirit and nature is that hypostatizing the polarity of these two entities is as impermissible as reducing one of them to the other."[56] A methodological dichotomy of natural and social sciences (social philosophy) is reiterated by Horkheimer. Natural science works with formulae, and the social philosopher reexperiences meanings. "The philosopher," Horkheimer writes, cannot talk about man, animal, society, world, mind, thought, as a natural scientist talks about a chemical substance: the philosopher does not have the formula. There is no formula. An adequate description, *unfolding the meaning* of any of these concepts, with all its shades and its interconnections with other concepts, is still a main task (italics mine).[57]

As Horkheimer repeats over and over again, the word with its half-forgotten layers of meaning and association is a guiding principle. These implications must be reexperienced and preserved. Instead of formal logic, Horkheimer asserts the need for Hegelian logic, which "is the logic of the object as well as of the subject; it is a comprehensive theory of the basic categories and relations of society, nature and history."[58]

Yet, despite the emphasis on "the basic categories and relations of society, nature and history," Horkheimer switches his attention to language as the key to the understanding of societal phenomena. Language becomes a primary datum for social analysis, not just an aspect of society, as is the case in *The German Ideology*.[59]

It is interesting to note the agreement between the Frankfurt School's preoccupation with language and that of neopositivism, albeit with a different emphasis. Horkheimer writes: "Philosophy is the conscious effort to knit all our knowledge and insight into a linguistic structure in which things are called by their right names."[60] For Wittgenstein, "all philosophy is a 'critique of language.'"[61] Unlike Wittgenstein, who investigated language and communication mainly, but not exclusively, to arrive at a universe of discourse consisting of clear and precise propositions, Horkheimer's interest in language centers on its emotive aspects. "Language reflects the longings of the oppressed and the plight of nature," he declares.[62]

Horkheimer opposes a separation of art and science because "philosophy is at one with art in reflecting passion through language and thus transferring it to the sphere of experience and memory."[63] Language has in common with art a mimetic character. Unlike Horkheimer, Wittgenstein advocated a strict scientific use and analysis of language. He wrote:

The correct method in philosophy would really be the following: to say nothing except what can be said, i.e., propositions
of natural science—i.e. something that has nothing to do with
philosophy—and then, whenever someone else wanted to say
something metaphysical, to demonstrate to him that he had
failed to give a meaning to certain signs in his propositions.[64]

These two positions represent two distinct lines of development
in the philosophy of language. Horkheimer's notion of language
has its roots in German romanticism, influenced by Marxian
socio-historic ideas and the philosophy of language of Karl
Kraus. Horkheimer writes:

The spoken word cannot deny its collective coinage, for language is a true reflection of a social structure. Karl Kraus's
influence exceeds that of a mere polemicist or satirist; only
rancor could deny him the rank of a poet. It was he who gave
impetus to the concept of a sociology of language in which the
starting point is the language itself rather than the social sciences. Karl Kraus's analytical treatise of the language serves
the social physiognomy. With the help of its language, Kraus
unmasks society. He stands in total opposition to the positivistic view of the sociology of language that discovers that true
meaning of language in its being a means of communication
. . ..[Kraus] perceives the dehumanization of man and his relationships through the bastardization of sentences and words:
he sees the destruction of the spirit through commercializa-
tion. The advent of fascism confirmed Kraus's predictions
based on his studies of the spoken word. The tools of official
sociology seem blunt and ineffective compared to his analysis
of language. There is an inexhaustive list of things the sociology of language can learn from Kraus; nor can psychology or
psychoanalysis ignore his ideas.[65]

CONCEPTIONS OF SCIENCE

Different conceptions of science and relationships to religion
correspond to the two types of reason, respectively. For subjective reason, science is the mere organization, classification, or

computation of data. These scientific operations are in the light of the classical systems of objective reason subordinate to speculation. Subjective reason abandons the fight with religion and recognizes two different modes of approaches (scientific and religious). As William James expressed it:

> the world can be handled according to many systems of ideas.
> . . . Science gives to all of us telegraphy, electric lighting, and diagnosis, and succeeds in preventing and curing a certain amount of disease. Religion in the shape of mind-cure gives to some of us serenity, moral poise, and happiness, and prevents certain forms of disease as well as science does.[66]

This means a retreat from the original militant position of the Enlightenment, which "furthered the abdication of religion in favor of reason as the supreme intellectual authority."[67] The complementary of the two modes of inquiry is emphasized by James when he asserts that "science and religion are both of them genuine keys for unlocking the world's treasure-house to him who can use either of them practically."[68]

Objective reason implies the convictions that an all-embracing and fundamental structure of being could be discovered and a conception of human destination derived from it. The Enlightenment still offered a comprehensive world view, a doctrine of man and nature, and a guide for moral conduct—"a correct pattern of living"—thereby fulfilling a function previously performed by religion. Later, diverse branches of philosophy, particularly epistemology and ethics, were separated. Spinoza's philosophy is an example of the earlier situation in which ethical conduct and insight into nature were intertwined. Seventeenth century philosophy was to replace theology with its comprehensive system by aspiring to be "the instrument for deriving, explaining, revealing the content of reason as reflecting the true nature of things and the correct pattern of living."[69] At that time, neither the church nor the rising philosophical systems separated wisdom, ethics, religion, and politics. There existed a combination of ethics and theory of knowledge, a state of affairs that was signified by "the right, the duty of the mind to discover the nature of things and to derive the right modes of activity from such insight."[70] Eventually, the conflict between religion and philosophy arrived at a stalemate, and religion and philosophy became separate branches of culture.

The retreat of objective or speculative reason, which first clashed with religion, was a parallel development with the unfolding idea of bourgeois tolerance and relativism. A situation arose in which "each cultural domain preserves its 'sovereignty' with regard to universal truth." This development of the division of labor in the realm of culture corresponds to a parallel development in the social division of labor.

The process of devitalization and emasculation of basic concepts such as reason was parallel taking place in political history and in the scientific enterprise. Horkheimer refers to a tradition of deep-seated distrust of (speculative) reason in the former as it had been expressed by John Dickinson of Pennsylvania at the American Constitutional Convention in 1787: "Experience must be our only guide. Reason may mislead us."[71] To be sure, this notion ran counter to the more speculative assumptions of Locke and Rousseau, against their notion that "the same spiritual substance or moral consciousness is present in each human being." Rational insight rather than empirical and verifiable evidence leads Locke to the belief that men are "by nature all free, equal, and independent."[72]

By contrast, the role of experiment as the only legitimate experience runs through pragmatist thought from Peirce to Dewey. Peirce, the founder of the school, pushed the issue farthest by stating that the proper procedure for philosophy is "experimental method by which all the successful sciences . . . have reached the degrees of certainty." Similarly for Dewey, "active experimentation is essential to verification."[73]

The loss of autonomy of all intellectual enterprise leads to a state of affairs in which all branches of culture are modeled after the production on the assembly line. "Thought must be gauged by something that is not thought, by its effect on production or its impact on social conduct, as art today is being ultimately gauged in every detail by something that is not art, be it box-office or propaganda value."[74] Reason has become oper-tionalized and its role reduced to a mere instrument in the domination of man and nature. Reason has become completely chained to the social process.

TOWARD A NEW "NATURPHILOSOPHIE"?

Horkheimer's general philosophy of science can most appro-priately be described as a new *Naturphilosophie*. German philosophy of nature of the second half of the eighteenth century arose as a reaction against contemporary French mechanistic and materialistic philosophies of science. In essence it was a reaction to the philosophies of both Descartes and Newton, for whom matter in motion and the machine analogy were the two basic principles, in terms of which both the working of the universe and the human mind were to be explained. The Car-tesian duality of mind and body or the duality of the world of spirit and the world of matter were considered inadequate ex-planatory principles for German thinkers. As Goethe expressed it:

> A system of nature was announced, and therefore we hoped to learn really something of nature,—our idol . . . . But how hol-low and empty did we feel in this melancholy, atheistical half-night, in which the earth vanished with all its images, the heaven with all its stars.[75]

Horkheimer attempts to integrate *Naturphilosophie* with Freud-ian psychoanalytic theory and to add to it a speculative historico-sociological dimension. It was hoped that thereby one would arrive at a comprehensive philosophy of history or that an all-embracing theory of society could be achieved, capable of explaining all aspects of late-industrial society, including its most extreme and consequent case, fascism. All the works of Horkheimer and Adorno, written jointly in the mid 1940s, are the products of this endeavor.

"Philosophy," Horkheimer argues, "must formulate the concept of science in a way that expresses human resistance to the threatening relapse into mythology and madness."[76] The question of who should formulate the new rules and new methods of this "new science," and how it is to be done, is left vague, except for the proclamation that at a certain point science may conceivably go beyond the method of experimentation. Indeed, the key issue is experimental method versus speculation, an issue long ago decided for science. Modern positivists are reprimanded because

> they do not care to found their own recognition of scientific methods, such as experimentation, on intuition or any principle that could be turned against science as it is successfully practiced and socially accepted.[77]

To found scientific method exclusively on intuition is unacceptable for modern science. Intuition as an initial phase in scientific procedure, followed by some verification, is probably the generally accepted rule. Mere philosophical intuition with no testing is rejected.

The cornerstone of Horkheimerian "science" seems to be "critical reflection," that is "to see through the notion of fact itself."[78] Horkheimer asserts that facts ascertained by quantitative methods are only surface phenomena that obscure rather than disclose the underlying reality. This stand again boils down to the Hegelian notion of differentiating between appearance and essence. Horkheimer rejects the identification of cognition [Erkenntnis] with science as well, because it represents a simplistic reductionism and makes science the servant of the prevailing production apparatus. Contents, methods, and all categories of science are ultimately societal products and cannot be made absolute categories.

The emergence of modern science with its increasing specialization and the concomitant rise of a bourgeois-capitalist society with its division of labor, resulted in the loss of totality, which was originally the totality of the ancient Greeks, had been continued in medieval totality, and was still present in early

Enlightenment. Horkheimer is the last in a long line of German thinkers to yearn for the lost totality and mourn over man's fragmentation. The fascination with Greek culture in general and with Greek totality and harmony in particular runs through the classical-humanistic tradition of German culture, as exemplified in the works of Winckelman, Goethe, Schiller, Friedrich Schlegel, Marx, and the Hungarian Lukács—trained in the German intellectual tradition. Walter Rehm writes on the "Griechensucht der Deutschen." He is probably right in asserting that "Greekdom has been a religion for Germans for a considerable period of time or at least a surrogate for religion." ("*Griechentum für den deutschen Menschen eine bemessene Zeit hindurch zur Religion wurde, zu mindest zu einer Art von Ersatzreligion.*")[79] Schiller the poet, as if anticipating ideas of modern sociology of knowledge, saw occupation as the single most important category for shaping man's thinking, albeit in a negative sense. In his words "eternally chained to only one single little fragment of the whole, Man himself grew to be only a fragment; . . . and instead of imprinting humanity upon his nature he becomes merely the imprint of his occupation."[80] Marx, drawing on the work of his predecessors, located the problem in the production process of capitalist society, as presented in his theory of alienation in the 1844 *Paris Manuscripts*. After more than a half century of oblivion, with the outbreak of the catastrophe of World War I, the problem reappears for thinkers. The pre-Marxist Lukács writes of the Greeks that "the circle whose closed nature was the transcendental essence of their life has, for us, been broken."[81]

THE ATTACK ON "SCIENTISM"

It is difficult at times to separate neopositivist and pragmatist philosophies of science from plain "scientism." Horkheimer, in his frontal attack against similar and yet diverse orientations of philosophies of science, lumps together Sidney Hook, Ernest

Nagel, and John Dewey and labels them as "positivists."[82] In this
black-and-white labeling, even Max Weber, the founder of a
sociology of *Verstehen*, becomes "a positivist at heart." Hook's
simplistic scientism, which explains the crisis of the age by "the
limitations of the authority of science" is aptly criticized. It is
more doubtful that Horkheimer is on solid ground when attacking Hook for his restatement of the well-known distinction between scientific and unscientific statements, the former being
based on the method of public verifiability, and the latter lacking it. We would also question the validity of his accusation of his
opponents in stating that "instead of interrupting the machine-
like functioning of research, the mechanism of fact-finding,
verification, classification, et cetera, and *reflecting* in their
meaning and relation to truth, the positivists reiterate that science proceeds by observation and describe circumstantially how
it functions (italics mine)".[83] Reflection seems to be a key term
for Horkheimer, although it is never defined or elaborated.

The philosophy and sociology of science of Critical Theory
must be criticized on two accounts that are interlocked. On the
first account, Critical Theory misunderstood the internal logic
of scientific developments in history. In his well-known statement, "If society has a technical need, that helps science forward
more than ten universities," Engels overstated the point of
societal determination. This "externalist" position is taken up
by Horkheimer, who attributes all characteristics of modern
science (the use of mathematics, symbolic logic, the experimental method, and the democratic consensus of scientists) to external factors, that is, the rise of bourgeoise society and the
bourgeoisie's drive to dominate and suppress man and nature.
Modern sociology and the history of science acknowledges an
intricate interplay between external (societal) and internal factors (or the internal logic) in the growth of science.[84]

Second, Critical Theory deviates from the classics of Marxism by reverting to a simplistic anti-scientism. As known, Marx
and Engels were lifelong students of the natural sciences. In the
division of labor between the two scholars, it was Engels who
devoted years to a thorough study of physics, chemistry, and

biology when writing *Anti-Dühring*, while Marx was working on *Das Kapital*. The division of labor has served many Marx-ologists in confronting the work of the two men. Recent scholar-ship has called attention to the fact that the recently discovered voluminous manuscripts of Marx prove that he too seriously studied the natural sciences of his time, such as physics, geo-logy, and biology, as early as the 1850s and continued to do so through the 1870s and 1880s. In 1968 the Institute of Marxism-Leninism in Moscow published a 1000-page manuscript of Marx on mathematics.[85] Thus the anti-mathematical bent of Critical Theory does not have much in common with real Marxism; its roots lie basically in the tradition of various German anti-science intellectual currents.

As discussed in this chapter, Horkheimer's concern was the reconciliation (*Versöhnung*) of man with nature. It should be noted that the two different philosophical orientations have existed concurrently in both Western and Oriental civiliza-tions—the former aimed at man's reconciliation with nature, the latter toward man's domination of nature. The idea of domina-tion of nature leads in Chinese thought from Hsün Tzu (third century B.C.) to Mao Tse-tung. Hsün Tzu, a Confucian thinker, puts forth a powerful plea for mastering nature:

> You glorify Nature and meditate on her;
> Why not domesticate her and regulate her?
>
> You obey Nature and sing her praises;
> Why not control her course and use it?
>
> You look on the seasons with reverence and await them;
> Why not respond to them by seasonal activities?
>
> You depend on things and marvel at them;
> Why not unfold your own abilities and transform them?
>
> You meditate on what makes a thing a thing:
> Why not so order things that you do not waste them?
>
> You vainly seek into the causes of things:
> Why not appropriate and enjoy what they produce?

> Therefore I say—To neglect man and speculate about
> Nature
> Is to misunderstand the facts of the universe.

In Needham's words, Hsün Tzu "struck a blow at science by emphasizing its social context too much and too soon."[86] Mao Tse-tung, himself an accomplished poet, expressed the same idea in a more prosaic and programmatic language:

> Natural science is one of man's weapons in his fight for freedom. For the purpose of attaining freedom in society, man must use social science to understand and change society and carry out social revolution. For the purpose of attaining freedom in the world of nature, man must use natural science to understand, conquer and change nature and thus attain freedom from nature.[87]

To sum up, Critical Theory's sweeping critique of modern science and technology seems to be a modern version of the old anti-science sentiments of German idealist philosophy masked as a critique of bourgeois-capitalist society. It represents a stand that is completely alien to Marxist position. Marx considered the capitalist development and the development of large scale industry based on modern technology a necessary step toward socialism for all its concomitant negative aspects, such as exploitation, wagework, and the increasing alienation and Verelendung of the proletariat. Through this development, most notably with the increase of the productive forces and the increased productivity of labor, the necessary material preconditions for the liberation of mankind were created. The disappearance of local and national frontiers and the creation of a world market are some other aspects of the triumphant bourgeois-capitalist society, for which technology, that is, applied science, is one of its major driving forces. As Marx and Engels expressed it in the Manifesto, "the bourgeoisie cannot exist without constantly revolutionizing the instruments of production, and consequently the relations of productions and the whole relations of society."[88] They lavishly praised this triumphant march of technological progress:

> The bourgeoisie, by the rapid improvement of all instruments of production, by the immensely facilitated means of communication, draws all nations, even the most barbarian, into civilization. . .It has created enormous cities, has greatly increased the urban population as compared with the rural, and has thus rescued a considerable part of the population from the idiocy of rural life.[89]

For Marx, the basic contradictions were (1) between the forces and relations of production and (2) between social production and private appropriation. Consequently, the forces of liberation must emerge and must be explained from a scientific analysis of capitalist society.

Marx, it will be recalled, envisaged the transition from capitalism to socialism as the conscious revolutionary act of the proletariat, which destroys the political apparatus of the capitalist state machinery but takes over and socializes the technological apparatus, the means of production. This latter act represents an element of historical continuity—a continuity of technological rationality, its liberation from irrational bondages, the realization of its unlimited development, and its unfolding in the new society. The Frankfurt School disagrees with this view and sees the roots of evil in the technological apparatus. For the Frankfurt School, technology represents the medium of Verdinglichung; the diabolical uses of science and civilization were inseparable. Horkheimer and Adorno wrote in the Dialektik der Aufklärung that "horror and civilization are inseparable. One cannot abolish horror and retain civilization."[90]

Refrain from action, primacy, and glorification of thought—reflection, to use the catch phrase of the Frankfurt School—is the major theme here. "Reason," Horkheimer argued,

> can realize its reasonableness only through reflecting on the disease of the world as produced and reproduced by man; in such self-critique, reason will at the same time remain faithful to itself, by preserving and applying for no ulterior motive the principle of truth that we owe to reason alone.[91]

For Marx, the *Aufhebung* of alienation was the abolition of class society with its domination of men over men. For Critical Theory, it is reflection and self-critique. As Horkheimer put it: "The possibility of a self-critique of reason presupposes . . . that at this stage of complete alienation, the idea of truth is still accessible."[92]

THE AUTHORITARIAN PERSONALITY: DIAGNOSIS AND THEORY

The Authoritarian Personality is considered one of the key works of modern empirical social science, "the union of German theory and American empiricism,"—a union that "proved highly productive."[93] In terms of basic orientation, the study signifies a shift in emphasis for Critical Theory in general and for its concern with fascism in particular. The shift does not indicate a decision to ignore the objective socio-economic factors, but rather a shift of the emphasis toward the subjective psychological aspects of the problem and on the possible amelioration of the situation through reeducation. In Horkheimer's words:

> It may strike the reader that we have placed undue stress upon the personal and psychological rather than upon the social aspects of prejudice. This is not due to a personal preference for psychological analysis nor to a failure to see that the cause of irrational hostility is in the last instance to be found in social frustration and injustice. Our aim is not merely to describe prejudice but to explain it in order to help in its eradication. . . Eradication means re-education, scientifically planned on the basis of understanding scientifically arrived at.[94]

In view of the Nazi holocaust, the order of the day is "to prevent or reduce the virulence of the next outbreak."[95] This theoretical and practical stand is a move away from the classical Marxian position of the primacy of the infrastructure, that is, a reversal of the thesis that "It is not the consciousness of men that determines their being, but, on the contrary, their social being that determines their consciousness." It is also a turning away from the pessimistic social philosophy of the *Dialektik*, that is, from the tenet of the inevitability of the collapse of bourgeois civilization to the belief in the possible reeducation of members of capitalist society.

The study is concerned with investigating the interrelationship between personality syndromes and susceptibility to prejudice. The problem is to establish the correlation between "deep-rooted personality traits and overt prejudice" and to measure these traits by means of an interdisciplinary approach.[96]

The authors state their major hypotheses thus:

> The research to be reported in this volume was guided by the following major hypothesis: that the political, economic, and social convictions of an individual often form a broad and coherent pattern, as if bound together by a 'mentality' or 'spirit'; and that this pattern is an expression of deep-lying trends in his personality.

> The major concern was with the *potentially fascistic* individual, one whose structure is such as to render him particularly susceptible to anti-democratic propaganda.[97]

As will be recalled, the authors had a definite theoretical model of the authoritarian personality in mind long before they embarked on this empirical study, as presented in the volume, *Studien über Autorität und Familie*. Erich Fromm also dealt with the problem of authoritarianism in his book, *Escape from Freedom*, also written in Frankfurt. He equated "sado-masochistic character," typical of the German lower middle class, with the authoritarian character and believed it to be most susceptible to Nazi ideology. As he states: "By the term 'authoritarian character', we imply that it represents the personality structure which is the human basis of fascism."[98] Comparing the content of the questionnaire developed for *Studien über Autorität und Familie* with that of *The Authoritarian Personality*, the latter can be seen as a logical extension of a program that had been launched in Frankfurt some ten years before. The authors acknowledge their heavy reliance on Freud: "For theory as to the structure of personality we have leaned most heavily upon Freud. . . ."[99] It is evident that the authors are aware of the difficult problem of the operationalization of Freudian psychoanalytic theory from the statement:

> A particular methodological challenge was imposed by the conception of *levels* in the person; this made it necessary to devise techniques for surveying opinions, attitudes, and values that were on the surface, for revealing ideological trends that were more or less inhibited and reached the surface only in indirect manifestations, and for bringing to light personality forces that lay in the subject's unconscious.[100]

This sounds like a Hegelianization of Freud: "opinions, attitudes, and values on the surface" corresponding to Hegel's "Erscheinung" and "personality forces that lay in the subject's unconscious" corresponding to the Hegelian "Wesen."[101]

Using a combination of diverse techniques, such as questionnaires, depth interviews, and projective tests, The Authoritarian Personality attempted to tap diverse levels of the personality structure from the "surface" level to the "unconscious " level. For the former, questionnaires—which were less costly—were used; for the latter depth interviews were used, the results of which, in turn, helped to refine the questionnaires at every stage of the project.

The study starts out with an inquiry into anti-Semitic ideology. As stated by the authors: "One of the most clearly anti-democratic forms of social ideology is prejudice, and within this context anti-Semitism provides a fruitful starting point for a social psychological study."[102] As a social movement, anti-Semitism is clearly one of the major threats to democracy. Anti-Semitism "is one of the most powerful psychological vehicles for anti-democratic political movements and it provides . . . perhaps the most effective spearhead for a frontal attack on our entire social structure. . . "[103] The problem was the investigation of beliefs about Jews as the basis for anti-Semitic attitudes toward Jews. Five subscales were devised to measure stereotyped beliefs about Jews—aggressiveness, offensiveness, threatening, seclusiveness, intrusiveness—in addition to the desirability of segregating them. The five subscales were then combined in the "Total Anti-Semitism (A-S) Scale," which was "intended to measure the individual's readiness to support or to oppose anti-Semitic ideology as a whole."[104] The scale was based on the conception of the ideology of

> stereotyped negative opinions describing the Jews as threatening, immoral, and categorically different from non-Jews, and of hostile attitudes urging various forms of restriction, exclusion, and suppression as a means of solving "the Jewish problem."[105]

The intercorrelation between the subscales was high, and the intercorrelation between each separate subscale and the total A-S scale ranged from 0.92 to 0.94, high enough to provide support "for the hypothesis that anti-Semitism is a general frame of mind."

The next stage was concerned with prejudice broadly conceived, that is, finding out whether anti-Semitism is part of a larger ethnocentric ideology. Ethnocentrism was first defined by William Sumner in his book, *Folkways* (1906), as the ethnically centered ideology that accepts members of the "ingroup" and rejects those of the "outgroup."[106] The structure of general ethnocentric ideology included as its main characteristic the ingroup-outgroup distinction as a basis for social thinking. Major outgroups were identified as Jews, Negroes, members of lower socioeconomic classes, and radicals. The authors sum up the ideology of ethnocentrism:

> Ethnocentrism is based on a pervasive and rigid ingroup-outgroup distinction: it involves stereotyped negative imagery and hostile attitudes regarding outgroups, stereotyped positive imagery and submissive attitudes regarding ingroups, and a hierarchical, authoritarian view of group interaction in which ingroups are rightly dominant, outgroups subordinate.[107]

An ethnocentrism scale was then devised with several sub-scales (Negro, Minority, and Patriotic) to measure pseudo-democratic and openly anti-democratic opinions and attitudes. The subscales were combined in the "Total Ethnocentrism (E)" scale, which was again administered to subjects. There was again a high intercorrelation among the subscales. The result of the statistical analysis of the subscales supported the hypothesis that "there is such a thing as general ethnocentric ideology."[108]

The third step focuses on political economic ideology as an expression of the political and economic forces of society and its relationship to ethnocentrism. Ideology is defined as "an organized system of opinions, values and attitudes."[109] Although it is customary to equate or at least to correlate both right and left extremism with ethnocentrism, the authors believe that "fascism, which represents the most extreme right-wing political and economic structure and ideology, is also the most virulent anti-democratic form of ethnocentrism."[110]

Since neither of these extreme positions constitutes any real threat to American society, the study focuses on liberalism versus conservatism. Based on earlier studies of Levinson and Sanford, "there is considerable evidence suggesting a psychological affinity between conservatism and ethnocentrism, liberalism and anti-ethnocentrism."[111] Therefore, an attempt was made to measure politico-economic ideology along a liberalism-conservatism dimension, by using a Politico-Economic Conservatism (PEC) scale. The findings showed a statistically significant, although quantitatively imperfect, relationship between conservatism and ethnocentrism, between liberalism and anti-ethnocentrism.

Next, religion was taken up, but the objective factors (denomination and church attendance) did not prove to be very significant. Then the "F-Scale" tried to measure implicit anti-democratic trends. On the basis of investigations up to that point, a number of variables, which made up the basic content of the F scale (F=fascism), were identified. The variables and their definitions are as follows:

1 *Conventionalism.* Rigid adherence to conventional, middle-class values.

2 *Authoritarian submission.* Submissive, uncritical attitude toward idealized moral authorities of the ingroup.

3 *Authoritarian aggression.* Tendency to be on the lookout for, and to condemn, reject, and punish people who violate conventional values.

4 *Antiintraception.* Opposition to the subjective, the imaginative, the tenderminded.

5 *Superstition and stereotypy.* The belief in mystical determinants of the individual's fate; the disposition to think in rigid categories.

6 *Power and "toughness."* Preoccupation with the dominance-submission, strong-weak, leader-follower dimension; identification with power figures; overemphasis on the conventionalized attributes of the ego; exaggerated assertion of strength and toughness.

7 *Destructiveness and cynicism.* Generalized hostility, vilification of the human.

8 *Projectivity.* The disposition to believe that wild and dangerous things go on in the world; the projection outwards of unconscious emotional impulses.

9 *Sex.* Exaggerated concern with sexual "goings-on."[112]

The question is, why and how does the "authoritarian personality," develop these traits? On the basis of her analysis of the interviews with 45 prejudiced and 35 unprejudiced individuals of the original sample of 2099, Else Frenkel-Brunswik presents the theory of developmental patterns that produce authoritarian and nonauthoritarian personalities. She sums up:

> When we consider the childhood situation of the most prejudiced subjects, we find reports of a tendency toward rigid discipline on the part of the parents, with affection which is conditional rather than unconditional, i.e. dependent upon approved behaviour on the part of the child. Related to this is a tendency ... to base inter-relationships on rather closely defined roles of dominance and submission, in contradistinction to equalitarian policies. . . .

Forced into a surface submission to parental authority, the child develops hostility and aggression which are poorly channelized. The displacement of a repressed antagonism toward authority may be ... the principal source of his antagonism toward outgroups. ...

Fear and dependency seem to discourage the ethnocentric child from conscious criticism of the parents. It is especially the prejudiced man who seems intimidated by a threatening father figure. Display of a rough masculine facade seems to be a compensation for such an intimidation. ...

The fact that the negative feelings against the parents have to be excluded from consciousness may be considered as contributing to the general lack of insight, rigidity of defense, and narrowness of the ego so characteristic of high scorers. ...

The parents of prejudiced subjects ... also tend toward preoccupation with problems of status ... What is socially accepted and what is helpful in the climbing of the social ladder is considered good, and what is socially inferior is considered bad. ...

[The prejudiced person] expects—and gives—social approval on the basis of external moral values including cleanliness, politeness, and the like. He condemns others for their nonconformity to such values. ... The functioning of his superego is mainly directed toward punishment, condemnation, and the exclusion of others, thus mirroring the type of discipline to which he himself was apparently exposed. ...

The difficulty with children growing up in such an environment as that pictured by our prejudiced subjects seem to have in developing close personal relationships, may be interpreted as one of the outcomes of the repression of hostile tendencies, which are not integrated or sublimated, but which become diffuse and free-flowing.[113]

The concluding chapter emphasizes as its most important finding the close correspondence of the subject's approach to and his outlook in such diverse areas as family and sexual adjustment, religion, and social and political philosophy. Stereotyped, hierarchical, and dichotomous thinking and behavior in terms of ingroup–outgroup relationships and superordinations and

subordinations is characteristic of the authoritarian personality—the origins of which go back to the parent-child relationship as the major influencing factor.

The authors acknowledge the limitations of the study because it focuses exclusively on psychological aspects and thereby
excludes historical factors and economic forces. The limitations
are due in part to the sample size (N = 2099). In their words:
"Only in a truly representative study would it become possible to
appraise quantitatively the amount of prejudice in our culture,
to determine the general validity of the personality correlates
outlined in this volume."[114] Yet the possibility and necessity
of treatment of symptoms of the disease, prejudice, is stressed,
because "We are sometimes very glad to be able to control a
disease even though we cannot cure it."[115] The study's main
achievement is seen, then, in the fact that its contribution to the
knowledge of the potential fascist personality "will make symp-
tomatic treatment more effective."

The next question is, what can be done about the disease
itself? The uses of individual psychotherapy (changing adult
personality) are negligible in view of the limited number of
therapists available. Early childhood training seems to be more
effective, because the correct program "even in the present cultural pattern, could produce nonethnocentric personalities. All
that is really essential is that children be genuinely loved and
treated as individual humans."[116] Yet the impact of such a program would be lessened by the influence of ethnocentric parents.
Therefore, it seems obvious that "the modification of the potentially fascist structure cannot be achieved by psychological
means alone. The task is comparable to that of eliminating
neurosis, or delinquency, or nationalism from the world."[117]
Once again the theme of Marx's eleventh thesis on Feuerbach re-
sounds: "These are products of the total organization of society
and are to be changed only as that society is changed."[118] But
the battle cry calls only for interdisciplinary research, and for
the efforts of all social scientists. The problem is one that
requires the efforts of all social scientists. Enlightened education is needed because fascism is imposed on people against

their basic interests, and "when they can be made fully aware of themselves and their situation they are capable of behaving realistically."[119]

To overcome resistance to "self-insight and resistance to social facts," individual psychotherapy must play the dominant role. Indeed, we are told, "individual psychotherapy can be improved and adapted for use with groups and even for use on a mass scale."[120] This assertion, when contrasted with the previous statement on the negligible usefulness of psychotherapy, reveals the authors' ambivalent attitude. Some of the reasons for this ambivalence are understandable from the point of view of their precarious position in American society, as discussed later.

The authors conclude in a reflective mood:

> Although there is reason to believe that the prejudiced are the better rewarded in our society as far as external values are concerned . . . there is good reason to believe that the tolerant receive more gratification of basic needs. . . . The evidence is that they are, basically, happier than the prejudiced . . . . If fear and destructiveness are the major emotional sources of fascism, *eros* belongs mainly to democracy.[121]

SOCIOLOGICAL METHOD AND PSYCHOLOGICAL METHOD

The relationship of sociology to psychology has been an uneasy and complex one throughout the history of the discipline. For Auguste Comte there was no room for psychology in his system of the sciences. Of course, psychology as an acknowledged field of scientific inquiry was nonexistent at that time. Gustav T. Fechner's book, *Elemente der Psychophysik*, the first work on scientific experimental psychology, was not published until 1860. The Institute of Psychology of Wilhelm Wundt, who is often considered the first psychologist, was founded in 1889 in Leipzig.[122] Durkheim's "anti-psychologism" has its special historical reasons. Psychology had just recently won academic recognition in his native France; and Durkheim, in his crusade to achieve equal recognition for sociology, had to combat this closely competing science of man, to demonstrate the superiority of the explanatory power of sociology, and to draw a sharp dividing line between the two fields. "In no case can sociology simply borrow from psychology any one of its principles in order to apply it, as such, to social facts," declared Durkheim.[123] His contemporary, another giant of modern sociology, Max Weber, laying the foundation for scientific sociology in neighboring Germany, hoped to arrive at a grand synthesis of *"Naturwissenschaften"* and *"Kulturwissenschaften"* by taking the idea of causality from the former and combining it with the notions of the uniqueness of historicism and the method of *"Verstehen,"* adapted from Dilthey's and Jasper's psychology.

Modern sociologists favor not a sociological reductionism *à la* Durkheim, but the idea of the complementarity of psychology and sociology. Some theorists even read this idea *into* the work of their predecessors; Talcott Parsons, for example, perceives Freud's "convergence with Durkheim."[124] Modern sociologists face an additional problem—the diversity of psychological orientations. The question arises: whose psychology should be accepted and integrated with social theory? Different theorists have made different choices. Parsons borrowed certain elements of Freudian theory, and Homans opted for behaviorism. The same question arises with Marxian social theory. Soviet Marxism followed the official line of the canonization of Pavlov. Freudian psychoanalysis, with its overemphasis on sex, appeared suspect and incompatible with Marxism. Only Leon Trotsky pleaded in defense of Freudian psychoanalysis. In 1922 he attempted to persuade Pavlov to use his influence in favor of tolerance and freedom of research in psychology. In a letter to Pavlov, Trotsky wrote:

> Your teaching about conditioned reflexes embraces, so it seems to me, Freud's theory as a particular instance. The sublimation of sexual energy . . . is nothing but the formation on a sexual basis of the conditioned reflexes n plus one, n plus two, and of the reflexes of further degrees.

Trotsky believed that "it would be too simple and crude to declare psycho-analysis as incompatible with Marxism and to turn one's back on it."[125] But representatives of Occidental Marxism came up with a variety of attempts to integrate Marx and Freud, the best known examples of which are the works of Wilhelm Reich, Erich Fromm, and Herbert Marcuse. In the work of Horkheimer and Adorno, one can discern stages of this integration, which is closely linked with their theory of fascism, which in turn is an integral part of their general philosophy of history.

CONCLUSION

In evaluating the contribution of the Frankfurt School toward the understanding of fascism, we must first view the subject through sociological and political science literature.

One of the earliest attempts at a sociological explanation of the rise of Nazism was made by Theodor Geiger. His classic study, *Die soziale Schichtung des deutschen Volkes*, deals with the problem of the relationship between the middle classes and the Nazis. His analysis of the voting statistics of the last years of the Weimer Republic established a correlation between the decreasing vote of the bourgeois parties of the center and the increasing votes of the Nazi party (NSDAP). His thesis is that the success of Hitler's movement does not stem from any idealism, but rather from material and economic frustrations, the hopelessness of the old middle class, small entrepreneurs, and the new middle class of white collar workers. Geiger's findings have been popularized and expanded in the political sociology of Lipset.[126]

After the war, German sociologists discussed the problem anew, although initially in the form of reflections rather than of scientific research. Leopold von Wiese expressed the continuing confusion about fascism among German sociologists, calling it "a metaphysical and enigmatic phenomenon which cannot be penetrated by the sociologist."[127]

The complex and puzzling character of the phenomenon of fascism is manifested in the strange fact that 50 years after the rise of Italian fascism, 40 years after the rise of German Nazism, and almost three decades after the fall of both (an event that opened a flood of archival material for scholars), a comprehensive, generally accepted theory of fascism is still not in sight.

Attempts of the social sciences to explain the complex phenomenon, fascism, fall into two categories: "pure" theories of fascism and "totalitarianism" theories. The pure theories research the socioeconomic and ideological components of fascism; the latter focus on similarities in the political domination of left and right extremist regimes, considering them a general malaise of twentieth century mass societies, especially of those societies beset with problems of modernization.[128]

Ever since Stalin and Hitler rose to power in 1929 and 1933, respectively, many theorists proposed a general theory of totalitarianism—a theory that would subsume both the fascist and Communist regimes in a theoretical frame of reference. Thus Leon Trotsky suggested that "Stalinism and fascism, in spite of a deep difference in social foundations, are symmetrical phenomena. In many of their features they show a deadly similarity."[129]

After having witnessed events in Russia, Schumpeter had a similar notion about Stalinist socialism that is different from "the civilization of which orthodox socialists dream," a socialism that "is much more likely to present fascist features."[130] Earlier, Karl Mannheim's *Ideology and Utopia* (1929) could only compare Italian fascism with Leninism and emerging Stalinism. He warned that "it would be misleading to overlook the differences in emphasizing the similarities."[131]

Totalitarianism theories emphasize the similarities in basic methods and processes of domination. Totalitarian regimes are then characterized by the total centralization and regimentation of all spheres of political, social, and intellectual life. Furthermore, exclusive claim to the leadership of a party and ideology is basic to them. Totalitarian politics can be summed up by a syndrome of basic characteristics: (1) an all-embracing and exclusive ideology, (2) centralized and uniform mass movement, (3) control of all means of communication through coercion, and (4) bureaucratic control of the economy and social relations.

The social sciences have not yet defined fascism with a precision acceptable to all. In Marxist-oriented theories of fascism, the agitprop aspect, in accordance with the daily requirements of the political line, has always dominated scholarly scientific considerations, as exemplified most blatantly in the "social fascism" theories that lump together all opponents of the Communist Party to denounce them as fascist or at least potentially fascist.[132]

National divergences seem to make the creation of a general theory of fascism an almost insurmountable problem. Even the two prototypes, Italian and German fascism, had significant differences. Karl Dietrich Bracher suggests that instead of fascism it would be better to talk about fascisms.[133] The success of all fascist movements very much depended on both the degree to which a more or less capitalistic economy could make the necessary changes for modernization and the historical-politically determined reaction of the populace. All fascist movements had been right wing antidemocratic movements, directed against liberal-democratic and socialist-communist political and social orders. Yet German fascism was unique in its extreme racist ideology, global demand for domination, imperialist drive, and technological efficiency.

With a move away from the Cold War period and with the post-Stalinist changes of Soviet type societies, the totalitarian theory approach seems to lose its appeal for many scholars. The distinguished political scientist, Peter Ludz, a long-time student of Communist societies, suggested that totalitarianism theories as a methodological and conceptual tool be abandoned altogether.[134]

Others still seem to adhere to the idea of totalitarianism as a useful concept, not merely a product of the Cold War scholarship and atmosphere, and advocate a differentiated application. For Bracher, totalitarianism and fascism theories can be complementary.[135]

The fascism theories of Critical Theory of Horkheimer and Adorno, formulated during the 1940s, represent a gradual shift from a particular type of "theory of fascism" to the totalitarianism theories of the social-philosophical variety. Thus Horkheimer's "The Jews and Europe" (and his unpublished "The Authoritarian State") tried to account for fascism in socioeconomic terms, with a specific emphasis on the Jewish component.[136] In *Dialectic of Enlightenment* and *Eclipse of Reason*, domination, the key concept of the totalitarianism theories, became the central category and was applied predominantly to Western capitalist societies. Only in the mid-1960s did Adorno's *Negative Dialektik* and Marcuse's *One Dimensional Man* develop their special kind of totalitarianism theories. These works deviated from other dominant theories of that approach in that they focused on the trend toward total domination of *all* advanced industrial societies on a global scale.

Basically, Horkheimer's less systematic utterances on a "totally administered world" (*verwaltete Welt*) agree with Adorno and Marcuse. Each of them arrived at different practical conclusions—Adorno at absolute nihilism, Marcuse at support of the student revolt, and Horkheimer at a yearning for another world.

Concerning fascism, Critical Theory's major shortcomings can be listed as follows: (1) different approaches and products of this period have never been integrated into a meaningful general theory of fascism or of totalitarianism; (2) there has been no empirical analysis of concrete socio-historical conditions, only extremely speculative reflections even in the intellectual history of ideas chapters. Lukács' *Zerstörung der Vernunft* (1954)—if we take out the polemical, that is, agitprop passages—is superior in its history of ideas analysis of German irrational thought and is more scholarly than the dubious thesis of enlightenment reverting into myth. Historically, reason and unreason ran parallel in Western thought, and the latter triumphed only in the countries in which socioeconomic conditions facilitated it.[137]

In spite of its shortcomings, *The Authoritarian Personality*

seems to be the most valuable and lasting accomplishment of
this period. Although highly controversial and criticized by
many on methodological and ideological grounds, it occupies a
firm place as a classic in modern social psychology and has
stimulated scores of follow-up studies since its publication in
1950.[138]

THE IMPACT OF EXILE

More than 100 years ago Engels wrote to Marx that "the emigration is an institution which must turn everybody into a fool, an
ass and a common knave, unless he manages to get completely
away from it. . . ."[139] In the twentieth century, many European
intellectuals have wrestled with the problems of the refugee
existence and its ensuing psychological state. All of them have
tried to resolve the problems and dilemmas in different, sometimes extreme ways. Ernst Toller, the writer, hanged himself in
his Manhattan hotel room; Edgar Zilsel, the philosopher of
science, also committed suicide, as did Kurt Tucholsky, Stefan
Zweig, and Walter Benjamin. An exhaustive treatment of the
problem lies beyond the scope of this study, but I touch on a few
representative examples that are illustrative in their ways.

Karl Korsch, the noted neo-Marxist thinker, was puzzled by
his encounter with the New World and found American social
reality "intellectually impenetrable [zu unübersichtlich]." Yet,
as if foreshadowing Marcuse's "one-dimensional society" and
"one-dimensional" thought, Korsch detected at least one crucial aspect of American capitalist society: its immense flexibility
and capacity to neutralize all real opposition and to absorb all
countertrends. His diagnosis of American society is perhaps the
most concise statement on the subject. He wrote in a letter to
Paul Partos,

> In Europe there is a legitimate opposition between the static
> "positive" and the dynamic "critical" theory. The first offers a
> rational technical solution to present problems while the latter

exposes the irrationality of those technical solutions in the face of real problems. In the United States, however, there is no room for such coexistence. There are a lot of presupposed activities such as continuous correction of researched facts; the discovery of new scientific territories and the application of new methods, and instant absorption of counter-cultural tendencies; a saturation of everything anomalous and illegal; the institutionalization of business, politics, corruption, power and criminality. Under these circumstances, new ideas in science do not precipitate conflicts or strains; they merely supply the daily ration of "motor-fuel."[140]

Bertolt Brecht, already a successful playwright and poet by the time he left Germany, was driven from one country to another by advancing Nazism. He moved from Berlin via Denmark to Sweden; after the invasion of Norway he settled in Finland until the Soviet Union invaded Finland. Then he made his way to California via Vladivostok, subjecting himself to a long trans-Siberian trip. After he arrived on the West Coast, he decided "to join the sellers," the Hollywood market "where lies are bought"; but everywhere he was faced with the request, "Spell your name," which to him symbolized homelessness and insecurity. His "Sonnet in Exile" sums up the refugee intellectual existence as perceived by a sensitive artist:

> Chased out of my country, I must now see how to open a new shop, some place where I can sell what I think. I must take the old paths, worn smooth by the steps of the hopeless ones! Already on my way, I don't yet know to whom I am going. Wherever I go, I hear 'Spell your name!' Oh, this 'name' was once one of the great ones.[141]

In 1947 he was driven out of the country by the House Un-American Activities Committee.[142]

Another of the "great names," Thomas Mann, started out on his American sojourn on a positive note; the New Deal era had inspired him to portray Roosevelt and his policies in his *Joseph*-tetralogy. In the early 1950s, however, Thomas Mann became frightened by McCarthyism. Homesickness for Europe coupled

with fear—of what he termed a "new fascism" in America
—made him return to Europe. Thomas Mann described his state
of mind in a letter in 1951: "I possess a kind of irrational fear of
having to be buried in this country that gave me nothing and
knows nothing of me."[143]

As for Critical Theory, Adorno's summary gives an insight
into the psychological state of "the intellectual from abroad."
Adorno reflects on the shock of new experiences, the frightening
vastness of everything, and its ultimate reduction into a thing:

> It is made unmistakably clear to the intellectual from abroad
> that he will have to eradicate himself as an autonomous being
> if he hopes to achieve anything or be accepted as an employee
> of the super-trust into which life has been condensed. The
> refractory individual who does not capitulate nor completely
> toe the line is abandoned to the shock that the world of things,
> concentrated into gigantic blocks, administers to whatever or
> whomever does not become a thing. Impotent in the machin-
> ery of the universally developed commodity relation, which
> has become the supreme standard, the intellectual reacts to the
> shock with panic.[144]

Only a study based on a combination of sociological and
psychological aspects of Horkheimer's and Adorno's American
experiences could provide a thorough explanation for many
facets of their work in America. Horkheimer and Adorno
encountered almost every aspect of American capitalist civilization with shock and dismay. Adorno puts the matter very well:

> Every intellectual in exile, without exception, is injured. . . .
> He lives in an environment, which must remain incomprehen-
> sible for him, even if he finds himself at home in the labor
> unions or in the traffic. . . . His language is expropriated and
> he is stripped of his historical dimension from which his
> cognition has drawn its strength."[145]

A yearning for European liberal-bourgeois society and the life
style of its cultured upper middle class members is an ever
recurring theme in Adorno's writings.

"In the realm of erotic sphere," Adorno writes,

> a transvaluation seems to take place. Under liberalism, up till
> recently, married men from good society, unsatisfied by their
> correct spouses of sheltered upbringing, were wont to in-
> demnify themselves with actresses, *bohémiennes*, sweet girls
> (*süsse Mädel*) and *cocottes*. The possibility of this irregular
> bliss has disappeared with the rationalization of society. The
> *cocottes* have died out, the sweet girls have never existed in
> the Anglo-Saxon and other countries of technological civiliza-
> tion.[146]

Every minute aspect of the new society is a new shock: "The
technization [*Technisierung*] makes gestures precise and rough,
and it does the same to men. Thus one forgets how to close a door
softly, carefully, and yet firmly. One has to slam the doors of
autos and refrigerators. . . ."[147] Adorno asks in a reflective mood:
"What does it mean for the subject that there are no windows
with wings to be opened but only windows to be pushed up and
down, no door-handles but doorknobs to be turned. . . ., no
fences around the garden."[148] In addition, there is the struggle
for existence, or rather the life-death struggle for survival, in
competition with the natives and with the fellow exiled intellectuals. Adorno remarks:

> The share of the social product for strangers is meager and
> drives them to a hopeless second competition among them-
> selves besides and beyond the general one. All that leaves
> marks on everyone. . . .The relationship among the 'outcasts'
> is even more poisoned than among the natives.[149]

Time is money. Personal greetings like taking off one's hat and
shaking hands are being replaced by the indifferent *hello* just as
letters are replaced by "interoffice communications" without
signatures. In this total estrangement, "the triumph of matter-
of-factness [*Sachlichkeit*] in human relations among human
beings which does away with all ideological ornament, has itself
become ideology for the treatment of human beings as things
[*Sachen*]."[150]

The problems of the refugee existence result in a state of mind that Adorno describes:

> Individuals are reduced to a mere sequence of instantaneous experiences which leave no trace. . . .What a man was and experienced in the past is as nothing when set against what he now is and has and what he can be used for. The well-meaning if threatening advice frequently given to emigrants to forget all their past because it cannot be transferred, and to begin a completely new life, simply represents a forcible reminder to the newcomer of something which he has long since learned for himself. History is eliminated in oneself and others out of a fear that it may remind the individual of *the decay [Zerfall] of his own existence*—which itself continues (italics mine).[151]

In sum, writings of the critical theorists during that period are basically existentially determined critical reflections, that is, the existential philosophy of a group of refugee intellectuals from Nazi Germany, who, observing evil ("The observation of evil is a fascinating occupation"), were paralyzed by the monster called fascism and frightened by the "decay of their own existence" as stated in the *Dialectic of Enlightenment*.

NOTES

1. Max Horkheimer (Ed.), *Studien über Autorität und Familie*, Paris, 1936.
2. Georgi Dimitrov, *Selected Works*, Sofia, 1960, p. 88.
3. Max Horkheimer, "Die Juden und Europa," *ZfS, VIII*, 1/2 (1939), p. 115.
4. *Ibid.*, p. 116.
5. *Ibid.*, p. 120.
6. See James Burnham, *Managerial Revolution*, New York, 1941.
7. Immanuel Kant, *Werke*, Vol. VI, Berlin, 1914, p. 318.
8. Horkheimer, "Die Juden," p. 126.
9. *Ibid.*, p. 128.
10. *Ibid.*, p. 128.

11. *Ibid.*, p. 129.

12. See Gershom Scholem, *Walter Benjamin—die Geschichte einer Freundschaft*, Frankfurt am Main, 1975, pp. 276–277.

13. Horkheimer, "Die Juden," p. 132. For a sociological discussion of Eastern Jews (*Ostjuden*) in Germany, see S. Adler-Rudel, *Ost-juden in Deutschland 1880–1940*, Tübingen, 1959.

14. *Ibid.*, p. 133.

15. *Ibid.*, p. 135.

16. Max Horkheimer and Theodor W. Adorno, *Dialektik der Aufklärung*, Amsterdam, 1947; Max Horkheimer, *Eclipse of Reason*, New York, 1947; and Theodor W. Adorno, *Minima Moralia*, Frankfurt am Main, 1951.

17. Theodor W. Adorno, "Reflexionen zur Klassentheorie," *Gesammelte Schriften 8*, Frankfurt am Main, 1972. Theodor Wiesengrund Adorno, born in Frankfurt am Main in 1903, was the son of a German-Jewish wine merchant and a singer, Maria Calvelli-Adorno della Piana, a gentile of Italian background. He studied philosophy, musicology, psychology, and sociology at Frankfurt University, where he met Max Horkheimer. After receiving a Ph.D. in 1924 with a dissertion on Husserl, Adorno went to Vienna to study composition with Alban Berg. From 1928 to 1932 he edited the Viennese musical journal, *Anbruch*. In 1931, Adorno completed his *Habilitationsschrift*, a study of the aesthetic theories of Kierkegaard. After Hitler came to power, Adorno left Germany and settled first in Oxford, England. He arrived in New York City in 1938 for a three-year stay. In 1941 he joined Horkheimer in California, where he lived until 1949, when he returned to Frankfurt am Main, in Germany. Adorno was Professor of Philosophy and Sociology at the Johann Wolfgang von Goethe University in Frankfurt am Main and Director of the reorganized Institute until his death in 1969.

18. Horkheimer, *Eclipse*, p. VII.

19. Horkheimer-Adorno, *Dialektik*, p. 5.

20. *Ibid.*, p. 50.

21. *Ibid.*, p. 8.

22. *Ibid.*, p. 74.

23. *Ibid.*, p. 15.

24. R. P. Wolff, B. Moore Jr. and H. Marcuse *A Critique of Pure Tolerance*, Boston, 1965, pp. 83–84.

25. Horkheimer-Adorno, *Dialektik*, p. 256.

26. *Ibid.*, p. 141.

27. *Ibid.*, p. 265.

28. *Ibid.*, pp. 261–262. Since the *Dialektik* was dedicated to Friedrich Pollock, a lifelong friend of Horkheimer and the political economist of the Institute, a few words are in order on the relationship between Critical Theory and political economy. As known, the critical theory of Marx was first and foremost a critique of bourgeois political economy. Marx's original studies were in philosophy; after having discovered that "the anatomy of bourgeois society is to be sought in political economy," he taught himself political economy. Horkheimer and Adorno did not follow Marx's example. The later Adorno is credited with having said that "economics is simply repulsive" to him. Although it is difficult to trace the exact nature of the impact of Pollock's work on Horkheimer and Adorno, it can be stated that the basic themes of Pollock's economic thought had provided the general "economic infrastructure" for Critical Theory.

   Pollock's early work on Soviet planning was based on his first experience during a trip to the Soviet Union in the late 1920s. In 1932 he asserted the impossibility of planning in a capitalist society. In 1941, his "theory of state capitalism" perceived similar trends in Nazi Germany, the Soviet Union, and the United States in that the state assumed the functions of the individual capitalists. The market is thus replaced by central planning requiring an enlarged and all-powerful bureaucratic apparatus that in turn arises out of the merging of state bureaucracy and the higher echelons of industrial management. Pollock follows to some extent James Burnham's theory of "the managerial revolution" overemphasizing the significance of the separation of ownership and management in late capitalist society—a highly un-Marxian thesis and a controversial one, too. According to Pollock, two political organizations correspond to this state capitalism: the authoritarian, such as Nazi Germany and the Soviet Union, and the democratic, such as the United States.

   Horkheimer's closest reliance on Pollock's theory of state capitalism can be detected in his essay, "The Authoritarian State," written in 1942 for a Benjamin-memorial volume and made available to the larger public only in 1972.

   For a recent reissuing of Friedrich Pollock's *Zeitschrift* articles, see *Stadien des Kapitalismus*, Helmut Dubiel (Ed.) München, 1975.

   See also for informative assessment of Pollock, Giacomo Marramao, "Zum Verhältnis von politischer Ökonomie und

The Middle Period of Critical Theory 123

Kritischer Theorie," in *Ästhetik und Kommunikation*, Heft 11, (April 1973), pp. 79–93.

29. Horkheimer, *Eclipse of Reason*, p. VI.
30. *Ibid.*, pp. 8–9.
31. *Ibid.*, p. 42.
32. *Ibid.*, p. 45.
33. *Ibid.*, p. 4.
34. *Ibid.*, p. 11.
35. *Plato's The Republic*, B. Jowett (Transl.) New York, n.d. p. 278.
36. Max Weber, *Economy and Society*, Guenther Roth and Claus Wittich (Eds.) Vol. I, New York, 1968, p. 85.
37. *Ibid.*, p. 85.
38. Horkheimer, *Eclipse*, p. 121.
39. Martin Heidegger, *An Introduction to Metaphysics*, New Haven, Conn, 1959, p. 199. See also Martin Heidegger, "Nur noch ein Gott kann uns retten. Spiegel Gespräch mit Martin Heidegger am 23. September 1966," in *Der Spiegel*, XXX, 23 (1976), pp. 193–219.
40. Horkheimer; *Eclipse*, p. 105.
41. *Ibid.*, p. 93.
42. *Ibid.*, p. 94.
43. *Ibid.*, p. 94.
44. *Ibid.*, p. 95.
45. *Ibid.*, p. 95.
46. *Ibid.*, p. 96.
47. Emile Durkheim, *The Rules of Sociological Method*, New York, 1964, p. 123.
48. *Ibid.*, p. 123. Further, on Durkheim's view of human nature, see Emile Durkheim, *Suicide*, New York, 1951, pp. 246–257; also Emile Durkheim, "The Dualism of Human Nature and its Social Conditions," in *Essays on Sociology & Philosophy*, Kurt H. Wolff (Ed.) New York, 1964, pp. 325–340.
49. Horkheimer, *Eclipse*, pp. 100–101.
50. Emile Durkheim and Marcel Mauss, *Primitive Classification*, Chicago 1972.
51. Horkheimer, *Eclipse*, p. 108.
52. Horkheimer-Adorno, *Dialektik*, pp. 19–20. The same proposition was made earlier by Lukács: "Civilization creates the rule of man over nature but in the process man himself falls under the

domination of the very means that enabled him to dominate nature." Georg Lukács, "Alte Kultur und neue Kultur," in *Kommunismus* 1/43 (1920), p. 1539.

53. *Ibid.*, p. 40.

54. Horkheimer, *Eclipse*, p. 169.

55. *Ibid.*, p. 171.

56. *Ibid.*, p. 171.

57. *Ibid.*, p. 166.

58. *Ibid.*, p. 168.

59. Marx and Engels wrote: "Language is as old as consciousness, language is practical consciousness as it exists for other men, and for that reason, is really beginning to exist for me personally as well; for language, like consciousness, only arises from the need, the necessity, of intercourse with other men. Where there exists a relationship, it exists for me: the animal has no 'relation' with anything, cannot have any. For the animal, its relation to others does not exist as a relation. Consciousness is therefore from the very beginning a social product, and remains so as long as men exist at all." Karl Marx and Frederick Engels, *The German Ideology*, New York, 1970, p. 51.

60. Horkheimer, *Eclipse*, p. 179.

61. Ludwig Wittgenstein, *Tractatus Logico-Philosophicus*, London, 1961, p. 37.

62. Horkheimer, *Eclipse*, p. 179.

63. *Ibid.*, p. 179.

64. Wittgenstein, *Tractatus*, p. 151.

65. Max Horkheimer, "Die Soziologie der Gegenwart (Sprachanalyse von Karl Kraus)," Karl-Kraus-Archives, Vienna.

66. William James, *The Varieties of Religious Experience*, New York, 1902, p. 120.

67. Horkheimer, *Eclipse*, p. 13.

68. *Ibid.*, p. 120.

69. Horkheimer, *Eclipse*, p. 14.

70. *Ibid.*, p. 16.

71. *Ibid.*, p. 24.

72. *Ibid.*, p. 27.

73. *Ibid.*, pp. 47–88.

74. *Ibid.*, p. 51. For a brief summary of the concept of science of logical positivism, see Hans Haeberli, *Der Begriff der Wissenschaft im logischen Positivismus*, Bern, 1955.

75. Steven Mason, *A History of the Sciences*, New York, 1962, p. 349.
76. Horkheimer, *Eclipse*, p. 77.
77. *Ibid.*, pp. 77–78.
78. *Ibid.*, p. 82. For a critical survey of the problem of intuition, see Mario Bunge, *Intuition and Science*, Englewood Cliffs, N.J., 1962.
79. Walter Rehm, *Griechentum und Goethezeit*, Bern, 1952, p. 12.
80. Friedrich Schiller, *On the Aesthetic Education of Man*, New York, 1965, p. 40. For a recent sociological study of occupations as determinants of *Weltanschauungen*, see Joseph Bensman and Robert Lilienfeld, *Craft and Consciousness. Occupational Technique and the Development of World Images*, New York, 1973.
81. Georg Lukács, *Die Theorie des Romans*, Neuwied am Rhein, 1963, p. 27. See also Marx on Greek art in Karl Marx, *Grundrisse. Der Kritik der politischen Ökonomie*, Berlin (East), 1953, pp. 30–31.
82. Horkheimer, *Eclipse*, passim. One could raise the question at this point when attacking positivism in sweeping general terms: "Which positivism? Whose positivism?" Positivism from its very beginning with Saint Simon and Auguste Comte up to that of, say, Rudolf Carnap, has undergone too many modifications for one to ignore all those changes. What does the work of two giants of positivist thought, such as Comte and Mach or Wittgenstein, have in common? The Comtean positivism has a philosophy of history ("law of the three stages"); it was instrumentalist ("Savoir pour prévoir et prévoir pour pouvoir") and empirical, emphasizing observation, experimentation, and comparison at least in program. Neopositivism is ahistorical, neutral in intrumentalism (separation of knowledge and praxis, except in its extreme scientist variant), and empirical. However, new elements have been added: the use of symbolic logic and the principle of verification.
83. Horkheimer, *Eclipse*, p. 76.
84. Thomas S. Kuhn, "The History of Science," in *International Encyclopedia of the Social Sciences*, Vol. 14, David L. Sills (Ed.) New York, 1968, pp. 74–83.
85. A selection of the Moscow publication was published in Germany; see Wolfgang Endemann (Ed.) *Karl Marx—Mathematische Manuskripte*, Kronberg/Taunus, 1974; further, see Kurt Reiprich, *Die philosophisch-naturwissenschaftliche Arbeiten von Karl Marx und Friedrich Engels*, Berlin (East), 1969, and Dirk J. Struik, "Marx and

Mathematics," in *Science and Society*, *XII*, 1 (Winter 1948), pp. 181–196.

86. Joseph Needham, *Science and Civilization in China*, Vol. 2, London, 1956, p. 28.

87. *Quotations from Chairman Mao Tse-tung*, Peking, 1966, pp. 204–205.

88. Karl Marx and Frederick Engels, *The Communist Manifesto*, New York, 1971, p. 12. As early as 1844, Marx summed up the role and effects of natural sciences as follows: "The *natural* sciences have developed an enormous activity and have accumulated an ever-growing mass of material. . . . But natural science has invaded and transformed human life all the more *practically* through the medium of industry; and has prepared human emancipation, although its immediate effect had to be the furthering of the dehumanization of man." See Karl Marx, *The Economic and Philosophic Manuscripts of 1844*, Dirk J. Struik (Ed.) New York, 1964, p. 142. See also Karl Marx, *Grundrisse*, London, Penguin Books, 1973, pp. 704–706; For sociological treatment of Marx's view of science and technology see J. D. Bernal, *Marx and Science*, New York, 1952 and Kostas Axelos, *Marx penseur de la technique*, 2 vols., Paris, 1974.

89. *Ibid.*, p. 13.

90. Horkheimer-Adorno, *Dialektik*, p. 256.

91. Horkheimer, *Eclipse*, p. 177.

92. *Ibid.*, p. 177.

93. John Madge, *The Origins of Scientific Sociology*, New York, 1962, p. 9. T. W. Adorno et al., *The Authoritarian Personality*, New York, 1950. This volume, close to 1000 pages, is one of the outcomes of a series of studies sponsored by the American Jewish Committee. Its Department of Scientific Research was headed by Horkheimer. Although his name appears only in the foreword and preface of the book, he retained a keen interest in the project throughout its entire course. As expressed by the authors: "Dr. Horkheimer played the crucial role in the initiation of the study, and he remained closely identified with it until the end; he contributed ideas, guidance, encouragement and untiring activity in support of our aims/xiii/."

94. Max Horkheimer and Samuel H. Flowerman, "Foreword to Studies in Prejudice," in *The Authoritarian Personality*, T. W. Adorno et al., New York, 1950, p. VII.

95. *Ibid.*, p. V.

96. *Ibid.*, p. VI.

97. Adorno et al., *The Authoritarian Personality*, p. 1.

98. Erich Fromm, *Escape from Freedom*, New York, 1965, p. 186.

99. Adorno et al. *The Authoritarian*, p. 5.

100. *Ibid.*, pp. 11–12.

101. See Ulrich Sonneman, "Hegel und Freud," in *Psyche*, 24, 3 (1970). pp. 208–218

102. Adorno et al, *The Authoritarian*, p. 57.

103. *Ibid.*, p. 57.

104. *Ibid.*, p. 94.

105. *Ibid.*, p. 71.

106. William G. Sumner, *Folkways*, Boston, 1906, pp. 12–15.

107. Adorno et al., *The Authoritarian*, p. 150.

108. *Ibid.*, p. 113.

109. *Ibid.*, p. 151n.

110. *Ibid.*, p. 151.

111. *Ibid.*, p. 152.

112. *Ibid.*, p. 228.

113. *Ibid.*, pp. 482–483. For a brief clarification of the scientific status of Freudian psychoanalytic theory, see R. R. Sears, *Survey of Objective Studies of Psychoanalytic Concepts*, New York, 1943; Jean Piaget, *Main Trends in Psychology*, New York, 1970.

114. *Ibid.*, p. 973.

115. *Ibid.*, p. 973.

116. *Ibid.*, p. 975.

117. *Ibid.*, p. 975.

118. *Ibid.*, p. 975.

119. *Ibid.*, p. 976.

120. *Ibid.*, p. 976.

121. *Ibid.*, p. 976.

122. Paul Fraisse and Jean Piaget (Eds.) *Experimental Psychology; Its Scope and Method*, Vol. I, *History and Method*, New York, 1967. See also Edwin G. Boring, *A History of Experimental Psychology*, 2nd. ed., New York, 1950.

123. Emile Durkheim, *The Rules of Sociological Method*, New York, 1964, p. iii.

124. Talcott Parsons, *Social Structure and Personality*, New York, 1970. p. 2. See also Ernest W. Burgess, "The Influence of Sig-

mund Freud upon Sociology in the United States," in *American Journal of Sociology*, 45 (Nov. 1939), 356–375.

125. Isaac Deutscher, *The Prophet Unarmed. Trotsky: 1921–1929*, New York, 1959, pp. 180–181, see also, Jean Marti, "La psychoanalyse en Russie 1901–1930," in Critique (Paris), XXII, 346 (March 1976), pp. 199–236; Wilhelm Reich, "Dialectical Materialism and Psychoanalysis," and "Psychoanalysis in the Soviet Union," in *Studies on the Left*, 6, 4 (1966), pp. 5–57; Michael Schneider, *Neurosis and Civilization. A Marxist/Freudian Synthesis*, New York, 1975. For a perceptive analysis of the history of Soviet psychology see John McLeish, *Soviet Psychology: History, Theory, Content*, London, 1975.

126. Theodor Geiger, *Die soziale Schichtung des deutschen Volkes*, Stuttgart, 1932: See also Seymour Martin Lipset, *Political Man*, Garden City, N. Y. 1963, pp. 149 ff.

127. Quoted in Heinz Maus, "Der achte Deutsche Soziologentag," *Die Umschau. Internationale Revue*, II, 1 (January 1947), p. 87.

128. Karl Dietrich Bracher, *Zeitgeschichtliche Kontroversen um Faschismus, Totalitarismus, Demokratie*, Serie Piper, München, 1976; K. D. Bracher, *The German Dictatorship*, New York, 1970; see also Wolfgang Sauer, "National Socialism: Totalitarianism or Fascism," in *American Historical Review*, LXXIII, 2 (1967), pp. 404–424; Wolfgang Wipperman, *Faschismustheorien. Zum Stand der gegenwärtigen Diskussion*, Darmstadt, 1972; and Reinhard Kühnl, "Problems of a Theory of German Fascism," in *New German Critique*, No. 4 (Winter 1975), pp. 26–50.

129. Leon Trotsky, *The Revolution Betrayed; What is the Soviet Union and Where is it Going?*, New York, 1972, p. 278.

130. Joseph A. Schumpeter, *Capitalism, Socialism and Democracy*, 3rd ed. New York, 1962, p. 375.

131. Karl Mannheim, *Ideology and Utopia*, New York, n.d., p. 145.

132. See Siegfried Bahne, "Sozialfaschismus in Deutschland. Zur Geschichte eines politischen Begriffs," in *International Review of Social History*, 10, 2 (1965), pp. 211–245.

133. Karl Dietrich Bracher, *Zeitgeschichtliche Kontroversen*, p. 27.

134. Peter C. Ludz, *The Changing Party Elite in East Germany*, Cambridge,/Mass. and London, 1972. See especially Chapter 1: "The Theoretical Frame of Reference."

135. Bracher, *Zeitgeschichtliche Kontroversen*, p. 33.

136. Max Horkheimer, "Autoritärer Staat," in *Gesellschaft im Über-*

gang; *Aufsätze, Reden und Vorträge 1942–1970*, Werner Brede (Ed.) Frankfurt am Main, 1972, pp. 13–35.

137. Georg Lukács, *Die Zerstörung der Vernunft*, Berlin (East), 1954; see also Hajo Holborn, "Der deutsche Idealismus in sozialgeschichtlicher Beleuchtung," in *Historische Zeitschrift*, 174, 2 (Okt. 1952), pp. 359–384.

138. *The Authoritarian Personality* was published in 1950, very bad timing indeed in view of the rising McCarthyism. Violent anticommunism was the order of the day, and many European intellectuals feared the reoccurrence of the German historical experience of the 1930s, leading to fascism in the U.S. The concentrated attacks directed against *The Authoritarian Personality* by fellow refugees and native scholars must be viewed in this context. The attacks on ideological, political, and methodological grounds certainly contributed to Horkheimer's and Adorno's decision to return to Frankfurt am Main. Even usually progressive intellectuals like David Riesman were caught up in the Cold War rhetoric and ideological confusion. Riesman wrote that the real danger for America lies not in the existence of a few million home-grown fascists but in Soviet Communism. He admitted that "there are undoubtedly some millions of fascist-minded people in the United States." However, "if there exists a danger of international repression in America today, it ensues more from the threat of totalitarian Soviet expansion than from sources in American 'authoritarian personality.'" David Riesman, "Some Observations on Social Science Research," in *Antioch Review*, 1 (1951), pp. 259–278. For critical evaluations, see Richard Christie and Marie Jahoda (Eds.) *Studies in the Scope and Method of the Authoritarian Personality*, Glencoe,/Illinois, 1954; Roger Brown, *Social Psychology*, Chapter 10, New York, 1965; for follow-up studies on authoritarianism, see R. Christie and P. Cook, "A Guide to the Published Literature Relating to the Authoritarian Personality through 1956," *Journal of Psychology*, 45 (1958), pp. 171–199. See also J. P. and R. C. Dillehay, *Dimensions of Authoritarianism. A Review of Research and Theory*, Lexington, Ky., 1967.

139. Karl Marx-Friedrich, Engels, *Werke*, Vol. 27, Berlin (East), 1963, p. 186.

140. Karl Korsch, "Über die amerikanische Wissenschaft," in *Alternative* (Berlin), 41 (April 1965), pp. 76–77.

141. Bertolt Brecht, *Gedichte 1941–1947*, Frankfurt am Main, 1964, p. 53.

142. Sander L. Gilman, "Bertolt Brecht and the FBI," in *The Nation*, (Nov. 30, 1974), pp. 560–562.

143. Quoted in Klaus Schröter, *Thomas Mann, in Selbstzeugnissen und Bilddokumenten*, RoRoRo Monographie, Reinbek bei Hamburg, 1964, p. 141.

144. Theodor W. Adorno, *Prisms. Cultural Criticism and Society*, London, 1967, p. 98.

145. Adorno, *Minima Moralia, Reflexionen aus dem beschädigten Leben*, 6th ed. Frankfurt am Main, 1969.

146. *Ibid.*, p. 31.

147. *Ibid.*, p. 42.

148. *Ibid.*, p. 43.

149. *Ibid.*, pp. 32–33.

150. *Ibid.*, p. 45.

151. Horkheimer and Adorno, *Dialektik der Aufklärung*, p. 255.

THREE

FRANKFURT SOCIOLOGY:
THEORY OF SOCIETY

POST WAR GERMANY

The European phase of World War II ended on May 8, 1945, with the victory of the allied antifascist forces; subsequently, Nazi Germany was divided among the victorious powers into four occupational zones. However, all democratic Germans feared the revival and continuation of the reactionary forces that helped Hitler to power. Even before the war was over, Thomas Mann, in a letter, earmarked de-Nazification as the order of the day:

> De-Nazification, in my opinion, does not mean that a mail carrier, who one day joined the party, may no longer carry the mail. . . but it does mean, above all, the ruthless expropriation of all profiteers of the defeated Nazi regime, of all those, who, under it and through it, grew rich and remained rich; it means to divest these well-fed parasites of their social and political influence—instead of drinking champagne with them as an expression of our class sympathy.[1]

Horkheimer and Adorno, too, it will be recalled, feared that developments might "lead to a victorious re-emergence of the neo-barbarism recently defeated on the battlefields."

By 1949, out of the postwar chaos, two Germanies emerged as separate political entities: the Federal Republic of Germany (*Bundesrepublik Deutschland*) and the German Democratic Republic (*Deutsche Demokratische Republik*). The former became a part of the Western NATO alliance, maintaining a capitalist economy and a bourgeois-democratic political system; the latter, with its socialist economic and political system, formed an integral part of the Eastern European socialist bloc. Ralf Dahrendorf describes the striking dissimilarity of the two states: "If one compares Frankfurt and Leipzig, Düsseldorf and Karl-Marx-Stadt, even East and West Berlin today, one is unlikely to conclude that these cities are all situated in the same country." The sociologist then wonders "how such differences could emerge in but twenty years." While the dominance of a political elite has characterized East German modernization, "the explosive development of its economy is the dominant and determinant feature of the short history of the Federal Republic of Germany." In East Germany, the "second industrialization" was accomplished again "from above," whereas West German society after 1948 made up allegedly for the errors Imperial Germany had committed. In 1965, however, when the postwar Adenauer restoration was drawing to a close, the liberal Dahrendorf could still detect many "counterrevolutionary" trends that in his view constituted a "return to premodern structures"—overemphasis on the family with parental prerogatives anchored in the constitution, the countertrend to secularization, and subsidies serving to perpetuate "anachronistic country life." Yet his overall balance sheet favored the postwar developments. He summed up the difference from Imperial Germany by asserting that "authoritarianism of the traditional kind has become impossible in Germany society." The social impact of the West German "economic miracle" was recognized in all institutions and spheres of German society. Dahrendorf singled out, as one of the most significant facts of change, the emergence of new "economic elites, which differ considerably in their composition from their historical predecessors." He considered as most important and positive the fact that a world of highly individual values has emerged.[2]

Yet critical observers point to the continuation of unresolved problems (unbewältigte Vergangenheit) from Imperial and Nazi Germany to the West German republic, one of which is the accelerated concentration of the means of production and wealth. The historian, Immanuel Geiss, asserts that in West Germany "the leading circles have remained essentially the same since the Wilhelmian Reich."[3]

It was this postwar Germany that Horkheimer and Adorno returned to in 1949 with the conviction that they should "be able to do more there than anywhere else both in theory and praxis." The Institute was reconstructed and opened in Frankfurt am Main in 1951, the same year that Horkheimer became the rector of Frankfurt University.

Before discussing the career of Critical Theory in Frankfurt am Main in the postwar decades, we must sketch the general condition of postwar German sociology. German sociology had to make a new start in 1945. In 1933 sociology was either exiled or had become part of the Nazi *Weltanschauung*. The Nazis hated and feared sociology, the science with the capacity to unmask social myths. In Adorno's words, "the National Socialists' hatred of sociology expressed nothing more than a simple fear of that knowledge that might reveal the real determining forces of society: differences of interest and the relationships of power."[4] Thus all empirical work was ruled out. The majority of sociologists, anticipating personal persecution because of their political views and/or racial origin, and looking forward to a serious curtailing of their scholarly pursuit, immediately left Germany—Karl Mannheim for England, Theodor Geiger for Denmark, René König for Switzerland, and members of the Frankfurt School for the United States. A minority of the remaining sociologists embraced Nazi ideology, and some members of the younger generation tried to avoid ideologically sensitive areas. Folklore (*Volkskunde*), with a strong ideological orientation, became a substitute for sociology. René König commented on the situation retrospectively:

> Those who remained in Germany had to remain silent unless they belonged to the group of rightist quasisociologists who made their accommodations with National Socialism, e.g., Hans Freyer, or those who unscrupulously joined the Nazis, such as Günther Ipsen, Andreas Walther, Karl Heinz Pfeffer, among others.[5]

The emerging new sociology faced four major obstacles. First, solving problems that took priority, such as providing the bare necessities of life, left little room in the early postwar years for intellectual endeavors. Second, 12 years of Nazi rule created a vacuum in academic life and an isolation from international developments that had become the order of the day that had to be overcome. Third, the lack of empirical tradition and the ambiguous status of sociology in academic life presented additional problems for the new beginnings. Even Adorno had to champion the cause of empirical research techniques, at least immediately after his return. Thus, while criticizing the extremes of a German sociology rooted one sidedly in the cultural science tradition (*geisteswissenschaftliche Soziologie*), Adorno emphatically declared that sociology is not a *Geisteswissenschaft* and called attention to the urgent need for correctives through empirical research.[6] There was still a tendency, we were told, to disguise plain societal phenomena under pretentious and pompous categories. One of the main tasks of empirical research was to eliminate those disguises. Similarly, Horkheimer reflected on the ambiguous status of sociology in German academia:

> In Germany. . . in contrast to America or France, sociology had never had an undisputed place in the scientific hierarchy. It is ranked among the social sciences, which, in this country, have traditionally included political science and economics and thus do not coincide with what is commonly known as social science in the United States.[7]

Fourth, from the very beginning the general public was clearly ambivalent or even hostile toward the acceptance of sociology as a discipline equivalent to other branches of science; this attitude was particularly accentuated after many students of sociology participated in the student protest movement in the late 1960s. Helmut Schmidt, a leading member of the *Bundestag* (German Parliament), probably expressed a widely held opinion of the German public in his statement:

> We do not need so many sociologists and political scientists as our universities presently produce. We need professionals who possess a real profession, one that society urgently needs, one that is practical today.[8]

Three major socio-historic events seemed to have determined the theoretical interest of the Frankfurt School after its return to Europe: first, the continued stabilization and increased affluence of all advanced capitalist societies, a development that made socialist revolution in the West unlikely. In Adorno's words, "philosophy, which once seemed obsolete, lives on because the moment to realize it was missed."[9] The times were characterized by the situation of "a practice indefinitely delayed."[10] Second, the traumatic experience of Auschwitz, expressed in Adorno's dictum, "No poetry after Auschwitz!" Third, the continuing purges by the rigid bureaucratic and terrorist Stalinist Soviet regime, which doused immediate hopes for building a genuine socialist society in the East. Marx and Engels "could not foresee what became apparent later in the revolution's failure even where it succeeded. . .."[11] The Frankfurt School's attitude toward the Soviet Union ranged from silence and contempt to the equation of red with brown totalitarianism, and to more open hostility, especially in the writings of Horkheimer.

Horkheimer's and Adorno's collaboration, established in California in the early 1940s, continued in Frankfurt in the 1950s and 1960s. They emphasized over and over again the identity of their thoughts and coauthored several volumes on sociology and philosophy, most notably *Soziologische Exkurse* (1956) and *Sociologica II* (1962), which come closest to what could be called systematic statements on the Frankfurt School of sociology.[12] Although Horkheimer and Adorno reiterated the unity and identity of their thought after they returned to Frankfurt am Main, the lion's share of the critique of positivist and empirical sociology and the codification of the Theory of Society, culminating in *Negative Dialektik*, was undertaken by Adorno. (Horkheimer was visiting professor at the University of Chicago from 1954 to 1959 and became professor emeritus in 1960.) Thus this chapter focuses primarily on Adorno's sociological and social philosophical writings, with occasional references to Horkheimer's writings in the 1950s and a brief discussion of his later philosophy.

TOWARD A CODIFICATION OF FRANKFURT SOCIOLOGY*

This discussion presents the attempted codification of Critical Theory as sociology, under the new label, "Theory of Society," after Horkheimer's and Adorno's return to Frankfurt. In this connection, an effort is made to establish the theory's relationship to traditional schools of sociology by examining the Frankfurt School's criticism of positivist and empirical sociological traditions on one hand and by presenting its theoretical and methodological position on the other. We seek to demonstrate the conceptual looseness of Frankfurt sociology and how it is manifested particularly by its proposition that the demarcation between art and science be blurred.

Any presentation of Frankfurt sociology, or Theory of Society, as the members preferred to call it after 1950, is beset with difficulties because Horkheimer and Adorno never arrived at a systematic codification of their sociological theories, as if thereby negating the tomes of traditional German academic scholarship, such as Simmel's *Soziologie* or Weber's *Wirtschaft und Gesellschaft*. At times one has the impression that Horkheimer and Adorno, while elaborating on a Theory of Society, considered sociology merely as an auxiliary discipline, contributing to the construction of the former. This attitude might be considered a remnant of Horkheimer's earlier position. As he put it in 1937: "To transform the Critical Theory of Society into a sociology is . . .an undertaking beset with serious difficulties."[13]

The Frankfurt School emphasized over and over again the inseparability of philosophy and sociology in many ways. First, both Horkheimer and Adorno held chairs of *philosophy* and *sociology* at Frankfurt University after their return to Germany. Second, blurring the conceptual and methodological frontier of

*The following terms were used interchangeably after 1950 by Horkheimer and Adorno for their social theories: Critical Theory, Critical Theory of Society, dialectical Theory of Society, Science of Society, sociology interested in essentials, dialectical doctrine of society, or simply Theory of Society. The latter term and the term Frankfurt Sociology are used in this discussion to distinguish it from Horkheimer's Critical Theory of the 1930s. Both Horkheimer and Adorno shunned the term sociology. Adorno once called it "a detestably sounding word (*ein abscheulich klingendes Wort)*'.

the neighboring sciences, they insisted on the use of key philosophical concepts such as totality and on the incorporation of elements of Dilthey's philosophical psychology or Freud's metapsychology. Any discussion of the pure sociology of the Frankfurt School under separate treatment violates its spirit. Dissecting the work of the Frankfurt School and discussing the pieces one by one is most objectionable to the faithful.

From its very beginnings, the aim of *Sozialforschung* was interdisciplinary research. An adherence to academic compartmentalization would have signified the acceptance of the division of labor of capitalist society and would have negated Critical Theory's aim to transcend this division of labor. After Horkheimer's grand program of 1937 failed, the anti-departmentalization bent was preserved in a modified "transcendental" version. As Adorno expressed it:

> As one speaks in the latest aesthetic debates of anti-drama and anti-hero, thus *Negative Dialektik* might be called anti-system. . . . Stringently to transcend the official separation of pure philosophy and the substantive or formally scientific realm was one of his [the author's] determining motives.[14]

THE CRITIQUE OF POSITIVIST SOCIOLOGY AND EMPIRICAL SOCIAL RESEARCH

The attempted codification of Frankfurt sociology was undertaken by Horkheimer and Adorno in a dialectical confrontation with the opposing theories of positivist and empirically oriented sociology, which they subjected to critical scrutiny and reexamination of basic tenets by focusing on the major issues raised during the course of its history. We briefly summarize the criticism by the Frankfurt School:

1. Sociology has moved toward an inevitable schism of theory, methods, and substantive areas.
2. Preoccupation with and concentration on limited research

areas and smaller problems have resulted in the loss of totality.

3. In the drive for exactness and quantification, the meaning of societal phenomena is lost.

4. Strict adherence to a natural science model in sociology means separating verifiable knowledge from ethics, that is, excluding the moral stand of the scientist by making sociology into a "value-free" science that is instrumental for dominant social powers as a tool of domination and manipulation.

5. The rigid separation of science and art results in the impoverishment of the sociological enterprise.

6. The emulation of a natural science model also excludes speculation, the source of invaluable insight into societal mechanisms.

In Adorno's opinion,

> all the methodological procedures which are subsumed under the label sociology as academic disciplines are interrelated only in a very abstract sense in that all of them deal in some way with societal phenomena. However, neither the object nor the method is uniform.[15]

As for its subject matter, there is nothing new in sociology; however the two doctrines of society, *sociology* and the *Theory of Society*, have different historical roots. The origins of the Theory of Society can be traced back to Plato. Philosophy and the Theory of Society were originally intertwined. One of the basic texts of Greek philosophy, Plato's *Republic*, put forth the doctrine of the good society, combined with a critique of Plato's contemporary society. Plato concluded that constitutional changes would only mean replacing the rule of the powerful with that of the more powerful. The real solution lies in the rational arrangement of the whole society, combined with the education of the citizenry for the Good. The cognition of the Good is the foremost task of philosophy, which in turn becomes the foundation of the good and just society. We have here the original intertwining of social theory, metaphysics (the doctrine of the true and eternal idea), and epistemology. Plato's concept has influenced all subsequent social theories; all designs of ideal society take existing society as their point of departure.

An illustration of the dialectical relationship between social theory and societal reality is how, with the dissolution of closed and hierarchically arranged feudal society, the static categories of evolution replace those of Being, and the history of philosophy replaces ontology as the basis for the construction of ideal society. With the development of exact natural sciences comes the demand for an exact science of society. Exactness as a criterion of relevance replaces the idea of a true and just society. This leads to the avoidance of "useless research of the inaccessible innermost nature or of the essential modalities in the generation of phenomena."[16]

The method of Auguste Comte's new science of society is observation, experimentation, and comparison with the premise that "societal movements are subject to unchangeable natural laws." The consciousness of the dynamic totality of society is replaced by positivistic methods. Society is the object of observation by an objective observer. Theory and praxis are separated because any intermixture of them would endanger both. Thus an element of resignation is implicit in positivistic sociology from the beginning. The perfectability of human society was already problematic in Comte's era. In spite of his idea of progress and his point of view of a philosophy of history in its innermost, "Comte's sociology is ahistorical."[17] It is quietistic as well, because of its view that if interventions, such as revolutions, contrary to the immanent laws of such societal developments were to occur, the society would necessarily be destroyed. At most, sociology helps shorten crises. Not "the domination of phenomena but modification of their spontaneous development is intended, which of course requires prior knowledge of their laws."[18] This position ultimately leads to the acceptance of the existing:

The mass of our race, being evidently destined, according to its unsurmountable fate, to always remain composed of men living in a more or less precarious manner off the current fruits of their daily labor, it is clear that the true social problem consists in ameliorating the basic condition of this immense majority. . . . By dissipating irrevocably all vain pretension and fully securing the ruling class [*classes dirigentes*] against all invasions of anarchy, the new philosophy is the only one which can direct a popular politics.[19]

Thus with the cult of the positive, reason dissolves into unreason. The admitted objective is to save bourgeois society and ensure a transition into a new social organization that is more progressive and stable. The impulse that "the ought could change being" (*das Sollen das Sein verändern könnte*) is replaced by "the acceptance of being as ought."[20] In that respect, continuity characterizes positivistic sociology running from Comte to Durkheim, Weber, and Pareto, we are told.

Yet in another sense, a lack of continuity characterizes sociology because its subject matter, society, is full of contradictions. Consequently, one must not be surprised by the fact that "the science dealing with society, societal phenomena, and *faits sociaux* cannot be formulated in a continuity."[21] Adorno argues that in every theoretical attempt that is aimed at harmony, such as the Parsonian grand system, there is an implicit effort to eliminate from society real contradictions, which are basically its constituent elements. In the same vein, the ideal "unity of science" represses (*verdrängt*) the contradictions of its object. A conceptual framework intended to incorporate everything societal, from the individual to the complex social formations, cannot account for the condition that the relationship of the individual to the society is full of contradictions because blind individual interests that are set free inhibit the construction of a society built on *collective* societal interests.

The "specific and frightening" inhomogeneity of sociology goes back to Comte, who, with his ideal of cognition based on natural science, wanted to formulate societal phenomena as if they were as coherent as a mathematical proof. Thus he regretted the sad state of affairs that sociology does not yet possess the reliability and exactness of the physical sciences, instead of reflecting on its peculiar nature and asking whether predictions in sociology are possible at all as they are in the physical sciences. On the other hand, for Comte, sociology was philosophy too. Yet, at the same time, he was "an enemy of philosophy," or at least of its speculative-metaphysical branch.[22]

The practical bent of Comte's new science was a reaction to the problems of postrevolutionary French society. As is well known, Comte divided his sociology into two parts: statics, dealing with order in society, and dynamics, devoted to problems of progress; however, his main interest was in the latter, that is, how controlled and directed "orderly progress" could be achieved. Comte's sociology had in common with that of Saint Simon a strong technocratic inclination, although the latter emphasized the dynamic element to a larger extent. In other words, social technology became the key idea for the new discipline. According to Adorno, even Marx shares some ambivalence with Saint Simon—or, for that matter, with Comte, for whom otherwise he had nothing but contempt—when Marx overemphasized the primacy of technique, that is the role of productive forces in the societal process.

Many problems of sociology are rooted in its twofold origins: the "philosophy" of Auguste Comte and the gradual development of empirical research techniques. An amalgamation of the two lines of development has never really been achieved. A major problem then seems to be the trend toward a widening gap between theory and method. Methodology tends to establish itself as an independent discipline in its own right, solely concerned with the verification, or falsification, the quantification and repeatability of subjective opinions, motivations, attitudes, and behavioral patterns, all of which are divorced from the sociological analysis of objective societal formations. The chief danger then consists of the growing autonomy of a specific methodological apparatus, spreading over the entire domain of sociology; in other words, of establishing the primacy of method over theory and subject matter. Developments have already led to the situation, we are told, that in sociology today "theory is regarded more as a necessary evil, as 'hypothesis construction' rather than something that should exist in its own right."[23] Adorno concludes on the pessimistic note: "This sociology could be called a 'sociology without society', just as fifty years ago one spoke of a 'psychology without soul.'"[24]

In regard to German postwar developments, Adorno in 1951 had already characterized the situation as one of schism. Members of the older generation attempt "total depictions of contemporary society's essential problems," whereas those of the younger "sceptical" generation concentrate on "specific and intermediate ranges of phenomena, which they regard as ascertainable and certain." In Adorno's words, the latter try "to out-Americanize the Americans" in their empiricism.

TOTALITY, DIALECTIC, AND UNIVERSAL GUILT

The problem of the loss of totality is closely tied to the rise of sociology as a "crisis science" in the nineteenth century and to its split with certain societal phenomena from the problem area of political economy. Yet the founding fathers, Auguste Comte and Herbert Spencer, still intended to establish sociology as a universal science. However, by making observation, experimentation, and comparison its sole method, positivistic sociology cannot transcend classificatory enumeration and cannot comprehend the interdependence of partial phenomena (family, religion, professions, etc.). This orientation inevitably leads to the loss of totality, the total concept of society. Earlier, Horkheimer, as will be recalled, did not assign a key role to that concept in his review of Mannheim's *Ideology and Utopia*. Now the accusation is made that

The consciousness of the dynamic totality of society is replaced by induction in positivist sociology. A whole can be

constructed only after the collection of protocol sentences is
completed. Even then the whole is to be understood in the
sense of a composition of the world out of its elements
(*Zusammensetzbarkeit der Welt aus Elementen*)."[25]

The dissection of objects according to societal sectors takes
place in sociology without an overview of their interdependence.

According to Theory of Society, the exclusive claims of
empirical social science find support insofar as subjective reactions are more easily determined and quantified than the structures of the total society, which resist direct empirical treatment.
The meticulous study of societal details is detested because,
when details are regarded as the strongest reality because of
their tangible immediacy, genuine perception will no longer be
possible. It remains problematic, in Adorno's view, that "one
can really proceed from the measurement of opinions and reactions of individuals to the grasping of the total structure and
the social essence."[26] The difference between the Theory of
Society rooted in Plato, Aristotle, and Hegel and the sociology
of Comte is not in the subject matter but in concepts, method,
and attitudes. The idea of the Theory of Society develops
out of "absolute principles of Being;" Comte's sociology is the
emancipation from theology, emulation of natural sciences,
that is, aimed at establishing regularities and causal connections.

Dialectical Theory of Society deals with societal totality,
with the laws of motion of society as a whole. It aims at gain-
ing insight into societal interconnections from basic structural
conditions, such as relations of exchange. Frankfurt sociology is thus a macrosociology with conceptualization and terminology such as totality, essence, and appearance, which are
Hegelian. Totality, a philosophical category, becomes a central
one for the Theory of Society; its use implies opposition to
academic compartmentalization. Totality is not an analytical
category that can be scientifically verified. "It is open to explication."[27]

Totality is a dialectical category of reciprocal interrelationships. "Societal totality," Adorno writes,

> has no life of its own beyond its constituent elements. It produces and reproduces itself through its moments. . . .As much as it [totality] is separated from the life, cooperation and antagonism of its elements, is as much as any element can be understood even in its functioning without insight into the whole which has its essence [expressed] in the movement. System and particularity are reciprocal and can be understood only from this reciprocity.[28]

Bourgeois society is an antagonistic totality. It exists solely through its antagonisms and cannot smooth them out.

Totality is a functional interrelationship as well, because all individuals depend on the totality they form. Furthermore, everyone is dependent on everyone else within the totality. The whole survives only through the unity of the functions that its members fulfill. Adorno answers the criticisms that totality is a prescientific and mythical category and that it is nothing but the trivial idea that in society everything is connected with everything else:

> Above and beyond all specific forms of social differentiation, the abstraction implicit in the system based on exchange value represents the domination of the general over the particular, of society over its captive membership (*über ihre Zwangsmitglieder*). It is not at all a socially neutral phenomenon, as the logistics of the process of reduction to units such as the social average labor time might suggest. Behind this reduction of men to agents and bearers of exchange value lies the domination of men over men. . . .The total interdependence has the concrete form that everyone is subordinated to the law of exchange if he does not wish to be destroyed, regardless of whether one, is led subjectively by the profit motive or not.[29]

Totality determines all the particulars, which are appearances, facts of immediate experience, in which the general is manifested.

Dialectics unfolds the difference between the particular and the general, dictated by the general.

> Totality has no life of its own beyond that which it comprises. It produces and reproduces itself through its particular moments. . . .and no particular element can be understood merely from its functioning without *insight into the whole*, which has its essence on the movement of the particular (italics mine).[30]

In other words, there is dialectical mediation between the particular and the general. Insight into totality (*Einsicht in das Ganze*) seems to be the important idea here.

In the dialectic of the Theory of Society, the general (totality, totality of society or object) takes primacy over the particular and determines it, that is, society precedes the subject. According to Adorno, "it is by the transition to the object's primacy that dialectics is rendered materialistic."[31] Yet, this primacy does not mean that the economic development of capitalist society inevitably leads to socialism; because "Marx's expectation that the primacy of forces of production in the historical process necessarily burst asunder the relations of productions was all too optimistic."[32]

In the dialectics of Hegel and Marx, negation of the negation results in a position on a higher level. After Auschwitz this is no longer possible; therefore, Adorno's negative dialectic is the "negation of the negation that will not become a positing (*Negation der Negation, welche nicht in Position übergeht*)."[33] Accordingly, totality is not regarded as an affirmative but as a critical category. As early as the mid-1940s, Adorno expressed his dismay with capitalist society by using the term totality: "The whole is the untrue (*Das Ganze ist das Unwahre*)."[34] All social relations in capitalist society are reified relations: therefore, "totality is . . .society itself as a thing-in-itself, with all its sins of reification."[35] Consequently, with the liberation of mankind from its state of sinfulness, the concept of totality is sublated (*aufgehoben*). As Adorno sees it, a liberated mankind would no longer be totality. Positivism is thus criticized because it lacks the experience of the blindly dominating totality and the driving inspiration of longing that at last society become "other."

It is interesting to note how closely Adorno's notion of totality corresponds with that of Franz Kafka, who provided perhaps the best depiction of many facets of modern capitalist society. Gustav Janouch reports on his conversation with Kafka:

> I showed Kafka some new books published by the firm of Neugebauer. As he was turning the leaves of a volume with illlustrations by George Grosz, he said:
> 'That is the familiar view of Capital—the fat man in a top hat squatting on the money of the poor.'
> 'It is only an allegory,' I said.
> Franz Kafka drew his eyebrows together.
> 'You say "only"! In men's thoughts the allegory becomes an image of reality, which is naturally a mistake. But the error already exists here.'
> 'You mean that the picture is false?'
> 'I would not quite say that. It is both true and false. It is true only in one sense. It is false in that it proclaims this incomplete view to be the whole truth. The fat man in the top hat sits on the necks of the poor. That is correct. But the fat man is Capitalism, and that is not quite correct. The fat man oppresses the poor man within the conditions of a given system. But he is not the system itself. He is not even its master. On the contrary, the fat man also is in chains, which the picture does not show. The picture is not complete. For that reason it is not good. Capitalism is a system of relationships, which go from inside to out, from outside to in, from above to below, and from below to above. Everything is relative, everything is in chains. Capitalism is a condition both of the world and of the soul.'[36]

The idea of a scientific truth must not be separated from the idea of a true society. The search and longing for a true life is the task of a dialectical Theory of Society. In our society "existence has become a universal guilt context." The need for emancipation from conditions of present-day society, emanates from this guilt experience, because "the guilt of life. . . is what compels us to philosophize."[37] It emanates from thought as well, because "thinking, itself an attitude, contains the need—the vital need, at the outset—in itself. The need is what we think from. . . ."[38]

The existential categories, experience of suffering, sin, and guilt context are more useful for Theory of Society than the theorems of formal logic and traditional epistemology. Formal logic versus dialectic and the elimination of contradictions versus demonstration of the meaning of socially determined contradictions are the irreconcilable opposing positions. "Dialectics as procedure means," we are told, "to think in contradictions, for the sake of the contradictions once experienced in the thing and against that contradiction."[39] Dialectical thinking shows the essence behind the appearance: it recognizes the general in the immediately experienced particularity. Appearance is then a manifestation of the essence and not just a semblance. To recognize the general in the particular is possible only with the knowledge of the general, which is totality, that is, "the sum total of contradictions."[40]

To be sure, there is no agreement on the meaning of the term totality in philosophy or in Marxist theory. Totality or the whole (das Ganze) in traditional philosophy included the unity of God, man (soul), and the world. Later, God was relegated to the realm of theology and man to the social sciences; no philosopher in our time could make correct statements about the physical universe, lacking this specialized knowledge. Karl Löwith refers to Alfred Whitehead as possibly the last philosopher who would attempt to develop a cosmology based on his thorough knowledge of physics and mathematics.[41] Kant's philosophy has been interpreted by Lucien Goldmann as the search for a concept of totality as the unifying theme of his philosophy.[42]

A perusal of the writings of Marxist thinkers reveals a variety of meanings and uses of totality. To begin with Marx, he still considered totality an analytical tool: the totality of relations of production constituting the economic structure of society, "the real foundation, on which arises a legal and political superstructure and to which correspond definite forms of social consciousness."[43] Lenin theorized along the same lines: "In order really to know an object we must embrace, study, all its sides, all connections and mediations."[44] In 1921, Lukács emphatically stated that it is not the primacy of economic motives in historical explanation that constitutes the decisive difference between Marxism and bourgeois thought, but the point of view of totality. Totality was still primarily a methodological category for Lukács, as defined by him at the 1947 Congress of Marxist philosophers in Milan. As he expressed it:

> The materialist–dialectical conception of totality means first of all the concrete unity of interacting contradictions. . ., second, the systematic relativity of all totality both upwards and downwards [which means that all totality is made of totalities subordinated to it, and also that the totality in question is, at the same time, overdetermined by totalities of a higher complexity. . .] and third, the historical relativity of all totality, namely that the totality character of all totality is changing, disintegrating, confined to a determinate, concrete historical period.[45]

With latter-day Marxists, the meaning of the term totality was shifted more toward ethics. In Lucien Goldmann's usage of the term, epistemology, ethics, and aesthetics are almost inextricably intermingled:

> Totality in its principal forms, the *universe* and the *human community* constitutes for me the most important philosophical category, as much in the field of epistemology as in ethics or esthetics. . . . I do not see this totality as something existent and given, but rather as a goal to be attained by *action*, which alone can create the human community, the *we*, and the totality of the universe, the cosmos.[46]

We cannot go into a discussion of the relationship of the term totality to the methodological concept of the whole or wholism as used by all nineteenth century sociologists.[47]

THE LOST MEANING

According to the Frankfurt School, the natural sciences and the sociology emulating them are sciences of domination

(*Herrschaftswissen*), to use Max Scheler's term. Theory of Society aims at grasping the *meaning* of social life. Its

> primordial motor. . . is not domination of nature and socie-
> ty. . . but the effort to penetrate cognitively societal life in
> regard to meaning as posited by men (*das gesellschaftliche
> Leben in Hinblick auf seinen von Menschen gesetzten Sinn
> erkenntnismässig zu durchdringen*).[48]

We are told that

> the limitation to controllable facts of experience and the com-
> plete exclusion of speculative thought seem to threaten not
> only the comprehension of the meaning of the societal, but the
> meaning of sociology itself.[49]

Two issues are raised here: the role of the subjective meaning and of speculative thought in sociology, that is, the idea of meaning is tied up with the methodological tool of interpreta-tion (*Deutung*). For Theory of Society, interpretation differs from the affirmative act of subjectively giving meaning by the knowing or acting subject to his action. The dialectical notion of meaning should show how societal essence shapes appear-ances.[50] Yet essence is not identical with meaning; it is not an entity sui generis. The Hegelian dictum that "the essence must appear in the semblance" is valid for Theory of Society. It is meaningless to speak of essence or relevant essences (*von wesentlichen Essenzen*) if they are not made manifest by interpretation (*Deutung*).[51] A real danger for sociology lies in its possible polarization into a mere collection of facts and un-substantiated declarations about insights into essences (*Wesen-schau*) in the manner of Husserl's phenomenology.

To be sure the subjective *meaning* of sociohistoric forma-tions and social actions has been a key idea for the social theories of Wilhelm Dilthey, Max Weber, Karl Mannheim, and Alfred Schutz. However, Max Weber at least insisted on the combina-tion of meaning with some kind of verification: "All interpreta-tions of meaning, like all scientific observations, strive for clarity and verifiable accuracy of insight and comprehension."[52] The use of meaning and *Deutung* in the Theory of Society represents a step backward toward an irrational uncontrolled intuitionism.

VALUES, THEORY, AND PRAXIS

Theory of Society's insistence on the unity of values, theory, and praxis, that is, the call for the right and just society, has its ultimate roots in the social philosophy of Plato, who combined a design of an ideal state with a critique of his contemporary society. Since cognition determines correct practice, Plato's objective was the unity of theory and practice that he proposed in the well-known philosopher–king solution:

> Until philosophers are kings, or the kings and princes of this world have the spirit and power of philosophy, and political greatness and wisdom meet in one. . .cities will never have rest from their evils, no, nor the human race. . .[53]

In other words, this is the earliest call for the unity of theory and *praxis*. Plato's idea of the just society emanated from and was closely connected with his metaphysics. With the dissolution of feudal society, which was a static and closed system, and with the rise of a dynamic bourgeois society, philosophy of history replaced ontology as the basis for the right society. Following the triumphant march of the natural sciences as instruments of the domination of nature, the demand for a science of society as an instrument for the domination of society arose. Social science emulated natural science by shifting its emphasis from the ideal of a just society to the drive for methodical exactness.

Comtean social philosophy, with its pronounced separation of values, theory, and praxis, abandoned the idea of radical intervention into societal mechanism. In Comte's words, "it is not a question of controlling the phenomena but solely of modifying their spontaneous development (*il ne s'agit point de gouverner les phenomenes, mais seulement d'en modifier le developpement spontane*)."[54] Consequently, the task of supplying useful knowledge for "piece-meal engineering" (Popper's term) to eliminate disturbances and to solve social problems was offered. Auguste Comte unequivocally outlined this task for sociology.[55]

The specificity of modern empirical social research is not rooted in the traditional *universitas litterarum*; its origins lie partly in market research, and it is closely allied with pragmatism. Its techniques are tailored to the needs of commercial and administrative tasks. It is aimed at *Herrschaftswissen* (science of domination) not at *Bildungswissen* (science aimed at pure knowledge). Historically, the outcome has not been the separation of theory and praxis but rather the separation of the social theorist from the use of his knowledge.

By contrasting instrumental social science with the interpretative and contemplative Theory of Society, the separation of the latter from academic sociology, from Marxist theory, and from its own stand in the 1930s becomes apparent. As for "bourgeois" academic sociology, its usefulness in social policy formation, usually called social technology or social engineering, has resulted in the large scale government and private financing of the empirical social research enterprise, especially in the United States after World War II. But instrumentality has also been a key idea for all Marxist theories, beginning with Marx's eleventh thesis on Feuerbach: "The philosophers have only interpreted the world differently, the point, however, is to change it."

The paralyzing effect of historical events led to the view expressed by Adorno: "the gaze upon disaster reveals a certain fascination" (*das Hinstarren aufs Unheil hat etwas von Faszination*) which serves as legitimation for escape from any praxis. Negative dialectics has a built-in, a priori antipraxis component. The works of Adorno were written with "no practical intention." Thought, by definition, must be negative because "positivity runs counter to thought."[56] Praxis presupposes the free and autonomous individual that is nonexistent today. At one point Adorno declares that "the aim of correct praxis would be its own elimination (*Das Ziel richtiger Praxis wäre ihre eigene Abschaffung*)."[57]

SCIENCE VERSUS ART

Adorno has always insisted on the inseparability of the pre-scientific and scientific realm and on the unity of art with all its methodological implications and consequences. It follows for Adorno that the traditional academic dichotomy (scientific vs. prescientific) reflects the split in positivist thought that classifies affairs and events as scientific and extrascientific. The prescientific sphere entails all elements of rationality and experience that are not and cannot be subsumed under the methodological requirements of "instrumental" reason.[58]

Adorno charges that the rule of the "quasidemocratic repeatability of cognitive operations and insights (*quasidemokratische Nachvollziehbarkeit von Erkenntnisoperationen und Einsichten*) " in the social sciences ignore the dominating power of false consciousness, which must be critically penetrated.[59] The social scientist who has grown up under the impact of a repressive culture industry that has become his second nature, to use Hegel's term, is unable and unwilling to develop a critical attitude. Furthermore, the uncritical attitude is promoted and reinforced by the distribution of funds only for research, which is intended to ascertain things within the existing system and does not lead to critical investigations of the structure and its implications for the system itself. The intention to sustain or to change existing societal arrangements penetrates sociology and determines the choice of its categories.

For Adorno, the method of survey research must be inadequate, because, if the subject's reaction is accepted at face value as the most reliable source of knowledge, the knowledge attained is superficial and misguided. This is particularly true of the realm of culture. How to measure culture remains an insoluble problem for sociology. The real objective should be the grasping of the objective spirit instead of the measurement of subjective reactions. The final aim even of quantitative research ought to be qualitative insight: "Quantification is not an aim in itself but the means for qualitative insight."[60]

Theory and empirical research must remain separate entities for Theory of Society, which sees no need to force them into a continuum, to tone down the divergences, and to bring them into harmonious unity. Rather, the real task would be to elaborate fruitfully on the tensions. Positivism is nothing but the puritanism of cognition with its abstinence from the cognitive dimension of reflexion.

The fiction of the consensus of the scientific community as guarantee of truth is categorically rejected: "The knowledge of objective societal lawfulness is by no means to be measured by *consensus omnium*."[61]

The Theory of Society considers art an invaluable source of insight into society because "art is cognition sui generis (*Kunst ist Erkenntnis sui generis*)."[62] Reflections on the evils of capitalist society by Adorno, the sensitive artist and humanist, and his worry over the future of mankind, is equated with scientific canons. Sociology is an art for the chosen few, for an intellectual elite, because "resistance against repressive total tendencies in contemporary society is reserved only for small minorities."[63] But what is the method for the artist-sociologist? In response to the demand of his positivist critics for an alternate model of sociological methodological procedures, Adorno points to the *Sprachkritik* of Karl Kraus as a possibility. Although Kraus' criticism was primarily directed against the grammatical violations in journalism, "his esthetic criticism has had a social dimension from the very beginning; deterioration of language meant for Kraus deterioration of social conditions."[64] The physiognomy of language unfolded by Kraus has presented more essential revelations about society than most empirical sociological findings because "it has shown seismographically the monster (*Unwesen*) from which social science has abstained and which it refused to treat."[65]

Thus interpretation, illumination, and reflection replace the accepted methods of science. Adorno's aim is to transcend traditional thought and methodology. As he stated of the critical theorist:

> He cannot accept the usual mode of thought which is content to register facts and prepare them for subsequent classification. His essential effort is to illuminate the realm of facticity—without which there can be no true knowledge—with reflections of a different type, one which diverges radically from the generally accepted canon of scientific validity.[66]

Consequently, it is not accidental that Adorno chose the essay form for most of his writings. The essay, a form of "intellectual poetry" (Lukács), seemed to be the most suitable form of expression for Adorno, an artist by training and sentiment. In Lukács' opinion, science is concerned with content, facts, and their interconnections; art is concerned with form, soul, and fate. Every writing depicts the world in symbols of relatedness to fate, that is, the fate problem determines the problem of form everywhere. The essay does not create a form, that is, something entirely new out of nothingness, but rearranges material that has already been there. The essayist-critic is an emissary judge with a calling, who is sent into this world "to announce and to judge (*richten*)." The essay is a tribunal, but it is not the verdict that is the essential and decisive element in it, but the process of trying (*das Richten*).[67] Just as Lukács saw in the essay the suitable form for judging the bourgeois culture of pre-World War I society, "the age of complete sinfulness" [*Zeitalter der vollendeten Sündhaftigkeit* (Fichte)], so did Adorno pass a verdict on capitalist society which culminated in Auschwitz.

THE CODIFICATION OF THE THEORY OF SOCIETY

Adorno defines Frankfurt sociology as

> insight into the essence of society, i.e., insight into what *is*, but in a critical sense. It measures societal reality against what it

pretends to be, in order to explore in the contradictions the potentiality and possibility of the changing of the entire social structure.[68]

Theory of Society must formulate its problems with the perspective of a just and true society. But, as if taking back his definition, Adorno admonishes:

> I ask you not to write down and take home what I have just said as *the* definition of sociology. It belongs to the attributes of a dialectical Theory of Society, that it cannot be reduced to definitions.[69]

What he means is that by establishing definitions thinking would be in accordance with traditional thought; that organizing things according to rigid concepts is alien to dialectical thought. Theory of Society is thus akin to Freudian psychoanalytic theory in that Freud turned to the "demolishing of the phenomenal world (*Abbruch der Erscheinungswelt*)" instead of concentrating on officially defined main problems. This turn enabled Freud to inquire into the essential problem, "the history of civilization as a history of repression."

The origins of Theory of Society go back to the political design of the Greeks and to the immediate reaction to the French Revolution. The doctrine of the Enlightenment, the teaching of Kant, that every human being should have the opportunity and the obligation to develop freely, culminating in the French Revolution, demonstrated that the released energy of political and economic forces had to result in enormous differences in income and property. Theory of Society arose when it became clear that the abolition of absolutism and feudal survivals did not fulfil the expectations. The Theory, begun with Babeuf and Fichte, never ceased to measure the society that emerged out of the French Revolution against its professed ideals. Saint Simon and Marx, next in line to the founding fathers, were convinced that the form of economic relations, the position of man in the labor process resulting from property relations, can be determined rationally. During the course of capitalist developments, the conscious rational decision was limited to the sphere of production. Horkheimer sees the basic difference between Theory of Society, the natural sciences, and natural scientific sociology as this: physics and biology are not expected to reflect on the forces whose organs they are. The manipulation of nature, without any reflection, is their aim.

Registering, classifying, and ascertaining social facts versus questioning the legitimacy of social arrangements are the issues that divide sociology and Theory of Society. For the Frankfurt sociologists, "only a critical spirit can make science more than a mere duplication of reality by means of thought."[70] Theory of Society, with the perspective of a free and just society and the full development of the individual, intends to break the spell of this duplication.

Essence is a key term for Theory of Society, and the most important criterion for selecting research problems is that they must be essential, even if they discover central problems that have not been defined and determined by the dominant interest groups and power cliques of society. But all positivists deny the distinction between appearances and essences. The "positivist rule of phenomenalism" asserts that there is no difference between essence (*Wesen*) and appearance or semblance (*Erscheinung*). Comte states the classical positivist position:

> All sound minds recognize today that our scientific studies are strictly limited to an analysis of appearances with a view to discovering their real laws, i.e., the constant relations of succession or likeness that exists between them, and that these studies cannot deal with the inner nature of the phenomena or with their cause efficient or final, or with the essential manner of their coming into existence.[71]

On the other hand, Hegel's doctrine asserts that observable phenomena are the manifestations of essences, of a reality that eludes ordinary cognition. According to Hegel, the essence appears in the phenomenon (*im Schein das Wesen erscheint*). The positivist doctrine of reducing research to phenomena accessible to sense perception and to available research techniques means the elimination of essential problems, the elimination of essences. Adjusting and tailoring research problems to existing methods and judging their relevance accordingly make social science inevitably the handmaiden of the sponsor.

The fallacy of all positivist-empirical sociology from Durkheim on down to its contemporary representatives is that it replaces real objectivity with that of a "collective consciousness." If the spirit of any given society, its collective consciousness, is taken for its essence, the distinction between true and false consciousness dissolves. Durkheim's doctrine of social facts as the sole legitimate basis of any sociological cognition excludes the possibility of any judgment of society in terms of truth criteria. The allegedly objective *faits sociaux*, the manifestations of collective consciousness, contain a latent momentum of subjectivism since the subject is designated as the chief criterion of truth because of the sensory certainty principle.

Empirical sociology measures only the surface phenomena of societal reality. Adorno writes: "The exclusive claims of empirical methods find support insofar as subjective reactions are more easily determined and quantified than the structures of the total society, which resist direct empirical treatment."[72] The real task, however, is to penetrate the surface and illuminate the essences. Quantitative social research must ultimately lead to qualitative insight. Quantification must not become an end in itself but the means to the latter. Theory of Society distrusts the facade of appearances.

The "structural interconnection" (*Verstrickungszusammenhang*) of a society in which all the individuals are included and manifested is essential.[73] Furthermore, the objective laws of the movement of society are the essentials that determine the fate of the individual. Auschwitz is a prime example of the essence of modern civilization. Adorno considered his famous dictum "No poetry after Auschwitz" imperative for all intellectual endeavor in the sense that he felt that no study of sociology could be possible without reflecting on Auschwitz and without concerning oneself with preventing new Auschwitzes. An essential research problem for empirical sociology would be to investigate the mechanism of mediation in the process of adjustment in a capitalistic society by those whose objective interests are basically contrary to the adjustment.[74]

Theory of Society is not satisfied with developing theoretical constructs for the classification of a "facade reality." Its aim is to penetrate that facade, to illuminate the real principles, the laws of essences (*Wesensgesetze*) that determine societal processes. As Adorno puts it: "As philosophy distrusted the deception of appearances, so does Theory of Society distrust the facade of society. . . .It will name that which holds society together. It would like to lift the stone under which the monster dwells (*brütet*)."[75] Theory of Society is distinct from the Baden School of neo-Kantianism, and adheres to the principle of the laws governing the structural movements of society. An example of laws of essence for a capitalist society would be the imperative for expansion, for growth. Stagnation is a danger signal of a coming crisis and decline.[76]

Essence is "that which lies concealed beneath the facade of immediacy, of the supposed facts, and which makes the facts what they are."[77] Essence can be recognized only in the contradiction between what things are and what they claim to be. Today the essence is a negative essence (*Wesen ist vorab Unwesen*). It is the law of doom (*das Gesetz des Verhängnisses*), which is obeyed by the historical process.[78]

Society, the central category of sociology, eludes definition. Only concepts that have no history can be defined. Society is not "a juridical concept that can be fixed by definition; it contains an infinite and historical richness."[79] Adorno approvingly cites Nietzsche: "All concepts which semiotically summarize an entire process defy any definition. One can define only something that has no history."[80] In a dialectical sense, society is neither the sum total of all individuals nor "a being in itself according to the model of an organism (*nach dem Bild des Organismus an sich Seiendes*)," but it constitutes a reciprocal interaction among individuals and an objectivity that makes itself independent of them and that stands against them.[81]

Society is a dynamic category and a functional one as well.

The dynamic aspect is manifested in the ongoing class struggle. Society remains today just what it was when the concept originated: a class struggle. The concept of society cannot be deduced from individual facts, nor is it subject to empirical verification. "Only a thorough-going Theory of Society can tell us what society really is."[82]

Modern society is the society of predominantly associative relationships (vergesellschaftete Gesellschaft); it is primarily determined by relations of exchange. Adorno here follows Tönnies and Weber in using the dichotomy of Gemeinschaft-Gesellschaft and combines it with the Marxist notion of a capitalist society based on commodity production. Vergesellschaftung takes place through the process of exchange, which is a basic social fact. The form of equal exchange is the essence of Vergesellschaftung. Exchange occurs in capitalist society through the form of the equivalent of money, the real unit behind which is the socially necessary average labor time.

Contemporary society is dominated by contradictions, the law of exchange, and an increasing instrumental rationality (Zweckrationalität). Human beings are mere agents of the commodity exchange principle behind which is the domination of man by man.[83]

Adorno, in reassessing the question of whether "Marx has become obsolete," asserts that capitalism found resources in itself that allowed it to postpone indefinitely the collapse of the system. These resources consist of the immense increase of technical potentials and the universal application of science to the domination of nature and society. The relations of production have become more elastic than Marx expected. The fact that proletarian class consciousness is virtually nonexistent in Western industrial societies does not negate the existence of classes that are objectively determined by the relationship to the means of production. The reason for the lack of class consciousness is that the Marxian prognosis of impoverishment (Verelendung) did not come true; instead the working class has been integrated into bourgeois society. Adorno sees that the difficulty in constructing a Marxist theory of classes in the situation arises because the objective economic explanation of this theory was connected with the labor theory of value. Technological progress has minimized the worker's share in the production of surplus value. That fact in turn affects the kernel of the Marxian labor theory of value. It is almost an impossibility to establish objectively the formation of classes without the labor theory of value. There is domination over the masses through the economic process, but the old societal oppression has taken on new anonymous forms and has become universal.

Adorno considers contemporary Western society as an industrial society in terms of its forces of production and a capitalist society in terms of the relations of production. Production is in the interest of profit maximization just as before. The establishment of a society assuring the dignity of man, once a utopia for Marx and Engels, has become a real possibility; but contradictions of a new kind in the international order, that is, the armaments race between East and West, make it impossible. In advanced capitalist societies a scarcity of goods and services does not have to exist, and working hours could be minimized. These were the two prerequisites for Marx for a higher stage of society. The rapid development of productive forces makes possible a life without want—which too was utopia for Marx and Engels. It could be realized today. Our advanced technology provides the objective conditions for society to become "an association of free individuals," that is, it could become "the realm of freedom" envisaged by Marx.[84]

The crucial question is then, why aren't there any social forces to utilize the objective possibilities? Why aren't there any real oppositional forces in late capitalist society? Marx's proletariat was outside bourgeois society and had no stake in its preservation. Early Critical Theory could still imagine a revolutionary potential in the proletariat.

As a reaction to the imminent revolutionary threat of the proletariat, steps were taken to integrate it into the system. Parallel with the objective process of integration, management of consciousness and even of the unconscious has taken place. Class consciousness is not connected with the objective existence of social classes in a mechanical manner. In the process of integrating the proletariat into the system, the "culture industry" has been instrumental in manipulating both the conscious and subconscious.[85]

The search for a revolutionary subject and the failure to find it resulted in the divergent positions of the Frankfurt theorists in the 1960s in Adorno's withdrawal into his ivory tower, in Horkheimer's yearning for God, and in Marcuse's temporary alliance with "the pseudo-revolution and its children," to use Habermas' term for the student protest movement.

INDIVIDUAL AND SOCIETY

Theory of Society insists that it must not be separated from neighboring disciplines, such as psychology, history, and economics, if the comprehension of the totality of societal conditions and forces is to be achieved. Yet it must not be dissolved into a conglomerate of sciences of man and society. Its specificity lies not in its subject matter but in its effort to relate its object to the laws of *Vergesellschaftung*. The important aspect about man is not that he is monadlike but rather that he is a social being (*Mitmensch*) prior to being an individual.

Comte deserves credit for his discovery that the individual is a product of society, but he mistakenly concluded that the individual must submit to society. The Frankfurt School perceives the individual–society relationship in a dialectical and historical fashion and, in agreeing with Hegel and Marx, believes that even the self-consciousness of the individual is ultimately social consciousness. In other words, this notion of the individual–society relationship rejects both the reduction to the individual, as Homans' sociology does, and the idea of the primacy of society, as Durkheim's sociology states. In Adorno's words, "There is no ego-consciousness without society just as there is no society beyond its individuals."[86] According to this dialectical relationship, "the fully developed individual is the

completion of a fully developed society. The emancipation of
the individual is not emancipation from society but the redemption of society from atomization."[87] Full development, of course,
can occur only in a just and humane society. According to
Theory of Society,

> The most important conclusion to be drawn from insight into
> the interaction of the individual and society. . .is that the
> human being is capable of realizing himself as an individual
> only in a just and humane society. This insight is already
> contained in the Platonic theme, that functional social inter-
> dependence is the precondition for the actualization of the
> Idea implanted in every human being. Only the just society
> will permit the human being to realize his Idea.[88]

For Theory of Society, assuming human dignity and the full
development of every individual must take priority and become
an integral part of theory construction. Early bourgeois society
nourished the idea of the autonomy of the individual. Later,
during the course of historical development in competitive
capitalism, this idea was reduced to an ideology. Theory of
Society is obliged to unmask this ideology.

Spencer predicted that societal developments would simultaneously increase integration and differentiation. Subsequent
developments have demonstrated that he was right: man has
been integrated more and more into society. Yet he was wrong in
that the division of labor that promoted differentiation at an
earlier phase of industrialization, today furthers uniformity. The
division of labor, which is maximized in mass production, has
broken down the work process into such tiny parts that one can
easily exchange one worker with another. Instead of differentiation, which was to lead to individuation and counterbalance
Vergesellschaftung through integration, uniformization has
taken place. This, of course, means a regression to earlier conditions. Furthermore, the individual–society relationship cannot
be separated from the relationship to nature. There is a constella-
tion of these three moments, that is, the division of labor, the
relationship of man to society, and the relationship of man to

nature. Theory of Society ought to investigate this reciprocal relationship from the perspective of the dynamics of history. It was Aristotle who first expressed the idea that, if not *vergesellschaftet*, man can be only a beast or a god. In German classical philosophy, Hegel summarized the same idea:

> True independence. . . consists solely in the unity and inter-pretation of individuality and generality in that it is just as much the general which gains for itself concrete existence through singularity as it is the individual and particular which finds the unshakable basis and true content for its reality only in the general.

He formulated the idea somewhat differently in the *Phenom-enology*: "Self-consciousness attains its satisfaction only in another self-consciousness."[89] It is then the reciprocal relation-ship and tension between the individual and society that pro-duces a dynamic totality.

Positivist sociology tends to reduce man to a species being of a higher order, a powerless representative of society.

Individuals and performances are made identical and commensurable through the universal spread of the principle of exchange value that is, the reduction of human labor to the abstract notion of average labor time. As Adorno writes:

> Above and beyond all specific forms of social differentiation, the abstraction implicit in the market system represents the domination of the general over the particular, of society over its captive members. . . .Behind the reduction of men to agents and bearers of exchange value lies the domination of men over men. . . . The form of the total system requires everyone to respect the law of exchange if he does not wish to be destroyed. . . .[90]

The spread of this principle drives the whole world to become identical, to become a totality.

Under the impact of the all-dominating totality, men cannot rationally determine their lives and the life of the whole. They are powerless against the system. Adorno sums up the individual—society relationship for our age:

> Men have come to be identified. . .in their innermost behaviour patterns with their fate in modern society. . . . So we have come full circle. Men must act in order to change the present petrified conditions of existence, but the latter have left their mark so deeply on people, have deprived them of so much of their life and individuation, that they scarcely seem capable of the spontaneity necessary to do so.[91]

Such diverse sociological orientations as the positivist sociology of Durkheim, the neo-Kantianism of Weber, and the dialectical Theory of Society seem to be in a close argument concerning the individual—society relationship. In Durkheim's theory, the individual finds himself in the presence of a force (society-totality) that is superior to him and "before which he bows."[92] For Weber, the increasingly bureaucratized mass society, capitalist and socialist alike, represents an "iron cage." In Theory of Society, the all-powerful negative totality determines every minute detail of social life, of the particular. In a totally reified society, "nothing particular is true," and "no single thing is at peace in the unpacified whole."[93] Yet, in spite of the formal agreement, there is substantial disparity. Durkheim accepts the domination of the whole over the individual as necessary and morally justified, whereas Weber perceives it with resignation and pessimism. Theory of Society views it with absolute despair.

Both Critical Theory and Theory of Society opposed the making of categories absolute (*Verabsolutierung*) and pleaded for permanent self-criticism. Yet they have violated both these dicta, as pointed out by critics. The experience of the holocaust was turned into an absolute historical and sociological category. The notion of the inevitable world historical process of Hegel and Marx, moving toward a goal, has been preserved, but the direction has been reversed in a negative sense. History becomes "progress toward hell (*Fortschritt zur Hölle*)."[94] The distinction between world *historical* totality and the *societal* totality was never made clear in Frankfurt thought. In a sense, particular socio-historic events of European civilization are being extrapolated into world-historical dimensions, into the fate of mankind. Adorno writes: "The world is a system of horror (Die Welt ist das System des Grauens)."[95] Hegel's Weltgeist is preserved, but it receives a negative sign. The idea of a negative Weltgeist is summed up thus:

> No universal history leads from savagery to humanitarianism, but there is one leading from the slingshot to the megaton bomb. It ends in the total menace which organized mankind poses to organized man, in the epitome of discontinuity. It is the horror that verifies Hegel and stands him on his head.[96]

EVALUATION

To assess the attempted codification of Critical Theory under the new label Theory of Society, one must define sociology. The majority of contemporary sociologists insist on the scientific nature of their discipline. Harry M. Johnson, the author of a standard textbook, Sociology: A Systematic Introduction, asserts that sociology has the following characteristics of a science: it is empirical, theoretical, cumulative, and nonethical.[97] To be sure, there are sociologists who disagree with this "consensus sociology." One representative, Joseph Bensman, sums up the dissenting position: "Sociologists. . . do not agree and never have agreed on a definition of sociology. For such a definition implies a program for work to be done (and the methods, materials, and ideas to be employed), a relationship to other disciplines, and. . .an attitude toward society."[98]

This discussion takes the position that sociology is a science that to some extent is characterized by parallel developments in other sciences.[99] There are, in fact, as noted, five major aspects of these developments in the physical and social sciences. First, the idea of discontinuity, which was introduced into both physics and biology in 1900. Both the quantum theory of physics and the mutation theory in biology replaced earlier theories of evolution of continuous transitions with notions of change as discontinuous jumps. In a similiar vein, few sociologists today would subscribe to the Spencerian theory of social evolution. An exception, Talcott Parsons, outlined a new grand theory of social evolution in the late 1960s, in spite of his earlier (1937) verdict that "Spencer is dead."[100] Second, *complementarity*, as exemplified in physics by Niels Bohr's theory of the electron as corpuscle and wave. In the social sciences, various approaches and seemingly opposing theories have increasingly been accepted to explain the same phenomenon.[101] Max Weber anticipated the idea of complementarity in his investigation of the interrelationship between the Protestant ethic and the rise of capitalist civilization. He concluded his classic study with the statement: "But it is, of course, not my aim to substitute for a one-sided materialistic and equally one-sided spiritualistic causal interpretation of culture and of history. Each is equally possible." Recently, Dahrendorf advocated the complementarity of consensus and conflict theories as two sides of the same coin for exploring societal reality.[102]

Third, *relativity*, introduced into physics by Einstein, has its equivalent in the social sciences, particularly in cultural anthropology. In a sense, the idea of relativism in sociology is as old as the discipline itself. According to Comte's law of the three stages, in the search for absolute knowledge, first and final causes must give way to the research of relations through empirical observation and logical reasoning. Karl Löwith rightly stated that "Comte's new philosophy is relativism in the literal sense, being concerned exclusively with relations."[103] The roles of Max Weber and Emile Durkheim should also be mentioned. Weber, in his comparative study of world civilizations, writes: "The question of the relative value of the cultures which are compared here will not receive a single word."[104]

Fourth, the turn to the study of *microcosm*. The nineteenth century idea that one can apply Newtonian macroscopic physics to the study of the nuclei or atoms and the idea that atomic physics is only a natural extension of a Newtonian model were discarded. It has been recognized that microscopic reality is a reality *sui generis*. Microscopic study in sociology is the study of small groups. Sociologists have discovered that, to understand social reality, they must study the small constituent components of that social reality and that they cannot carry over any universal Newtonian or Parsonian law into the study of the microscopic realm. Simmel's pioneering role for subsequent small-group research has been acknowledged. George C. Homans correctly emphasized the importance of Simmel's work by calling him "an ancestor of what is known today as small-group research".[105] The rise to dominance of the middle-range theories should also be mentioned in this connection.

Fifth, *indeterminancy* and *statistical causality*. The idea of indeterminancy in microphysics, usually associated with the name of Werner Heisenberg, asserts that the position and momentum of an electron cannot be determined simultaneously. In social sciences, indeterminancy is most prevalent in the realm of psychic phemomena. Statistical causality, based on probability theory, has replaced nineteenth century mechanistic and absolute causality in microcosm. In sociology, Max Weber had already paved the way in this direction when he replaced the notion of inevitability with probabilistic models. In his definition of law and power, Weber wrote:

> Law exists when there is a probability that an order will be upheld by a specific staff of men who will use physical or psychical compulsion with the intention of obtaining conformity with the order, or of inflicting sanctions for infringement of it. . . . In general, we understand by "power" the chance of man or of a number of men to realize their own will in a communal action even against the resistance of others who are participating in the action.[106]

In this century, the introduction of inferential statistics as a methodological tool has been crucial to the development of social sciences. In general, a mathematization of both physical and social sciences, which is usually considered a sign of maturity for all sciences, has taken place.[107] The increasing use of models and logical constructs is a dominant trend in all sciences as well. Furthermore, there is general agreement among sociologists on two additional canons of modern science: on verification and on the principle that the community of scientists be the sole judge of the validity of scientific findings. The fact that these parallel developments have taken place independently should be emphasized. It may be added parenthetically that as early as 1914 Max Planck called the attention of physicists to the use of statistics in the social sciences.[108]

Having outlined what are considered the scientific criteria by the community of social scientists, albeit with some dissenting voices, we may now examine the sociological theories of the Frankfurt School in the postwar decades and attempt to evaluate them in light of established canons of scientific sociology.

The elevation of insight and reflection to a prime sociological method and the concomitant rejection of the "quasidemocratic" consensus omnium are grounded in an elitist intellectual attitude that is incompatible with the generally agreed on rules of scientific procedures. Adorno had nothing but contempt for "organized scepticism," another cornerstone of the "ethics of science." Scepticism has been intimately intertwined with the rise of modern science, which process, in turn, went hand in hand with the overthrow of dogmatism and authority both in the religious and the political realms. Herbert Butterfield traces this attitude back to Joseph Glanvill, who first insisted on "the importance of scepticism in science and on the system of methodical doubt."[109] For Adorno, "bourgeois scepticism is obtuse."

Regarding the critique of positivist and empirical sociology, Horkheimer and Adorno raised many true and valid critical points; their overall criticism, however, lacks originality. American academic sociology, for example, has had its own native critics ever since the days of Thorstein Veblen, the most important being Robert Lynd, Edwin H. Sutherland, and C. Wright Mills. (The complete ignorance of the work of Mills demonstrates the narrow horizon of the Frankfurt theorists.)[110]

The assessment of Theory of Society of the post-1950 period

on a comparative basis with canons of modern sociology leads to the conclusion that Theory of Society violates the canons of scientific sociology significantly and therefore cannot qualify as sociology. Although the emphasis of the category of totality would make Theory of Society another macrosociological orientation, its insistence on blurring the dividing line between science and art and its elevation of insight (Einsicht) and reflection to a primary source of sociological knowledge are incompatible with scientific sociological methodology. Science is cumulative; it progresses ad infinitum through the process of addition of new knowledge. The classic statement was presented by Max Weber, in whose words "science is chained to the course of progress," while works of art, "if they are genuine fulfillments, can never be surpassed." The related issue, the search for meaning, has its roots in the doctrine of Dilthey, which was adopted by Weber, except that both Dilthey and Weber attempted to work out some kind of "verification" procedure for it, whereas the Frankfurt theorists categorically rejected those efforts as dangerous and leaning toward positivism.

Theory of Society can be called an amalgamation of artistic reflections (Kulturkritik), combined with Marxian categories and elements, and a pessimistic philosophy of history. If we accept the notion of existential determination of social theories, in this case we might speak of "existential overdetermination," or of Adorno's "biographical imprisonment," to use Habermas' term.

The reasons for Adorno's stand on the issues discussed are twofold. To a great extent, they are rooted in his early musical training and the impact of the modern music of the Vienna School on him. In 1924, after having completed his doctoral thesis on the aesthetic theories of Kierkegaard, Adorno met Alban Berg, one of the leading masters of modern music, and decided to study composition with him in Vienna. From this relationship, Adorno received a lasting impact. Even 40 years later he found it difficult to write about Berg because he could not gain adequate distance from his teacher. This influence of music of the Vienna School is manifold in Adorno's work. He acknowledges certain techniques and idiosyncrasies of his style as carryovers from his Viennese days. One important element in Adorno's work can also be traced back to the influence of those times: the fear and anxiety (*Angst*) of modern, alienated man. Hanns Eisler, who was also a student of Schönberg, remembers his teacher: "He expressed the feelings of people crowded in air-raid shelters, long before the bombers were invented."[111] This feeling, of course, implies a total attitude of the masters of modern music of the Vienna School toward life and society. Angst, fatalism, and the feeling of powerlessness are the key terms. In and from an air raid shelter one cannot change the world. The sole and main objective remains: survival. Subsequent historical events and the experiences of a refugee intellectual existence certainly intensified Adorno's initial feeling to such heights as in the despair of the *Minima Moralia*, subtitled *Reflections from an Injured Life*, and the nihilism of *Negative Dialektik*.

In a candid intellectual autobiographical essay written shortly before his death, Adorno assesses the influence of his artistic (musical) background as something permeating every aspect of his thinking, including matters of social science methodology. He wrote: "Something specifically musical impeded my progress from theoretical considerations to empiricism. . . .I approached the specific field of the sociology of music more as a musician than as a sociologist."[112]

Indeed, Adorno remained an artist throughout his entire life. He proudly reaffirmed his idea of the unity of science and art in the late 1960s, when, at the height of the German student protest movement, pressed to take a practical stand, he declared: "I am a man of theory, and feel theoretical thought to be extremely close to the purpose of the artists."[113] Second, throughout his life Adorno's main concern was to preserve the intellectual integrity and continuity of his personality. He left Hitler's Germany at the age of 31 and arrived in America at the age of 35 after a four-year stay in England. Uncritical empirical sociology in the service of commercial interest and adjustment to the new home in America were considered by Adorno as

identical threats to his integrity. In the intellectual-
autobiographical essay, written shortly before his death, Adorno
revealed many aspects of his relationship to America in general
and to American sociology in particular. He writes:

> My development up to the age of thirty-four was thoroughly
> speculative. I considered it to be my . . . assignment to inter-
> pret phenomena—not to ascertain, sift, classify facts and make
> them available as information. That corresponded not only to
> my idea of philosophy but also of sociology. To the present day
> I have never rigorously separated the two disciplines.[114]

The thought and attitudes of Adorno were decisively shaped by
his bourgeois social background and its concomitant life style,
his training in music in Vienna, and the socio-historic experiences of his encounter with American civilization. We have
discussed the impact of his artistic experience in Vienna on his
thinking. In addition to the analysis of intellectual existence in
exile at the end of Chapter 1, some specific aspects relating to
Adorno's situation as a refugee intellectual might be added.

As stated earlier, Adorno encountered every aspect of
American civilization with shock. Being suddenly transplanted
from "baroque" and gemütlich Vienna with its nineteenth century atmosphere, via Oxford, England, to the slums of Newark,
New Jersey, necessarily brought forth shock and panic. Adorno
worked on a radio research project in Newark. As he recalls:

> The Princeton Radio Research Project had its headquarters at
> that time neither in Princeton nor in New York, but in Newark,
> New Jersey, and indeed, in a somewhat pioneering spirit, in an
> unoccupied brewery. When I travelled there through the tun-
> nel under the Hudson I felt a little as if I were in Kafka's Nature
> Theater of Oklahoma. I was very much taken by the embar-
> rassment about the choice of a site that would scarcely have
> been conceivable by the lights of the European academic
> community.[115]

In another interview for Hamburg Radio, Adorno described how
he suffered in America when he was forced to bring his ideas

"down to earth." He solved the problem by pursuing a sort of "schizophrenic" intellectual existence: he divided his work into esoteric and exoteric parts. He composed his esoteric writings in German for his desk drawer without any hope of publication, and the exoteric material in English for publication.[116] The recent publication of the correspondence between Thomas Mann and his publisher Samuel Fischer, the owner of the respected Fischer Verlag in Frankfurt am Main, is revealing in this respect and sheds additional light on the matter. In a letter, Thomas Mann responded less than enthusiastically to Adorno's request to speak on his behalf with S. Fischer. The Fischer Verlag, residing in Stockholm during the war, rejected the manuscript of Adorno's *Minima Moralia*, which was published only after his return to Frankfurt am Main in 1951.[117] On another occasion, Thomas Mann wrote to Adorno after receiving his book *Prismen. Kulturkritik und Gesellschaft*: "I will read *Kulturkritik und Gesellschaft* when I am more alert. In order to read you, one must not be tired."[118]

Adorno's intellectual-autobiographical remarks tell the story of his manuscript of *The Philosophy of Modern Music*, which his American editor returned with the comment "badly organized." Adorno remarks: "I said to myself, in Germany at least this could never have happened to me, in spite of all that has happened in Germany."[119] He cites language as one of the main reasons for his return to Germany in spite of Auschwitz:

> My return to Germany was motivated not just simply by a subjective need, by homesickness. There was also the objective reason: the language. Not only the fact that one can never express himself with all the nuances and the rhythm of chain of thought in a newly acquired language, but the German language obviously has an elective affinity (*Wahlverwandtschaft*) to philosophy, particularly to its speculative moment.[120]

In Adorno's case, the complexity and problematic character of the language is saddled with an additional difficulty, that of writing in a "borrowed" language. Writing on Heinrich Heine, the German-Jewish poet, a contemporary of Karl Marx, Adorno gives the best summary of this issue:

> The fluency and clarity which Heine appropriated from current speech is the very opposite of native "at-homeness" [Geborgenheit] in a language. Only he who is not truly at home inside a language uses it as an instrument.[121]

This statement stands not only for Heine, but serves as a confession for Adorno as well. It cogently expresses the situation for Horkheimer, too, which was discussed in Chapter 1. Herein lies in all probability the answer to the question of the peculiarities of Adorno's language and style, often ridiculed by his critics as "Adorno-Deutsch."[122]

THE WELTANSCHAUUNG OF HORKHEIMER'S LATER PERIOD

It is often pointed out that the optimism and militancy of early Critical Theory turned into the pessimism, the elitism, and the resignation of late Critical Theory, after Horkheimer and Adorno returned to Germany. Some observers write of the break in Critical Theory or even about the treason of critical theorists who made an accommodation with postwar German society and became integrated into its academic structure. From Budapest, Georg Lukács made this devastating comment on the postwar Frankfurt School:

> A considerable part of the leading German intelligentsia, including Adorno, have taken up residence in the "Grand Hotel Abyss" which I described in connection with my critique of Schopenhauer as "a beautiful hotel, equipped with every comfort, on the edge of an abyss. . . . And the daily contemplation of the abyss between excellent meals and artistic entertainments can only heighten the enjoyment of the subtle comforts offered."[123]

Lukács called this intellectual attitude "conformism disguised as non-conformism."

The lack of mediation between theory and praxis gave early Critical Theory a degree of ambiguity. In this respect, there is no real break in Critical Theory, but rather a continuity. When asked about his turn to pessimism in the 1960s, Horkheimer is said to have answered that it is better to speak of a *return*.[124] Horkheimer's 1937 program had already asserted the predominance of ethical elements over the accumulation of specialized knowledge:

> However extensive the interaction between Critical Theory and the special sciences whose progress the theory must respect and on which it has for decades exercised a liberating and a stimulating influence [sic!], the theory never aims simply at an increase of knowledge as such, *Its goal is man's emancipation from slavery* (italics mine).[125]

The predominance of the ethical over the sociological and epistemological elements in early Critical Theory leads to the absolute reduction of all branches of knowledge, first to ethics, to questions of morality, then to theology and "the yearning for God." The postwar phase was introduced by Horkheimer's programmatic statement:

> The real individuals of our time are the martyrs who have gone through infernos of suffering and degradation in their resistance to conquest and oppression, not the inflated personalities of popular culture, the conventional dignitaries. . . the anonymous martyrs of the concentration camps are the symbols of the humanity that is striving to be born. The task of philosophy is to translate what they have done into language that will be heard, even though their finite voices have been silenced by tyranny.[126]

Twenty years later Adorno reiterates the point that later Critical Theory obeys the subject's pressure for expression. "The need to let suffering (*Leiden*) speak is the premise of all truth. For suffering is objectivity, which presses on the subject, and what he perceives as the most subjective, its expression, is objectively mediated."[127]

In 1968, a two-volume collection of Horkheimer's
Zeitschrift articles was republished under the editorship of
Alfred Schmidt, a second-generation critical theorist. This publication was subtitled *A Documentation* to indicate its historic
character and emphasize its disassociation from the author's
present stand. Horkheimer's preface reads:

> The reason for my hesitation to republish these articles of the
> *Zeitschrift*, unavailable for a long time, was not to a small
> degree due to the conviction that an author should always
> publish thoughts with which he can identify without reserva-
> tion.[128]

Horkheimer notes that the socio-historic situation has substan-
tially changed from the time his early writings were published.
It was an era in which proletarian revolutions seemed to be
imminent. Today the proletariat has been integrated into the
capitalist system. In Horkheimer's view, the teaching of Marx
and Engels is inadequate either for the explanation of internal
developments or for that of the external relationship among
nations. He concludes: "Socialism, which was once the idea of
the realization of the content of democracy, has been perverted
in the countries of diamat into an instrument of manipulation.[129]

Horkheimer claims to share many of the impulses and
ideals of the student rebels of the 1960s, their yearning for the
better, for the right society. However, the decisive difference
between him and the students is in the use of force. Late in life
Horkheimer professed to stand for conservatism, pessimism,
and the free world. True conservatism, he asserted, which takes
seriously the spiritual tradition (*geistige Überlieferung*) is a
revolutionary sentiment. Metaphysical pessimism, which is an
implicit moment of any genuine materialistic thought, has
always been dear to him. The free world is an island, the end of
which, in the ocean of terror systems, would mean the end of
civilization of which Critical Theory is a part. The thinker must
defend the free Western World. "It is the honor and duty of every
thinker," he contends, "to measure the free world on its own

professed ideals, to have critical attitude toward it and to defend it against fascism of any variety, Hitlerite, Stalinist or
other."[130]

It seems easy for Horkheimer, champion of the "free world,"
to identify even with emperor Wilhelm II of the German Reich.
Strangely enough, the one-time director of the "Studies in Prejudice" writes:

> In the West in the twentieth century, the responsibility of each
> individual citizen is. . . multifold. The threat to freedom from
> outside is evident. Already in the first decade of the twentieth
> century, Wilhelm II, who was not otherwise overly endowed
> with the gift of prophecy, spoke of the menace of the yellow
> race. Despite the maintenance of economic relations with the
> East, it should be taken very seriously today.[131]

According to Horkheimer, philosophy (Critical Theory) must
confront the East. The competition with the East, he argues,
concerns not only the increase of productivity but also that of
truth, which was once considered by the West as its most intimate mission.

Consequently, the later Horkheimer embraces some kind of
theism reminding one of Auguste Comte's stages of intellectual
career, moving from science to the Religion of Humanity. For
Horkheimer, truth cannot be separated from theism. It is futile to
want to hold on to an absolute meaning without God. There is no
glory to a good deed or to the rescue of the unjustly persecuted
without reference to the divine. Yet this theism differs from any
organized religion; it is transcendental. It does not consist of
any particular religious system, nor is it religious scholarship,
but rather an expression of yearning, a yearning after perfect
justice, which can never be realized on earth. Theology gives us
hope that injustice will not reign forever in this world. Questions of ethics and morality are then reduced to theology. Everything related to morality goes back, in the last instance, to
theology. Horkheimer and Schopenhauer share the view that
one of the greatest component elements in the teaching of both
Judaic and Christian religions is original sin.

It has determined history up to the present and still determines it for thinkers. It is possible only under the premise that God created man with a free will. Man's first act has been to commit the original sin; on this basis the whole history of mankind can be explained theologically.[132]

The scepticism of Critical Theory was mainly due to the historical experiences of critical theorists with fascism, Stalinism, and what they called late-capitalist American civilization. However, the germ of this all-pervasive scepticism of later Critical Theory was present in Horkheimer's writings in 1935. In a short article about the illusionary character of perfect justice, he wrote:

> The productive kind of criticism of the status quo, which found expression in earlier times as a belief in a heavenly judge, today takes the form of a struggle for more rational forms of societal life. But just as reason after Kant, even though it knows better, cannot avoid falling into shattered but nonetheless recurring illusions, so too, ever since the transition from religious longing to conscious social practice, there continues to exist an illusion which can be exposed but not entirely banished. It is the image of a perfect justice.
>
> It is impossible that such justice should ever become a reality within history. For even if a better society develops and eliminates the present disorder, there will be no compensation for the wretchedness of past ages and no end to the distress in nature.[133]

Horkheimer could even justify *Humanae Vitae*, the papal encyclical that prohibits the use of any artificial birth control method for Catholics. When asked why he agreed with the Pope on this issue, he defended his position thus:

> Critical Theory, and I have spoken as critical theorist, has a double task. It has to designate that which has to be changed, but it also has to point to that which has to remain. It has the task to point to the price we have to pay for this or that measure, for this or that progress. . . We have to pay for the pill with the death of erotic love. . . . The pill kills the yearning, because love is based on yearning for the loved one. It is not free of the sexual [sic!]. The greater is the yearning for uniting

with the loved person, the greater is love. The pill makes
Romeo and Juliet museum pieces.[134]

It is easy to understand how the longing for traditional German
bourgeois family life is intimately linked to this *Weltan-schauung*, which is neither critical nor theory any longer. The
mother who pursues an occupation, Horkheimer declares, is
something entirely different from the one whose life objective
centered on raising children. Occupation reifies thinking. If the
woman is emancipated, she no longer radiates the love she did
before. Nietzsche was absolutely right in stating that woman
loses with emancipation the most important thing she has, the
non-reified, not merely pragmatic thinking.[135]

A somewhat ambivalent elitism was an omnipresent
ingredient of Critical Theory. It was ambivalent because concern
for the masses has always accompanied fear and/or ignorance of
the masses for the Frankfurt theorists. Elitism was important on
both the theoretical and the practical levels. The very specific
role of the critical theorist, standing above and beyond the
masses, was already evident in 1937. Horkheimer considered
the intellectual elite of critical theorists as a "numerically small
group of men" with whom truth may reside. To be sure, Marx
envisaged a leading role for theorists when he predicted that

> in times when the class struggle nears the decisive hour,. . . a
> portion of the bourgeoisie goes over to the proletariat, and in
> particular, a portion of the bourgeois ideologists, who have
> raised themselves to the level of comprehending theoreti-
> cally the historical movement as a whole.[136]

The succumbing of the masses to fascism gave critical theorists
enough reason to distrust the masses. Yet, on balance, one must
not forget that, whereas Horkheimer and Adorno deplored the
"enigmatic readiness of the technologically educated masses to
fall under the sway of any despotism," French workers and
intellectuals of the Resistance were engaged in a life and death
struggle with fascism. Horkheimer and Adorno had nothing to
say about the masses of Soviet and Yugoslav partisans fighting

Hitler's invading armies, or about Chinese peasants who were fighting Japanese imperialism as well as their own native oppressors.

MARX TURNED UPSIDE DOWN

Horkheimer names his teacher, Hans Cornelius, a neo-Kantian empiricist, artist and liberal critic of bourgeois society, and Schopenhauer, the conservative critic of society, as early influences on his thinking. The critical aspect of Schopenhauer's philosophy facilitated Horkheimer's transition to Marxism because

> the Marxian teaching was essentially a protest against the situation that the ideals of the bourgeois revolution—*liberté, egalité, fraternité*—. . . have been realized only for a small minority in a society that professed those ideals as its own.

Horkheimer concludes: "Thus the two thinkers converged for me."[137]

The possibility of a revolution in Germany influenced critical theoretical work from 1933 until about 1940. "When Hitler came to power, many people hoped for his revolutionary overthrow. This hope was probably an illusion, a dream. Still, it dominated my work during that period from 1933 on."[138] Now under the different circumstances, in Horkheimer's view, oppositional attitude is necessarily tied to conservative thought.

> We want not only to prevent the decline of the autonomous personality, but, in accordance with Marx, we want that freedom of the entrepreneur [*Unternehmer*] which is limited today to a small group, to be extended to the whole society.[139]

This stand is obviously based on a distortion of the Marxian vision of a future society that is "a community of free individuals carrying on their work with the means of production in common, in which the labour-power of all the different individuals is consciously applied as the combined labour-power of the community.''[140] This arrangement of society represents something other than extending the freedom of the entrepreneur to the whole society, because for Marx, the capitalist himself is a slave to his reified consciousness.

Horkheimer criticizes Marx on several accounts. Marx was wrong in prophesying the inevitability of the historical trend toward the realm of freedom; the trend is toward total administration (*Tendenz zur absoluten Verwaltung*). Nor did Marx see the historical dialectic between freedom and justice. For Horkheimer, justice, equality, and freedom are mutually exclusive concepts:

> Justice and freedom are dialectical concepts: the more justice, the less freedom and the more freedom, the less justice. Fraternité, egalité and liberté is a wonderful promise. But if you want to maintain equality you have to curtail freedom and if you want to have freedom you cannot have equality.[141]

Another misinterpretation is Horkheimer's claim that Marx was reluctant to describe or depict the "good society." However, as early as 1848, Marx and Engels suggested certain "pretty generally applicable" measures for the new society after the overthrow of the bourgeois rule, such as the abolition of property rights, inheritance, the equal obligation of all to work, and so on. Earlier, in more romantic form, they envisaged a

> communist society, where nobody has an exclusive sphere of activity but each can become accomplished in any branch he wishes; society regulates the general production and thus makes it possible for me to do one thing today and another tomorrow, to hunt in the morning, fish in the afternoon, rear cattle in the evening, criticize after dinner.[142]

FRANKFURT SCHOOL AND JUDAIC THOUGHT

The later philosophy of Horkheimer and Adorno contains some basic elements of Judaic thought and tradition. The impact of

Judaism, although latent and not a cornerstone of the early phase, can be traced in Frankfurt thought throughout its 50-year history. A sketch of certain basic biographical and intellectual-biographical facts can enhance the understanding of the thought of both Horkheimer and Adorno.

As related in Chapter 1, Horkheimer was born into a respected, well-to-do, and assimilated, yet tradition-conscious Jewish family, and the impact of his family background and the memory of childhood experiences remained essential for him for the rest of his life. It was certainly not accidental, but rather symbolic, that he delivered his last lecture, a few weeks before his death, on Judaism, in the *Israelitische Cultusgemeinde* (Jewish Cultural Community) in Zürich.[143]

The essence of traditional Judaic thought is usually summed up in four major themes.[144] First, ethical monotheism, that is, the unconditional character of the ethical demand. In Leo Baeck's words, "Judaism is not only ethical, but ethics constitutes its principle and its essence." Second, awareness of the historical mission, the consciousness of being the chosen people, that is messianism. Third, justice and goodness, expressed in the untranslatable term *zedakah*. Fourth, concern with social justice.

In discussing the impact of the Judaic heritage on Frankfurt thought, one must consider the role of Jewry in European society after the French Revolution in general and the interrelationship between Marxian socialist thought and the Judaic legacy in particular. Most scientific and philosophical accomplishments of Jews in Europe since the French Revolution were produced by assimilated Jews who strove to identify themselves with liberal and radical movements in order to be completely absorbed in European culture. Two reactions of the Jews to their emancipation in the post French revolutionary era in Europe were the attempted total assimilation into the existing order and the intellectual critique, the endeavor to measure "that order with its own professed ideas." Horkheimer rightly remarks: "Assimilation and critique are two moments of the same process of emancipation."[145] Thus many assimilated Jews in the German

Reich were more faithful to the emperor (*Kaisertreu*) than other *Bürger* but not less sensitive against the Eastern Jews (*Ostjuden*) who still pursued the old ways of life. On the other hand, many "non-Jewish Jews" who were great revolutionaries of modern thought turned to socialism as the *Weltanschauung* and "science" of a total progress to which they could transfer old messianic hopes. Isaac Deutscher sums up the situation in his seminal essay, "The Non-Jewish Jew:"

> The Jewish heretic who transcends Jewry belongs to a Jewish tradition. You may, if you like, see Akher as a prototype of those great revolutionaries of modern thought: Spinoza, Heine, Marx, Rosa Luxemburg, Trotsky, and Freud. You may, if you wish, place them within a Jewish tradition. They all went beyond the boundaries of Jewry. They all found Jewry too narrow, too archaic, and too constricting. They all looked for ideals and fulfillment beyond it, and they represent the sum and substance of much that is greatest in modern thought, the sum and substance of the most profound upheavals that have taken place in philosophy, sociology, economics, and politics in the last three centuries.[146]

One could add to his list of names no lesser figures than Einstein, Schönberg, Lukács, and Deutscher himself. According to Deutscher, all these Jewish heretics have certain things in common. First, they are determinists who believed that there are basic regularities, that is, the universe is governed by laws. Second, living on the borderlines of various civilizations, they conceived of reality as dynamic and not static. Third, they held that knowledge is inseparable from praxis. Fourth, they believed in the ultimate solidarity of man in universal human emancipation.[147]

There is considerable disagreement in regard to the complex and intricate issue of Marx's Jewishness, which even Jewish scholars debate. Shlomo Avineri, the Israeli political scientist, labels Marx as an "inveterate anti-Semite."[148] Some publicists have gone so far as to republish the Marxian essay on "The Jewish Question" under the title, *A World Without Jews*, a title Marx never used. Another group of Jewish scholars, ranging

from Martin Buber to Karl Löwith and from Ernst Bloch to
Hannah Arendt, perceive an underlying biblical passion for
justice in the lifework of Marx. They argue that his passionate
and messianic drive for justice and the Marxian vision of a
utopian society with absolute reconciliation of all antagonisms
between social classes, between man and man, and man and
nature are definitely an integral part of the Judaic heritage.

Karl Löwith, the eminent German philosopher of Jewish
background, traces the inspiration of the Communist Manifesto
back to Jewish messianism and prophetism. He writes:

> The fundamental premise of the Communist Manifesto is not
> the antagonism between bourgeoisie and proletariat as two
> opposite facts; for what makes them antagonistic is that the
> one class is the children of darkness and the other the children
> of light. Likewise, the final crisis of the bourgeois capitalist
> world which Marx prophesies in terms of a scientific predic-
> tion is a last judgment, though pronounced by the inexorable
> law of historical process. . . .He was a Jew of Old Testa-
> ment stature. . . .It is the old Jewish messianism and
> prophetism—unaltered by two thousand years of economic
> history from handicraft to large-scale industry—and Jewish
> insistence on absolute righteousness which explains the
> idealistic basis of Marx's materialism. Though perverted into
> secular prognostication, the Communist Manifesto still retains
> the basic features of a messianic faith: "the assurance of things
> to be hoped for."[149]

The themes—ethical commitment, messianism, concern with
social justice—can be easily traced throughout the history of
Frankfurt thought from the 1930s to its demise in the late 1960s.
The cornerstone of Judaic thought, the will for social justice,
drove young Horkheimer toward Marxism as the only realistic
alternative to the menacing totalitarianism of the right, that of a
Hitler in the Germany of the 1930s. The brutal practices of the
left totalitarianism of Stalin repelled him from Marxism in the
1940s, ten years later. Thus it was not Horkheimer's theoretical
"drifting," but the dialectical interaction between social reality
and theoretical response that accounts for the shifts in Critical
Theory. Social theory depends to some extent on the personality

of the theorist, but in the final analysis, his perspective depends on his interaction with his environment, on his relationship with other human beings. His life and theoretical activity are part of his age; he is part of a larger social and historical whole or totality.

Frankfurt thought has always stressed the need and later the yearning—but only the yearning—for a just society based on reason. The ban on images follows the Second Commandment: "Thou shall not make unto thee any graven image, or any likeness *of any thing* that *is* in heaven above."[150] The later Horkheimer explicitly refers to this aspect of Judaic heritage and expresses the difference between Marx's Jewish legacy and his own thought in this way: "In my opinion, Marx was influenced by Judaic messianism while for me the main thing is the ban on images, i.e., that God can not be depicted, but is the object of yearning."[151] Indeed, in spite of the intellectual predominance of Jews in modern European history and their "over-representation" in almost every branch of intellectual life, there are few great Jewish painters. The German-Jewish writer of Prague, Franz Kafka, perhaps the most sensitive observer of many phenomena of modern capitalist society (alienation, bureaucracy), commented: "We Jews are no painters. We cannot depict things statically. We see them always in transition, in movement, in change."[152] The paintings of Marc Chagall, who might represent a possible exception, are full of movement, floating, and change.

Horkheimer's ambivalent attitude toward Israel might find its explanation in his "overidentification" with European culture as well as in his lifelong rejection of nationalism of any kind. He was of the opinion that the rise of Zionism (one of the most recent nationalist movements) was facilitated by a loss of faith in the possibility of a cultural-political pluralism, accentuated and accelerated by the extreme nationalism and militarization of the twentieth century. In Horkheimer's words:

> The Zionist movement, which distrusted the chance of pluralism and the culture of the autonomous individual in

Europe, represented a reaction of Jewry upon the possibilities opened up in the last century, a reaction that was radical and was a resignation at the same time. It is the saddest aspect of recent history both for Europe and Jewry that Zionism was proven right.[153]

Horkheimer recognized the immediate and immense historic significance of the establishment of a Jewish state, but he could not quite reconcile this fact with the Old Testament prophecy about the Promised Land. Horkheimer reflected on this problem in one of his last lectures when he spoke of his difficulty in accepting the fact that the Jewish state of Israel should have been established where it is instead of in another part of the world.

The Bible states, after all, that the righteous people of all nations will be led by the Messiah to the land of Zion. I still think about how the state of Israel—which I definitely stand up for—should interpret this prophecy of the Old Testament. Is Israel then the Zion of the Bible? As things stand, the solution to this problem might lie in the fact that the persecution of the Jews. . .continues in spite of Israel. Israel is a land in distress just as the Jews have always been a people in distress. For that reason one has to stand up for Israel. The decisive fact for me is that Israel gives asylum to many people. But as far as I am concerned, it remains questionable that the existence of Israel is the fulfillment of the prophesies of the Old Testament.[154]

To understand fully the Judaic impact on the thought of Horkheimer and Adorno since the 1940s, one must go beyond the common themes of traditional Judaism and look into the diversity of modern Jewish experience and responses to the historical experience of Auschwitz. George Steiner distinguishes four types of Jews in our epoch: the Orthodox, the Zionist, the American, and the European survivor. The orthodox view the holocaust as but one tragic chapter in the millennial dialogue between God and his chosen people. The Zionists look at Israel as the positive outcome of the mass murder. Instead of burdening themselves with remembrance of the disasters, they look forward; their history has just begun. The relationship of American Jews to recent history is radically different from the European. For them, the holocaust justified the emigration to America. They can understand the holocaust in an intellectual sense, but "it has no immediate personal relevance. . . .In America, Jewish parents listen at night for their children; but it is to make sure the car is back in the garage, not because there is a mob out. It cannot happen in Scarsdale."[155] To survivors like Steiner, Horkheimer or Adorno, the Israeli might say: "Why aren't you here?" The answer to this question lies in the nature of the fourth type of Jewishness, which "will appear unacceptable or self-defeating to the Orthodox and the Israeli." It will also seem remote and overdramatized to most American Jews.

> The idea that Jews everywhere have been maimed by the European catastrophe, that the massacre has left all who survived (even if they were nowhere near the actual scene) off balance, as does to the tearing off of a limb.[156]

The traumatic experience of Auschwitz and the fear that it might just happen again shapes the psychological state of mind of the accidental survivor of the holocaust. It is best described by George Steiner, who might provide a clue to understanding the many writings of the later Horkheimer and Adorno. Steiner writes:

> Due to my father's foresight (he had shown it when leaving Vienna in 1924), I came to America in January, 1940, during the phony war. We left France, where I was born and brought up, in safety. So I happened not to be there when the names were called out. I did not stand in the public square with the other children, those I had grown up with. Or see my father and mother disappear when the train doors were torn open. But in another sense I am a survivor and not intact. If I am out of touch with my own generation, if that which haunts me and controls my habits of feelings strikes many of those I should be intimate and working with in my present world as remotely sinister and artificial, it is because the black misery of what happened in Europe is to me indivisible from my own identity.

Precisely becuse I was not there, because an accident of good
fortune struck my name from the roll.[157]

The subtitle of Adorno's *Minima Moralia*, *Reflections from an
Injured Life*, suggests a similar feeling. Adorno conveys
thoughts that are almost identical to Steiner's in describing the
survivor experience in *Negative Dialektik:*

> Perennial suffering has as much right to expression as a tor-
> tured man has to screaming: hence it may have been wrong to
> say that after Auschwitz you could no longer write poems. But
> it is not wrong to raise the less cultural question whether after
> Auschwitz you can go on living—especially whether *one who
> escaped by accident, one who by rights should have been
> killed*, may go on living (italics mine).[158]

In regard to Judaic influences, Adorno's case is extremely complex. He clearly stated his adherence to the ban on images:

> The materialist yearning to comprehend the thing aims at the
> opposite: it is only in the absence of images that the full object
> could be conceived. Such absence converges with the theolog-
> ical ban on images. Materialism brought that ban into secular
> form by not permitting one to picture utopia positively: this is
> the content of its negativity.[159]

Arnold Künzli, the Swiss author of a monumental psychological
study of Marx, criticizes Adorno for his "unreflected and dogmatic assertion of an absolute ban."[160] He attributes Adorno's
"negative dialectic" to his break with Judaism and asserts that
Adorno projects his own personal guilt feelings into a general
human condition of a world historical dimension. As is well
known, Adorno dropped Wiesengrund, the family name of his
Jewish father, on his arrival in America and henceforth used the
name Adorno, of his non-Jewish mother. The Wiesengrund
name was relegated to the meaningless middle initial, W.,
which could stand for Walter, Williams, or anything. Künzli
asks: "Does not the *Negative Dialektik* contain moments of personal guilt feelings of a man who survived though he was

destined to die?"[161] Adorno's utterance about himself as the "one who escaped by accident, one who by rights should have been killed" seems to confirm this assertion.

NOTES

1. Unpublished letter of Thomas Mann to Frank Kingdon, Feb. 15, 1945, in Thomas Mann Archives, Zürich, Switzerland.

2. Ralf Dahrendorf, *Society and Democracy in Germany*, Garden City, N. Y., 1969, pp. 412–418.

3. Immanuel Geiss and Volker Ullrich (Eds.), *Fünfzehn Millionen beleidigte Deutsche oder Woher kommt die CDU?* Reinbek bei Hamburg, 1940, p. 7. For the history and sociology of postwar West German society, see Ernst-Ulrich, Huster, *et al.*, *Determinanten der westdeutschen Restauration 1945–1949*, Frankfurt am Main, 1973; Urs Jaeggi, *Kapital und Arbeit in der Bundesrepublik*, Frankfurt am Main, 1973. See also G. Hallgarten and J. Radkau, *Deutsche Industrie & Politik, von Bismarck bis heute*, Frankfurt am Main-Köln, 1974; Enzo Collotti, *Storia delle due Germanie, 1945–1968*, Torino, 1968. For a succinct discussion of the political–intellectual atmosphere, see Iring Fetscher, "Philosophie der Politik in Deutschland," in *Contemporary Philosophy, A Survey*, Raymond Klibansky (Ed.), Firenze, 1971, pp. 279–291.

4. Theodor W. Adorno, *Gesammelte Schriften*, Band 8, Frankfurt am Main, 1972, p. 500.

5. René König, "Die Situation der emigrierten deutschen Soziologen in Europa," *KZfSS*, XI, 1 (1959), pp. 113–131. See also Heinz Maus, "Bericht über die Soziologie in Deutschland 1933 bis 1945," in *KZfSS XI*, 1 (1959), pp. 72–92.

6. Adorno, *Gesammelte Schriften*, Band 8, p. 481.

7. Max Horkheimer, *Survey of the Social Sciences in Western Germany*, Washington, D. C., 1952, p. vii.

8. *Die Zeit* (Hamburg), (Oct. 29, 1968), p. 2.

9. Theodor W. Adorno, *Negative Dialektik*, Frankfurt am Main, 1966, p. 13.

10. *Ibid.*, p. 13.

11. *Ibid.*, p. 314.

12. Institut für Sozialforschung, *Soziologische Exkurse*, Frankfurt am Main, 1956; Max Horkheimer and Theodor W. Adorno, *Sociologica II*, Frankfurt am Main, 1962.

13. Max Horkheimer, "Traditionelle und kritische Theorie," *ZfS*, VI, 2 (1937), p. 289.

14. Adorno, *Negative Dialektik*, p. 8.

15. Adorno, *Gesammelte Schriften*, Band 8, p. 196. A major part of the Frankfurt School's critique of positivist sociology was carried out in the so-called *Positivismusstreit* in the 1960s with the participation of Theodor W. Adorno, Hans Albert, Ralf Dahrendorf, Jürgen Habermas, Harold Pilot, and Karl. R. Popper. A systematic discussion of the *Positivismusstreit* cannot be attempted here; only Adorno's contribution to it is utilized. Theodor W. Adorno et al., *Der Positivismusstreit in der deutschen Soziologie*, Neuwied-Berlin, 1969; see also, T. W. Adorno et al., *The Positivist Dispute in German Sociology*, London, 1976.

16. *Soziologische Exkurse*, pp. 17–18.

17. *Ibid.*, p. 12.

18. Cited in *Soziologische Exkurse*, p. 13.

19. *Ibid.*, p. 13.

20. *Ibid.*, p. 14.

21. Theodor W. Adorno, *Vorlesung zur Einleitung in die Soziologie*, Frankfurt am Main, 1973, p. 10.

22. *Ibid.*, p. 12.

23. *Soziologische Exkurse*, p. 108.

24. *Ibid.*, p. 16.

25. *Ibid.*, p. 12.

26. Theodor W. Adorno, *Stichworte*, Frankfurt am Main, 1969, p. 121.

27. Adorno, *Gesammelte Schriften*, Band 8, p. 292.

28. *Ibid.*, p. 549.

29. *Ibid.*, p. 294.

30. *Ibid.*, pp. 549–550.

31. Adorno, *Negative Dialektik*, p. 191.

32. Adorno, *Gesammelte Schriften*, Band 8, p. 363.

33. Adorno, *Negative Dialektik*, p. 396.

34. Theodor W. Adorno, *Minima Moralia*, Frankfurt am Main, 1969, p. 57.

35. Adorno, *Gesammelte Schriften*, Band 8, p. 292.
36. Gustav Janouch, *Conversations with Kafka*, New York, 1971, pp. 151–152. For a perceptive analysis of Kafka's works, see Wilhelm Emrich, *Franz Kafka. A Critical Study of his Writings*, S. Zeben Buehne (Transl.), New York, 1968.
37. Adorno, *Negative Dialektik*, p. 355.
38. *Ibid.*, p. 397.
39. *Ibid.*, p. 146.
40. Theodor W. Adorno, *Aufsätze zur Gesellschaftstheorie*, Frankfurt am Main, 1970, p. 105.
41. "Wozu heute noch Philosophie? Spiegel-Gespräch mit dem Philosophen Karl Löwith, *Der Spiegel*, *23*, 43 (Oct. 20, 1969), pp. 204–211.
42. Lucien Goldmann, *Immanuel Kant*, London, 1971.
43. Karl Marx, *A Contribution to the Critique of Political Economy*, New York, 1970, p. 20.
44. V. I. Lenin, *Selected Works*, Vol. IX, New York, 1943, p. 66. See also Georg Lukács, *Geschichte und Klassenbewusstsein*, Berlin, 1923, p. 39.
45. György Lukács, *A marxista filozófia feladatai az új demokráciában* (*The Tasks of Marxist Philosophy in the New Democracy*), Budapest, 1948, pp. 11–12. See also Silvie Rücker, "Totalität als ethisches und ästhetisches Problem," in *Text + Kritik*, 39/40 (Okt. 1973), pp. 52–64; István Mészáros, *Lukács' Concept of Dialectic*, London, 1972.
46. Lucien Goldmann, *Immanuel Kant*, p. 50.
47. See Ernest Nagel, "On the Statement 'The Whole is More than the Sum of Its Parts' " in *The Language of Social Research*, Paul F. Lazarsfeld and Morris Rosenberg (Eds.), New York, 1955, pp. 519–527.
48. Horkheimer and Adorno, *Sociologica II*, p. 14.
49. *Soziologische Exkurse*, p. 107.
50. Adorno, *Gesammelte Schriften*, Band 8, p. 320.
51. *Ibid.*, pp. 315 and 320.
52. Max Weber, *Economy and Society*, Vol. I, p. 5.
53. *Plato's The Republic*, B. Jowett (Transl.) New York, n.d., p. 203.
54. Auguste Comte, *Cours de philosophie positive*, Vol. IV, Paris, 1908, p. 214.
55. *Ibid.*, pp. 106–107.

56. Adorno, *Negative Dialektik*, p. 28.

57. Theodor W. Adorno, *Stichworte*, p. 178.

58. Adorno, *Gesammelte Schriften*, Band 8, pp. 299–300.

59. *Ibid.*, p. 327.

60. *Ibid.*, p. 324.

61. *Ibid.*, p. 327.

62. *Ibid.*, p. 337. See also Robert Nisbet, *Sociology as an Art Form*, New York, 1976.

63. *Ibid.*, p. 327.

64. *Ibid.*, pp. 329–331.

65. *Ibid.*, p. 329.

66. Theodor W. Adorno, *Prisms*, London, 1967, p. 7.

67. Georg Lukács, *Soul and Form*, Cambridge, Mass., 1974, pp. 1–18, and Theodor W. Adorno, "Der Essay als Form," in *Noten zur Literatur I*, Frankfurt am Main, 1965, pp. 9–49.

68. Theodor W. Adorno, *Vorlesung*, p. 16.

69. *Ibid.*, pp. 16–17.

70. *Soziologische Exkurse*, p. 18.

71. Comte, *Cours de philosophie positive*, Vol. II, p. 338.

72. Adorno, *Stichworte*, p. 121.

73. Adorno, *Vorlesung*, p. 22.

74. Adorno, *Gesammelte Schriften*, Band 8, p. 287.

75. Horkheimer and Adorno, *Sociologica II*, p. 205.

76. Adorno, *Vorlesung*, p. 43.

77. Adorno, *Negative Dialektik*, p. 167.

78. *Ibid.*, p. 167.

79. Adorno, *Vorlesung*, p. 30.

80. *Ibid.*, p. 31.

81. *Ibid.*, p. 41.

82. Adorno, *Gesammelte Schriften*, Band 8, p. 11.

83. Marx stated the problem thus: "The reciprocal and all-sided dependence of individuals who are indifferent to one another forms their social connection. This social bond is expressed in *exchange value*. . . . The power which each individual exercises over the activity of others or over social wealth exists in him as the owner of *exchange values*, or *money*. The individual carries his social power, as well as his bond with society in his pocket. . . Each individual possesses social power in the form of a thing. Rob the thing of this social power and you must give it to persons

to exercise over persons. Relations of personal dependence. . .
are the first social forms, in which human productive capacity
develops only to a slight extent. . . . Personal independence
founded on *objective* [*sachlicher*] dependence is the second
great form, in which a system of general social metabolism, of
universal relations, of all-round needs and universal capacities
is formed for the first time. Free individuality, based on the
universal development of individuals and on their subordina-
tion of their communal, social productivity as their social
wealth, is the third stage." Karl Marx, *Grundrisse. Introduction
to the Critique of Political Economy*, London, 1973, pp. 157–158.

84. Theodor W. Adorno, "Spätkapitalismus oder Industrie-
gesellschaft?" in *Gesammelte Schriften*, Band 8, pp. 354–370.

85. It may be noted that these processes are in line with Marxian
theory, which asserts that "the state is nothing but the executive
committee of the ruling class." The bourgeoisie was expected to
use all its power to stabilize the system. If Marx is right that "the
class which has the means of material production at its disposal
has control at the same time over the means of mental production," it is obvious that these "means of mental production" are
used to manipulate consciousness.

  Several layers of middle classes have been created in the postwar period as buffer zones between the top and bottom of the
stratification pyramid, or diamond, in advanced industrial
societies. Furthermore, today even the *Lumpenproletariat* is
integrated into the system by the creation of the extended welfare
system. A significant segment of academic intellectuals,
sociologists, psychologists, and economists specializes in
developing theories and organizational structures for "manipulating the poor;" and another middle class, "the welfare bourgeoisie," implements these poverty and welfare programs.
For good discussions of this problem, see Joseph Bensman and
Arthur Vidich, *The New American Society*, Chicago, 1971, especially chapters 10, 11, and 12; Frances Fox Piven and Richard A.
Cloward, *Regulating the Poor*, New York, 1971.

86. Adorno, *Negative Dialektik*, p. 270.

87. Max Horkheimer, *Kritik der instrumentellen Vernunft*, Frankfurt
am Main, 1967, p. 130.

88. *Soziologische Exkurse*, p. 48.

89. G. W. F. Hegel, *Werke*, Band 2, p. 146.

90. Adorno, *Gesammelte Schriften*, Band 8, p. 294.

91. *Ibid.*, p. 18.

92. Emile Durkheim, *The Rules of Sociological Method*, New York, 1964, p. 123.

93. Adorno, *Negative Dialektik*, pp. 153–154.

94. Adorno, *Minima Moralia*, p. 314.

95. *Ibid.*, p. 145.

96. Adorno, *Negative Dialektik*, p. 312.

97. Harry M. Johnson, *Sociology: A Systematic Introduction*, New York, 1960, p. 2.

98. Joseph Bensman, "Foreword" to Bernard Rosenberg, *The Province of Sociology. Freedom and Constraint*, New York, 1972, p. v.

99. Based on lectures of Professor Alexander Vucinich in the "Sociology of Intellectuals" course and the "Sociology of Science" seminar at the University of Illinois. I draw on them a great deal in what follows. I also use Louis de Broglie, *The Revolution in Physics*, New York, 1953; Ludwig von Bertalanffy, *Problems of Life*, New York, 1960, pp. 176ff; Robert K. Merton, *On Theoretical Sociology*. New York, 1967; Jean Piaget, *The Place of the Sciences of Man in the System of Sciences*, New York, 1974; and J. Piaget, *Logique et Connaissance Scientifique*, Paris, 1967, and *Sagesse et illusions de la philosophie*, Paris, 1968.

100. For a concise statement, see Talcott Parsons, "A Paradigm of Evolutionary Change," in *Societies. Evolutionary and Comparative Perspectives*, Englewood Cliffs, N.J., 1966, pp. 21–24.

101. According to Max von Laue, "The history of physics is forever furnishing new examples of how two completely independent theories, developed by different schools—for example, optics and thermodynamics, or the wave theory of X-rays and the atomic theory of crystals—unexpectedly coincide and *freely* combine." *History of Physics*, New York, 1950, pp. 8–9.

102. Max Weber, *The Protestant Ethic and the Spirit of Capitalism*, New York, 1958, p. 183. Ralf Dahrendorf, "Out of Utopia," in *American Journal of Sociology LXIV*, (1958). The idea of complementarity has been emphasized by other writers: Robert W. Friedrichs considers "system" and "conflict" or "priestly" and "prophetic" sociology as the two dominant paradigms of the discipline as "necessary elements in a larger dialectical *gestalt*." (Robert W. Friedrichs, *A Sociology of Sociology*, New York, 1972, p. 297.) Lewis Coser advocates the complementarity of functionalism and Marxism: "Even though, and perhaps just because, theorizing in the dominant mode of normative func-

tionalism has permitted American sociology to reach a level of sophistication hitherto unattained in any other sociological enterprise, it is time to help redress the balance by emphasizing the explanatory value of neglected conceptualizations of the factors of interests and power. This is, I take it, why Marx's sociology should again be accorded serious attention both as a corrective for certain prevailing emphases and as a major theoretical scheme in its own right." (Lewis A. Coser, *Continuities in the Study of Social Conflict*, New York, 1967, p. 140.) Pierre van den Berghe advocates a sociology "that achieves an adequate balance between stability and the various sources of endogenous and exogenous change, between consensus and conflict, and between equilibrium and disequilibrium." (Pierre van den Berghe, "Dialectic and Functionalism: Toward a Theoretical Synthesis," *American Sociological Review*, XXVIII, 5 [Oct. 1963], pp. 695–705.)

103. Karl Löwith, *Meaning in History*, Chicago, 1962, p. 70.

104. Max Weber, *The Protestant Ethic. . .*, p. 29. Weber, discussing the "specific and peculiar rationalism of Western culture," emphatically stated that "what is rational from one point of view may well be irrational from another." *Ibid.*, p. 26. Cf., Emile Durkheim, *The Rules of Sociological Method*, New York, 1938, pp. 41ff.

105. George C. Homans, "Social Behavior as Exchange," *The American Journal of Sociology*, LXII, May 1958, p. 597.

106. Hans Gerth and C. Wright Mills, (Eds.) *From Max Weber: Essays in Sociology*, New York, 1958, p. 180.

107. On this, see Salomon Bochner, *The Role of Mathematics in the Rise of Science*, Princeton, N. J., 1966.

108. Max Planck, *Physikalische Abhandlungen und Vorträge*, Vol. 3, Braunschweig, 1958, p. 79.

109. Herbert Butterfield, *The Origins of Modern Science*, New York, 1962, p. 196. The significance of the demarcation between science and speculative reflection was summarized by Piaget: "Although speculative reflection is a fertile and even necessary heuristic introduction to all inquiry, it can only lead to the elaboration of hypotheses, as sweeping as you like, to be sure, but as long as one does not seek for verification by a group of facts established experimentally or by a deduction conforming to an exact algorithm (as in logic), the criterion of truth can only remain subjective, in the manner of an intuitive satisfaction, of 'self-evidence,' etc. When it is a question of metaphysical problems involving the coordination of values judged to be of essen-

tial importance, problems which thus introduce factors of conviction or faith, speculative reflection remains the only method possible; but remaining bound up with the whole personality of the thinker, it can only lead to a wisdom or rational faith, and is not knowledge from the point of view of objective or interindividual criteria of truth." Jean Piaget, *Sagesse et illusions de la philosophie,* Paris, 1968, pp. 20-21.

110.   See Robert S. Lynd, *Knowledge for What? The Place of Social Science in American Culture,* Princeton, 1939, and C. Wright Mills, *The Sociological Imagination,* New York, 1959.

111.   Quoted in Georg Lukács, *Schriften zur Ideologie und Politik,* Frankfurt am Main, 1967, p. 627. Cf. Adorno's statements: "All post-Auschwitz culture, including its urgent critique, is garbage." In his view our culture stinks, because "its mansion is built of dogshit (*gebaut aus Hundsscheisse*)." *Negative Dialektik,* p. 357.

112.   Adorno, *Stichworte,* p. 119.

113.   Gespräch mit Theodor W. Adorno," *Der Spiegel,* May 5, 1969, pp. 204–209.

114.   Adorno, *Stichworte,* pp. 113–114.

115.   *Ibid.,* p. 117.

116.   "Gespräch mit Theodor W. Adorno," in *Auszug des Geistes. Bericht über eine Sendereihe,* Radio Bremen (Ed.), Bremen, 1962, pp. 126–128.

117.   Thomas Mann, *Briefwechsel mit seinem Verleger Gottfried Bermann Fischer, 1932–1955,* Frankfurt am Main, 1973, pp. 462, 473, and 478.

118.   Thomas Mann's unpublished letter to T. W. Adorno, February 12, 1952, in Thomas Mann Archives, Zürich, Switzerland.

119.   Adorno, *Stichworte,* p. 108.

120.   *Ibid.,* p. 110.

121.   Theodor W. Adorno, "Die Wunde Heine," in *Noten zur Literatur I,* Frankfurt am Main, 1965, pp. 148–149.

122.   An almost unsurmountable difficulty arises with translations. The translators of Adorno's *Prisms,* his first book rendered into English, entitled the introduction, "Translating the Untranslatable." W. R. Beyer, a Marxist critic, pointed to such "banalities presented in an artificial language" as: "Should one separate the immanent problems of science from its real ones, which are pallidly reflected in their formalisms, a fetishization of science would inevitably be the result." (*Man würde die Wis-*

senschaft fetischisieren, trennte man ihre immanenten Probleme radikal ab von den realen, die in ihren Formalismen blass widerscheinen.); or "There can be no emphatic notion of the truth without its containing the notion of an ideal social order, even though it might not stand up as a true image of things to come," (Im emphatischen Begriff der Wahrheit ist die richtige Einrichtung der Gesellschaft mitgedacht, so wenig sie auch als Zukunftsbild auszupinseln ist); or "Philosophical problems will not be solved by forcibly ignoring them, then discovering them later with the effect of a dernière nouveauté.' (Philosophische Fragen werden nicht dadurch erledigt, dass man sie erst gewaltsam vergisst und dann mit dem Effekt der dernière nouveauté wiederentdeckt).

Adorno's term durchvergesellschaftete Gesellschaft is another unsolvable example. See Wilhelm Raimund Beyer, Die Sünden der Frankfurter Schule, Berlin (East), 1971, pp. 45, 143, and passim.

See also Adorno's numerous utterances on the problem of language, e.g., "Only thoughts which cannot understand themselves are true (Wahr sind nur die Gedanken die sich selber nicht verstehen)." For Adorno, philosophy is something floating (schwebendes), is a "true sister of music," and must be composed. (Negative Dialektik, pp. 42, 55, and 113.) He is alleged to have said on one occasion: "I don't want to be understood." Quoted by Martin Puder, "Die Frankfurter Schule und die Neue Linke," in Neue Deutsche Hefte, 18, 1 (1971), p. 115.

According to Paul Lazarsfeld: "It is impossible to reproduce in another language the type of German in which . . . all . . . papers by Adorno are written. The length of the sentences, the rhythm of the words and the piling up of nouns—often the same nouns repeated with slightly different meanings—has an hypnotic effect on the reader. . . ." in Qualitative Analysis. Historical and Critical Essays, Boston, 1972, p. 169. Adorno's language, "the beautiful tongue" (die schöne Zunge), and its implications inspired two of Germany's most prominent writers to the following poems: Günter Grass, "Adornos Zunge," in Gesammelte Gedichte, Neuwied-Berlin, 1971, p. 121; Hans Magnus Enzensberger, "schwierige arbeit," (für theodor w. adorno), in Blindenschrift, Frankfurt am Main, 1965, pp. 58–59.

123. On the "break" in Horkheimer's thought, see Michael Theunissen, Gesellschaft und Geschichte, Berlin, 1969, pp. 14ff. For Lukács' critique, see Georg Lukács, Die Theorie des Romans, Neuwied am Rhein, 1963, p. 17.

198

The Frankfurt School

124. Max Horkheimer, *Die Sehnsucht nach dem ganz Anderen*, Hamburg, 1970, p. 5.

125. Max Horkheimer, "Philosophie und kritische Theorie," *ZfS*, VI, (1937), p. 626.

126. Max Horkheimer, *Eclipse of Reason*, New York, 1947, p. 161.

127. Adorno, *Negative Dialektik*, p. 27.

128. Max Horkheimer, *Kritische Theorie*, Vol. 1, Frankfurt am Main, 1968, p. x.

129. *Ibid.*, p. xi.

130. *Ibid.*, p. xi.

131. Max Horkheimer, "On the Concept of Freedom," *Diogenes* (Paris), No. 53 (1966), p. 79.

132. Horkheimer, *Die Sehnsucht*, p. 65.

133. Max Horkheimer, "Nachbemerkung," *ZfS*, IV, 2 (1935), p. 307.

134. Horkheimer, *Die Sehnsucht*, pp. 73–74.

135. *Ibid.*, p. 81.

136. Karl Marx and Frederick Engels, *The Communist Manifesto*, New York, 1948, p. 19.

137. Max Horkheimer, *Verwaltete Welt? Ein Gespräch*, Zürich, 1970, p. 9.

138. *Ibid.*, p. 26.

139. *Ibid.*, p. 28.

140. Karl Marx, *Capital*, Frederick Engels (Ed.) , Vol. 1, 3rd ed. New York, 1970, p. 78.

141. Horkheimer, *Die Sehnsucht*, p. 86.

142. Karl Marx and Frederick Engels, *The German Ideology*, New York, 1970 p. 53. Ralf Dahrendorf compiled a list of references to future society in the works of Marx and Engels; see Ralf Dahrendorf, *Die Idee des Gerechten im Denken von Karl Marx*, Hannover, 1971, pp. 167–182. See also Schlomo Avineri, "Marx's Vision of the Future," in *Dissent* (Summer 1973), pp. 323–330; Iring Fetscher, "Marx, Engels and the Future Society," in *Survey*, 38 (Oct. 1961), pp. 100–110; Thilo Ramm, "Die künftige Gesellschaftsordnung nach der Theorie von Marx und Engels," *Marxismusstudien II*, Iring Fetscher (Ed.) Tübingen, 1957, pp. 77–119.

143. "Das Judentum und die Krise der Religion," *Israelitisches Wochenblatt* (Zurich), 73, 25 (June 22, 1973), p. 24. See also Ernst Ludwig Ehrlich, "Max Horkheimers Stellung zum Judentum,"

Emuna (Frankfurt am Main), *VIII*, 6 (Nov.–Dec. 1973), pp. 457–460.

144. For the following, see Leo Baeck, *The Essence of Judaism*, New York, 1970. See also Julius Guttmann, "The Principles of Judaism," in *Conservative Judaism, XIV*, 1 (Fall 1959), pp. 1–24; For a systematic presentation, see Albert H. Friedlander, *Leo Baeck. Teacher of Theresienstadt*, New York, 1968, and A. H. Friedlander, "Leo Baeck und seine Auffassung vom Leid," in *Emuna, X*, 1/2 (March–April 1975), pp. 36–42; further, Hans Liebeschütz, *Von Georg Simmel zu Franz Rosenzweig*, Tübingen, 1970, Chapter 2.

145. Max Horkheimer, *Zur Kritik der instrumentellen Vernunft*, Frankfurt am Main, 1967, p. 307. See also Jacob Katz, *Emancipation and Assimilation. Studies in Modern Jewish History*, Westmead, Farnborough, Hants, England, 1972.

146. Isaac Deutscher, *The Non-Jewish Jew and Other Essays*, New York, 1968, p. 26. For a critical discussion of Deutscher's views on Israel, see Michael Landmann, *Das Israelpseudos der Pseudolinken*, Berlin, 1971, especially the essay "Antwort an Isaac Deutscher," pp. 36–78.

147. Ibid., pp. 35–37.

148. Shlomo Avineri, "Marx and Jewish Emancipation," in *Journal of the History of Ideas, XXV*, 4 (July–Sept. 1964), pp. 445–450; See also Edmund Silberner, "Was Marx an Antisemite?," in *Historica Judaica* (New York), *XI* (1949), pp. 3–52.

149. Karl Löwith, *Meaning in History*, Chicago, 1962, p. 44. See also Martin Buber, *Paths in Utopia*, Boston, 1960. For more details, see Gustav Mayer, "Der Jude in Karl Marx," in *Neue jüdische Monatshefte, II* (April 25, 1918), pp. 327–31; E. J. Lesser, "Karl Marx als Jude," in *Der Jude* (Berlin), *VIII*, 3 (1924), pp. 173–181; Hans Lamm, "Karl Marx und das Judentum," in *Karl Marx 1918–1968. Neue Studien zu Person und Lehre*, Mainz, 1968, pp. 11–66; George Lichtheim, "Socialism and the Jews," in *Dissent* (July–Aug. 1968), pp. 314–342; Robert Misrahi, *Marx et la question juive*, Paris, 1972; Robert S. Wistrich, *Revolutionary Jews. From Marx to Trotsky*, London, 1976. Prof. M. Landmann commented on the common messianistic roots of Socialism and Zionism, the former representing the universalistic and the latter the particularistic legacy of Messianism. See Michael Landmann, *Anklage gegen die Vernunft*, Stuttgart, 1976, p. 218.

150. *The Holy Bible*, p. 72.

151. Horkheimer, *Die Sehnsucht*, p. 77.

152. Janouch, *Conversations*, p. 152. For a detailed discussion on the subject, see Pierre Jaccard, "Kunst und Religion. Das Verbot bildlicher Darstellungen im alten Judentum und im Islam," *KZfSS*, 21, 3 (Sept. 1969), pp. 453–462; Alfred Vagts, "Die Familie Marc und der Durchbruch zur Malerei, *Bulletin des Leo Baeck Instituts*, 9, 33 (1966), pp. 85–96.

153. Horkheimer, *Zur Kritik*, p. 309.

154. Horkheimer, *Die Sehnsucht*, pp. 77–78.

155. Georg Steiner, *Language and Silence*, New York, 1972, p. 144. For a similar treatment of the problem, see Manés Sperber, "Churban oder Die unfassbare Gewissheit," in *Die Kontroverse: Hannah Arendt, Eichmann und die Juden*, München, 1964, pp. 9–32.

156. *Ibid.*, p. 144.

157. *Ibid.*, p. 140.

158. Adorno, *Negative Dialektik*, p. 353.

159. *Ibid.*, p. 205.

160. Arnold Künzli, *Aufklärung und Dialektik*, Freiburg, 1971, p. 146.

161. *Ibid.*, p. 146.

CONCLUSION

At the beginning of this study conflicting evaluations of the Frankfurt School of sociology and philosophy were discussed. They ranged from complete rejection (René König) of Critical Theory to its acceptance as a possible basis for a future dialectical sociology (Helmut Schelsky). Anglo-American sociologists' knowledge of the Frankfurt School ranges from very slight to confused.

In an attempt to arrive at an evaluation of the Frankfurt School, this study tried to examine critically the writings of Max Horkheimer and Theodor W. Adorno. The investigation focused on three key issues: first, the original program to offer a general theory of modern capitalist society; second, Critical Theory's claim to represent a continuation of the original critical theory of Marx; third, the scientific validity of Critical Theory in the light of generally accepted canons of the natural and social sciences.

In summary, the findings conclude that Critical Theory failed on all three accounts.

First, the accomplishment of Critical Theory falls short of the original program and promise, partly because of historical circumstances. The idea of interdisciplinary research was present throughout the 50-year history of the institute, yet it remained programmatic. Its logic and detailed mechanism were never worked out, nor was a thorough integration of monographs, produced by individual members of the institute, or a theoretical codification of knowledge gained from them, ever accomplished, perhaps because Horkheimer and Adorno had neither the training nor the interest to investigate socioeconomic bases empirically. They detested empirical research, which in their view deals only with the surface phenomema of society and not with its essence. (Although Critical Theory emphasized historicism from the very beginning, there was not one historian among the members of the institute during its 50-year career.)

Second, Critical Theory dissociated itself from the basic tenet of Marxism: the unity of theory, empirical research, and revolutionary praxis. The ambivalence of early Critical Theory toward praxis led to Adorno's withdrawal into an ivory tower and his glorification of it, as well as to Horkheimer's "yearning for God and another world." The crucial issue here, of course, is the abandonment of the Marxist method for the sake of metaphysical speculation. Fifty years ago Georg Lukács pointed to "method" as the most important aspect of the Marxian legacy. "Let us assume for the sake of argument," Lukács argued,

> that recent research had disapproved once and for all every one of Marx's individual theses. Even if this were so, every serious "orthodox" Marxist would still be able to accept all such modern findings without reservation and hence dismiss all of Marx's theses in toto—without having to renounce his orthodoxy for a single moment. Orthodox Marxism, therefore, does not imply the uncritical acceptance of the results of Marx's investigations. It is not the "belief" in this or that thesis, nor the exegesis of a "sacred" book. On the contrary, orthodoxy refers exclusively to *method*. It is the scientific conviction that dialectical materialism is the road to truth and that its method can be developed, expanded and deepened only along the lines laid down by its founders.[1]

The Marxian prognosis about the polarization of classes in a capitalist society (bourgeois versus proletariat), with the *Verelendung* of the latter and the final apocalyptic clash of two opposing camps, did not take place, and the likelihood that it would had faded by the 1930s. Advanced capitalism has managed to survive, resolving its contradictions and crises, through reforms in the United States and through counterrevolutionary measures in Germany in the 1930s. Yet, to conclude from historical events that one must give up the Marxian method entirely, that is, abandon the investigation of the socioeconomic base altogether and escape into the realm of speculative thought, would be a most blatant violation of the Marxian legacy, intolerable to a sociological current that is allegedly the heir of that tradition.

   Third, the Frankfurt School failed to grasp the philosophy of the modern natural and social sciences. It rejected such methodological pillars of modern science as experimentation, quantification, and verification and advocated a new *Natur-philosophie*, a "science" that is qualitative and contemplative. It also replaced scientific sociology with an elitist artistic reflection (*Kulturkritik*) on the evils of capitalist society and the horrors of fascism.

Many shortcomings of the Frankfurt School were rooted in the existential conditions of these intellectuals. To use Mannheim's term, their ideas were "*seinsgebunden.*" After beginning a critical analysis of German and Western European societies, they were abruptly transplanted to America. They never entered into close contact with any segment of the American intellectual community, nor did they succeed in understanding the social and intellectual tradition of the country.

The most celebrated and debated philosophy of the immediate postwar years was French Existentialism. Georg Lukács gave his critical evaluation of that philosophy in his essay, "Existentialism or Marxism?" (1947)—an evaluation that has relevance beyond its topical significance. "An epoch-making philosophy," Lukács wrote,

> has never yet arisen without a really original method. This was so for all the great philosophers of the past, Plato and Aristotle, Descartes and Spinoza, Kant and Hegel. What is the originality of Existentialism's method?"[2]

Twenty-five years have passed since Lukács raised the question. French Existentialism faded out; time seems to have confirmed Lukács' assessment of it as a "passing fad." Indeed, we could now ask Lukács' question of Critical Theory, "What is the originality of Critical Theory's method?" The answer is very disappointing. In a real sense, there has been no one Critical Theory, but rather the critical theories of Horkheimer, Adorno, and Marcuse. One could go even further and speak of critical *theories* of Horkheimer et al. in the 1930s, 1940s, and 1960s.[3] The only consistent elements of the critical theories are their ethical stance, their anxiety about the fate of mankind, their humanist concern about the future of Western civilization.

One of the main conclusions of this study is that, in the last analysis, Critical Theory is another existential philosophy. If we accept Hegel's dictum that "philosophy comprehends its time in ideas," it applies to existentialism, as it certainly does to Critical Theory, which was a specific expression of a certain socio-historic condition and the situation of a social group, the marginal bourgeois-Jewish intelligentsia.

Existentialism has always been a crisis philosophy, a theoretical expression of collapse, of a restructuring situation. Its focus is on the individual, his alienation, and his state of "thrown-outness" (*Hinausgeworfenheit*), to use Heidegger's term. The first recorded crisis situation was the Biblical age, with the prophets as existentialist philosophers, particularly Job, who cried out in dark times about the loss of wealth, power, home, happiness, and about his suffering (*Leid*). Young Marx, as one of the modern "existentialists," needs no further elaboration. The father of modern existentialism, Soren Kierkegaard (1815–1855), certainly influened Adorno. Adorno wrote his *Habilitationsschrift* on Kierkegaard, who remained a lifelong influence for him. By the end of the century a new founder of existentialism appeared: Friedrich Nietzsche (1844–1900). Influenced by Schopenhauer, he had a decisive impact on both Horkheimer and Adorno.[4] The unmasking process begins with Schopenhauer and continues with Sigmund Freud, another major influence for Critical Theory. In a broad sense, the kaleidoscope of modern existentialism includes thinkers and writers of a diverse political and intellectual spectrum that ranges from Heidegger, Jaspers, Scheler, Buber, and Rosenzweig to Rilke, Kafka, Sartre, Camus, Horkheimer, and Adorno.

At times Horkheimer and Adorno perceived their thoughts in that sense, and labeled their theories existentialist. Horkheimer's programmatic essay, "Traditional and Critical Theory" (1937), emphatically declares that "Critical Theory of society is, in its totality, the unfolding of a single *existential judgment*." (Italics mine.)[5] In the same vein, the *Dialectic of Enlightenment*, the main work of Critical Theory in the mid-1940s, says: "History is repressed in oneself and others out of fear that it might remind the individual of the *disintegration of his own existence*, which itself is being brought about by the repression of history." (Italics mine.)[6] Thus some key terms of existentialist philosophy, that is, *Verdrängung*, *Angst*, *Existenz*, are compressed in one single sentence.

Our conclusion seems to be in basic agreement with that of Jürgen Habermas on Adorno and that of Alfred Schmidt on Horkheimer. In 1963 Habermas called Adorno "a philosophizing intellectual (*ein philosophierender Intellektueller*)."[7] We might add, "a sociologizing intellectual." Six years later, after Adorno's death, Habermas aptly summarized the problematic character of Adorno's legacy:

> After the theoretical veil, which was held by Adorno's genius over our methodological nakedness, has fallen, we again stand naked as far as methodology goes (*Methodisch stehen wir nackt da, nachdem der theoretische Schleier, den Adorno's Genie vor unsere methodologische Blösse hielt, gefallen ist*).[8]

Alfred Schmidt, the closest disciple of Horkheimer, wrote in his obituary on Horkheimer about the

> factual difficulties which confront the interpreter of the Horkheimerian life-work, because it is broken [*brüchig*] and marked by the struggles and catastrophes of the century. . . . It contains the . . . general motives of a philosophy, which. . . cannot be expressed in concise theses and which does not lend itself to a reduction to a position which is expoundable.[9]

Asked recently about the theoreticians of the Frankfurt School, Ernst Bloch made the following extremely harsh statement:

> I would call the Institute of Social Research [*Institut für Sozialforschung*] of the Frankfurt School the Institute of Social Falsification [*Institut für Sozialfälschung*]. I have never accepted their pessimism. They are neither Marxists nor revolutionaries. What they offer is only a pessimistic theory of society. At one time, I had some rapport with Adorno although we never agreed on the concept of utopia. As far as Horkheimer is concerned, he became a reactionary.[10]

The collected articles of Horkheimer published in 1968 were entitled *Kritische Theorie. Eine Dokumentation*. Indeed, Critical Theory is the document of the disintegration of old Central European bourgeois society and the tragic fate of a group of intellectuals of that society.

NOTES

1. Georg Lukács, *Geschichte und Klassenbewusstsein*, Berlin, 1923, pp. 13–14.

2. György Lukács, *A polgári filozófia válsága* (The Crisis of Bourgeois Philosophy), Budapest, 1947, p. 130.

3. The repeated assertions of Horkheimer and Adorno about the identity of their thought can be accepted only for the 1940s, but not for their life work. A systematic contrasting of the thought of Horkheimer and Adorno was beyond the objective of this study. Yet one major difference should be mentioned—the different reception of the German philosophical heritage: the dominant impact of Schopenhauer on Horkheimer on one hand and that of Hegel on Adorno on the other.

4. Adorno wrote to Walter Benjamin in 1938: "God knows there is only one truth . . . and . . . there is more about this truth in Nietzsche's *Genealogy of Morals* than in Bukharin's ABC." Theodor W. Adorno, "Letters to Walter Benjamin," Harry Zohn (Transl.) *New Left Review*, 81 (Sept.–Oct. 1973), p. 72.

5. Max Horkheimer, *Critical Theory*, p. 227.

6. Horkheimer-Adorno, *Dialektik*, p. 216.

7. Jürgen Habermas, "Ein philosophierender Intellektueller," in *Philosophisch-politische Profile*, Frankfurt am Main, 1971, pp. 176–184. See also Claus Grossner, "Anfang und Ende der Frankfurter Schule (Theodor W. Adorno/Max Horkheimer," in *Verfall der Philosophie*, Hamburg, Reinbek bei Hamburg, 1971, pp. 106–122 and Eugene Fleischmann, "Fin de la Sociologie dialectique? Essai d'apprecation de l'Ecole de Francfort," *Archives Européennes de Sociologie*, XIV, 2 (1973), pp. 159–184.

8. Cited in Claus Grossner, *Verfall der Philosophie*, Reinbek bei Hamburg, 1971, p. 15.

9. Alfred Schmidt, *Zur Idee der Kritischen Theorie*, München, 1974, p. 137.

10. Interview with Ernst Bloch by Jean-Michel Palmier, "La Traversee du siecle d'Ernst Bloch. Voyage à 'Blochingen'," *Les Nouvelles Litteraires* (April 29 1976), pp. 8–9 and (May 6, 1976), pp. 8–9.

BIBLIOGRAPHY

The following abbreviations are used in the bibliography:

ZfS   *Zeitschrift für Sozialforschung*
SPSS   *Studies in Philosophy and Social Sciences*
KZfSS *Kölner Zeitschrift für Soziologie und Sozialpsychologie*

Adler-Rudel, S. *Ostjuden in Deutschland 1880–1940.* Tübingen: J. C. B. Mohr (Paul Siebeck,) 1959.

Adorno, Theodor W. *Aufsätze zur Gesellschaftstheorie und Methodologie.* Frankfurt am Main: Suhrkamp Verlag, 1970.

———. *Drei Studien zu Hegel.* Frankfurt am Main: Suhrkamp Verlag, 1970.

———. *Gesammelte Schriften*, Vol. 8, Frankfurt am Main: Suhrkamp Verlag, 1972.

———. "Letter to Walter Benjamin." Harry Zohn, *New Left Review, 81* (Sept.–Oct. 1973), p. 72. (Transl.).

———. *Minima Moralia. Reflexionen aus dem beschädigten Leben,* Frankfurt am Main: Suhrkamp Verlag, 1961.

———. *Negative Dialektik.* Frankfurt am Main: Suhrkamp Verlag, 1966.

———. *Noten zur Literatur I.* Frankfurt am Main: Suhrkamp Verlag, 1965.

———. *Prismen. Kulturkritik und Gesellschaft.* Frankfurt am Main: Suhrkamp Verlag, 1955.

———. *Stichworte: Kritische Modelle 2.* Frankfurt am Main: Suhrkamp Verlag, 1969.

———. *Vorlesung zur Einleitung in die Soziologie.* Frankfurt am Main: Junius Drucke, 1973.

———. et al. *The Authoritarian Personality.* New York: Harper & Row, 1950.

Theodor W. Adorno zum Gedächtnis. Eine Sammlung. Hermann Schweppenhäuser (Ed.) Frankfurt am Main: Suhrkamp Verlag, 1971.

"Dr. Theodor W. Adorno, Philosopher, Dies at 65." *The New York Times* (Aug 7, 1969), p. 35.

Apel, Karl-Otto. "Wissenschaft als Emanzipation? Eine Auseinandersetzung mit der Wissenschaftskonzeption der 'Kritischen Theorie,'" *Zeitschrift für allgemeine Wissenschaftstheorie, I*, 2 (1970), pp. 173–195.

Arendt, Hannah, *Crises of the Republic.* New York: Harcourt Brace Jovanovich, 1972.

Avineri, Shlomo. "Marx and Jewish Emancipation," *Journal of the History of Ideas*, *XXV*, 5 (July–Sept. 1964), pp. 445–450.

———. "Marx's Vision of the Future." *Dissent* (Summer 1973), pp. 323–330.

Axelos, Kostas. *Marx penseur de la technique*, 2 vols. Paris: Union Générale d'Editions, 1974.

Ayer, Alfred Jules. *Language, Truth and Logic*. New York: Dover Publications, 1952.

Ayer, Alfred Jules, et al. *The Revolution in Philosophy*. London: Macmillan, 1960.

Baeck, Leo. *The Essence of Judaism*. New York: Schocken Books, 1970.

Bahne, Siegfried. "Sozialfaschismus in Deutschland. Zur Geschichte eines politischen Begriffs." *International Review of Social History*, *10*, (1965), pp. 211–265.

Bauman, Zygmunt. *Towards a Critical Sociology. An Essay on Commonsense and Emancipation*. London: Routledge & Kegan Paul, 1976.

———. *Zarys marksistowskiej teorii spoleczentswa*. Warsaw: PWN, 1964.

Benjamin, Walter. *Angelus Novus. Ausgewählte Schriften 2*. Frankfurt am Main: Suhrkamp Verlag, 1966.

———. *Zur Kritik der Gewalt und andere Aufsätze*. Frankfurt am Main: Suhrkamp Verlag, 1965.

Bensman, Joseph. "Foreword," in Rosenberg, Bernard, *The Province of Sociology. Freedom and Constraint*. New York: Thomas Y. Crowell, 1972.

———. and Robert Lilienfield. *Craft and Consciousness. Occupational Technique and the Development of World Images*. New York: Wiley, 1973.

———. and Arthur Vidich. *The New American Society*, Chicago: Quadrangle, 1971.

Berger, Peter (Ed.). *Marxism and Sociology. Views from Eastern Europe*. New York: Appleton-Century-Crofts, 1969.

Bernal, J. D., *Marx and Science*. New York: International Publishers, 1952.

Bertalanffy, Ludwig von. *Problems of Life*. New York: Harper Torchbooks, 1960.

Beyer, Wilhelm R. *Die Sünden der Frankfurter Schule*. Berlin (East): Akademie Verlag, 1971.

Bienenfeld, F. R. *The Germans and the Jews*. London: Secker and Warburg, 1939.

Bloch, Ernst. *Geist der Utopie*. München-Leipzig: Duncker & Humblot, 1918.

Bloch, Jochanan. *Judentum in der Krise: Emanzipation, Sozialismus, Zionismus*. Göttingen: Vandenhoeck and Ruprecht, 1966.

Bochner, Salomon. *The Role of Mathematics in the Rise of Science*. Princeton, N. J.; Princeton University Press, 1966.

Böckelmann, Frank. *Über Marx und Adorno. Schwierigkeiten der spätmarxistischen Theorie*. Frankfurt am Main: Makol Verlag, 1972.

Böhler, Dietrich. "Kritische Theorie—kritisch reflektiert." *Archiv für Rechts—und Sozialphilosophie*, LVI, 4 (1970), pp. 511–525.

Bollhagen, Peter. *Soziologie und Geschichte*. s'Gravenhage, Netherlands: boek en druk n.v., 1973.

Boman Thorleif. *Hebrew Thought Compared with Greek*. New York: W. W. Norton, 1970.

Boring, Edwin G. *A History of Experimental Psychology*. 2nd ed., New York: Appleton-Century-Crofts, 1950.

Boyers, Robert (Ed.). *The Legacy of the German Refugee Intellectuals*. New York: Schocken Books, 1972.

Bracher, Karl Dietrich. *Die Krise Europas: 1917–1975*. Berlin: Propyläen Verlag; Propyläen Geschichte Europas, Bd. 6, 1976.

———. *The German Dictatorship*. New York: Praeger, 1970.

———. *Zeitgeschichtliche Kontroversen um Faschismus, Totalitarismus, Demokratie*. München: R. Piper & Co. Verlag; Serie Piper, 1976.

Braunreuther, Kurt (Ed.) *Zur Kritik der bürgerlichen Soziologie in Westdeutschland*. Berlin (East): VEB Deutscher Verlag der Wissenschaften, 1962.

Brecht, Bertolt. *Arbeitsjournal 1938–1942*, Vol. I. Werner Hecht, (Ed.). Frankfurt am Main: Suhrkamp Verlag, 1973.

———. *Gedichte 1941–1947*. Frankfurt am Main: Suhrkamp Verlag, 1964.

Breines, Paul. *Lukács and Korsch 1910–1923. A Study in the Genesis and Impact of Geschichte und Klassenbewusstsein and Marxismus und Philosophie*. Unpub. diss., The University of Wisconsin, 1972.

———. "Marcuse and the New Left in America." In *Antworten auf Herbert Marcuse*, Jürgen Habermas (Ed.). Frankfurt am Main: Suhrkamp Verlag, 1969, pp. 133–150.

Brenner, Hildegard. "Theodor W. Adorno als Sachwalter des Ben-jaminschen Werkes." In *Die neue Linke nach Adorno*, Wilfried F. Schoeller (Ed.). München: Kindler Verlag, 1969, pp. 158–175.

Brzezinski, Zbigniew K. "Totalitarianism and Rationality." *The American Political Science Review*, L, 3 (1956), pp. 751–763.

Brown, Roger. *Social Psychology*. New York: The Free Press, 1965.

Bruun, H. H. *Science, Values and Politics in Max Weber's Methodology*. Copenhagen: Munksgard, 1972.

Buber, Martin. *Paths in Utopia*. Boston: Beacon Press, 1960.

Bubner, Rüdiger. "Was ist kritische Theorie? (M. Horkheimer, J. Habermas)." *Philosophische Rundschau*, XVI, 3–4 (1969), pp. 213–49.

Buck-Morss, Susan F. "T. W. Adorno and the Dilemma of Bourgeois Philosophy." *Salmagundi*, 36 (Winter 1977), pp. 76–98.

Bühl, Walter. "Dialektische Soziologie und soziologische Dialektik." *KZfSS*, *21*, 4 (1969), pp. 717–751.

Bukharin, Nikolai. *Historical Materialism. A System of Sociology*. Ann Arbor: The University of Michigan Press, 1969.

Bunge, Mario. *Intuition and Science*. Englewood Cliffs, N. J.: Prentice-Hall, Inc., 1962.

———. "Über philosophische Fragen der modernen Physik." *Deutsche Zeitschrift für Philosophie*. *IV*, (1956), pp. 467–496.

Burgess, Ernest. "The Influence of Sigmund Freud upon Sociology in the United States." *American Journal of Sociology*, 45 (Nov. 1929), pp. 356–375.

Burnham, James. *The Managerial Revolution*. New York: The John Day Co., 1941.

Butterfield, Herbert. *The Origins of Modern Science*. New York: Collier Books, 1957.

Chesnokov, D. I. *Istoricheskii materializm i sotsial'nye issledovniaia* (Historical Materialism and Social Research). Moscow: 1967.

———. *Istoricheskii materializm kak sotsiologija marksizmalenin-izma* (Historical Materialism as a Marxist-Leninist Sociology). Moscow: Mysl, 1973.

Christie, R. and P. Cook, "A Guide to the Published Literature Relating to the Authoritarian Personality through 1956," *Journal of Psychology*, 45 (1958), pp. 171–199.

———. and Marie Jahoda, (Eds.). *Studies in the Scope and Method of the Authoritarian Personality*. Glencoe, Ill.: The Free Press, 1954.

Clemenz, Manfred. *Gesellschaftliche Ursprünge des Faschismus*. Frankfurt am Main: Suhrkamp Verlag, 1972.

Cohen, Herman. *Jüdische Schriften*, 3 vols. Berlin: C. A. Schwetschke & Son, 1924.

Colletti, Lucio. "Marxism as a Sociology." *From Rousseau to Lenin. Studies in Ideology and Society.* London: NLB, 1972.

Collotti, Enzo. *Storia delle due Germanie, 1945–1968.* Torino: Einaudi, 1968.

Comte, Auguste. *Cours de philosophie positive,* Vol. IV. Paris: Bachelier, 1908.

Coser, Lewis A. *Continuities in the Study of Social Conflict.* New York: The Free Press, 1967.

Crombie, A.C. (Ed.). *Turning Points in Physics.* New York: Interscience, 1959.

Dahrendorf, Ralf. *Marx in Perspektive. Die Idee des Gerechten im Denken von Karl Marx.* Hannover: Verlagsbuchhandlung J.H.W. Dietz, 1952.

———. "Out of Utopia." *American Journal of Sociology,* LXIV, 2 (1958), pp. 115–127.

———. *Society and Democracy in Germany.* Garden City, N. Y.: Anchor Books, 1969.

Davis, Devra Lee. "Theodor W. Adorno: Theoretician Through Negations." *Theory and Society. II,* 3 (Fall 1975), pp. 389–400.

Dawydow, Juri. *Die sich selbst negierende Dialektik.* Frankfurt am Main: Verlag Marxistische Blätter, GmbH., 1971.

Deak, Istvan. *Weimar Germany's Left-Wing Intellectuals: A Political History of the Weltbühne and Its Circle.* Berkeley and Los Angeles: University of California Press, 1968.

Deborin, Abram and Bukharin, Nikolai. *Kontroversen über dialektischen und mechanistischen Materialismus.* Frankfurt am Main: Suhrkamp Verlag, 1969.

de Broglie, Louis. *Physics and Microphysics.* New York: Grosset & Dunlap, 1966.

———. *The Revolution in Physics.* New York: The Noonday Press, 1953.

Descartes, René. *Discourse on Method and Other Writings.* Baltimore: Penguin Books Ltd; Penguin Classics, 1968.

Deutscher, Isaac. *The Non-Jewish Jew and Other Essays.* New York: Hill and Wang, 1968.

———. *The Prophet Unarmed. Trotsky: 1921–1929.* New York: Vintage Books, 1959.

Dimitrov, Georgi. *Selected Works.* Sofia: Foreign Languages Press, 1960.

Dubiel, Helmut. "Dialektische Wissenschaftskritik und interdiszipli-
näre Sozialforschung. Theorie- und Organisationsstruktur des
Frankfurter Instituts für Sozialforschung [1930 ff.]." *KZfSS*, *26*, 2
(1974), pp. 237–266.

Duker, Abraham G. and Meir, Ben-Horin. *Emancipation and Counter-
Emancipation.* Ktav Publishing House Inc., 1974.

Durkheim, Emile. "The Dualism of Human Nature and its Social Conditions." In *Essays on Sociology & Philosophy.* Kurt H. Wolff (Ed.).
New York; Harper Torchbooks, 1964.

————. *The Rules of Sociological Method.* New York: MacMillan,
1964.

————. *Socialism.* Alvin W. Gouldner (Ed.). New York: Collier Books,
1962.

————. *Suicide. A Study in Sociology.* George Simpson (Ed.). New
York: The Free Press, 1951.

Durkheim, Emile and Marcel Mauss. *Primitive Classification.* Chicago:
The University of Chicago Press, 1972.

Ehrlich, Ernst Ludwig. "Max Horkheimers Stellung zum Judentum,"
Emuna (Frankfurt am Main), *VIII*, 6 (Nov.–Dec. 1973), pp. 457–
460.

Emrich, Wilhelm. *Franz Kafka. A Critical Study of his Writings.* S.
Zeben Buehne (Transl.). New York: Frederick Ungar Publishing
Co., 1968.

Engels, Frederick. *Ludwig Feuerbach and the Outcome of Classical
German Philosophy.* New York: International Publishers, 1941.

————. *The Peasant War in Germany.* New York: International Publisher, 1973.

Enzensberger, Hans Magnus. *Blindenschrift.* Frankfurt am Main: Suhrkamp Verlag, 1965.

Epistémologie et Marxisme. Paris: Union Générale d'editions, 1972.

Eyck, Erich. *A History of the Weimar Republic. From the Collapse of the
Empire to Hindenburg's Election,* 2 vols. New York: Atheneum,
1970.

Fackenheim, Emil L. *Encounters Between Judaism and Modern
Philosophy.* New York: Basic Books, 1973.

Farganis, James. "A Preface to Critical Theory." *Theory and Society*, *II*,
4 (Winter 1975), pp. 483–508.

Fehér Ferenc. "Negative Philosophy of Music—Positive Results." *New
German Critique,* 4 (Winter 1975), pp. 99–111.

Ferber, Christian von. *Die Gewalt in der Politik.* Stuttgart: Verlag W.
Kohlhammer; Urban Taschenbücher, Bd. 804, 1970.

Ferrarotti, Franco. *Il Pensiero Sociologico da Auguste Comte a Max Horkheimer;* Milan: Mondadori, 1974.

Fetscher, Iring. "Marx, Engels and the Future Society." *Survey, 38* (Oct. 1961), pp. 100–110.

————. "Philosophie der Politik in Deutschland," in *Contemporary Philosophy. A Survey.* Raymond Klibansky (Ed.). Firenze: 1971.

Fijalkowski, Jürgen. "Theorie-Begriffe in der deutschen Soziologie der Gegenwart." *KZfSS, XIII,* (1961), pp. 88–109.

Finkelstein, Louis (Ed.). *The Jews. Their Role in Civilization.* New York: Schocken Books, 1971.

Fischer, George. *Science and Ideology in Soviet Society.* New York, 1976.

Fleischmann, Eugene. "Fin de la Sociologie dialectique? Essai de l'Ecole de Francfort." *Archives Européennes de Sociologie, XIV,* 3 (1973), pp. 159–184.

Fleming, Donald, and Bernard Bailyn, (Eds.). *The Intellectual Migration. Europe and America, 1930–1960.* Cambridge, Mass.: Harvard University Press, 1969.

Fraisse, Paul and Jean Piaget (Eds.). *Experimental Psychology: Its Scope and Method,* Vol. I. *History and Method.* New York: Basic Books, 1967.

Frenzel, Ivo. "Zur Kritischen Theorie Max Horkheimers." *Neue Rundschau, 80,* 3 (1969), pp. 527–533.

Freud, Sigmund. "Mourning and Melancholia." *The Standard Edition of the Complete Psychological Works of Sigmund Freud,* Vol. 14. London: Hogarth Press and the Institute of Psychoanalysis, 1957, pp. 243–258.

Friedlander, Albert H. *Leo Baeck. Teacher of Theresienstadt.* New York: Holt, Rinehart, Winston, 1968.

————. "Leo Baeck und seine Auffassung vom Leid." *Emuna, X,* 1/2 (March–April) 1975), pp. 36–42.

Friedrichs, Robert W. *A Sociology of Sociology.* New York: The Free Press, 1967.

Fromm, Erich. *Escape from Freedom.* New York: Avon, 1965.

Gay, Peter. "German Jews in German Culture, 1888–1914." *Midstream XXI,* 2 (Feb. 1975), pp. 23–65.

————. *Weimar Culture. The Outsider as Insider.* New York: Harper & Row, 1970.

Geiger, Theodor. *Die soziale Schichtung des deutschen Volkes.* Stuttgart: Enke Verlag, 1932.

Geiss, Imanuel and Ullrich Volker, (Eds.). *Fünfzehn Millionen beleidigte Deutsche oder Woher kommt die CDU?* Reinbek bei Hamburg: Rowohlt Verlag, 1970.

Gerth, Hans. "Theodor W. Adorno, 1903–1969." *Radical America, III,* 5 (Sept. 1969), pp. 1–2.

———. "The Nazi Party: Its Leadership and Composition." *AJS, XLV* (Jan. 1940), pp. 517–41.

Gerth, H. H. and C. Wright Mills (Eds.). *From Max Weber: Essays in Sociology.* New York: Oxford University Press; A Galaxy Book, 1958.

"Gespräch mit Theodor W. Adorno." In *Auszug des Geistes. Bericht über eine Sendereihe.* Radio Bremen (Ed.). Bremen: Verlag B. C. Heye & Co. 1962, pp. 126–128.

Giddens, Anthony. *Capitalism and Modern Social Theory. An Analysis of the Writings of Marx, Durkheim and Max Weber.* New York: Cambridge University Press, 1971.

———. *Positivism and Sociology.* London: Heinemann, 1975.

Gilman, Sander L., "Bertolt Brecht and the FBI." *The Nation,* (30 Nov. 1974), pp. 560–562.

Goldmann, Lucien. *Immanuel Kant.* London: New Left Books, 1971

———. "La mort d'Adorno." *La Quinzaine litteraire,* 78 (Sept. 1969), pp. 26–27.

———. *Lukács et Heidegger.* Paris: Denoël/Gonthier, 1973.

———. Marxisme et Psychologie." *Critique (June—July 1947),* pp. 115–124.

Goldmann, Nahum. *Deutsche und Juden.* Frankfurt am Main: Suhrkamp Verlag, 1967.

Gouldner, Alvin W. *The Coming Crisis of Western Sociology.* New York: Basic Books 1970.

———. *The Dialectic of Ideology and Technology. The Origins, Grammar and Future of Ideology.* New York: The Seabury Press, 1976.

Grass, Günter. *Gesammelte Gedichte.* Nuwied-Berlin: Luchterhand, 1971.

Grenz, Friedemann. *Adornos Philosophie in Grundbegriffen.* Frankfurt am Main: Suhrkamp Verlag, 1974.

Grossner, Claus. *Verfall der Philosophie.* Reinbek bei Hamburg: Christian Wegner Verlag, 1971.

Grünberg, Carl. "Festrede, gehalten zur Einweihung des Institutes für

Sozialforschung an der Universität Frankfurt a.M. am 22. Juni 1924." *Frankfurter Universitätsreden* (1924), pp. 3–6.

Guerin, Daniel. *Fascism and Big Business*. New York: Pathfinder Press, 1973.

Gumnior, Helmut and Rudolf Ringguth. *Max Horkheimer in Selbstzeugnissen und Bilddokumenten*. Reinbek bei Hamburg: Rowohlt Taschenbuch GmbH, 1973.

Gurvitch, Georges. *La Sociologie de Karl Marx*. Paris: Flammarion, 1962.

Guttmann, Julius. *Philosophies of Judaism. A History of Jewish Philosophy fom Biblical Times to Franz Rosenzweig*. New York: Schocken Books, 1973.

————. "The Principles of Judaism." *Conservative Judaism*, XIV, 1 (Fall 1959), pp. 1–24.

Habermas, Jürgen. *Philosophisch-politische Profile*. Frankfurt am Main: Suhrkamp Verlag, 1971.

Haeberli, Hans. *Der Begriff der Wissenschaft im logischen Positivismus*. Bern: Verlag Parl Haupt, 1955.

Hallgarten, G. and J., Radkau. *Deutsche Industrie und Politik von Bismarck bis heute*. Köln: Europäische Verlagsanstalt, 1974.

Hegel, G. W. F. *Sämtliche Werke*, Vol. 2. Hermann Glockner (Ed.). Stuttgart: F. Frommann, 1927.

von Heiseler, Johannes H. et al. *Die "Frankfurter Schule" im Lichte des Marxismus*, Frankfurt am Main: Verlag Marxistische Blätter GmbH, 1970.

Heidegger, Martin. *An Introduction to Metaphysics*. New Haven: Yale University Press, 1959.

Heidegger, Martin. "Nur noch ein Gott kann uns retten. Spiegel-Gespräch mit Martin Heidegger am 23, September 1966." *Der Spiegel*, XXX, 23 (1976), pp. 193–219.

Helberger, Christof. *Marxismus als Methode*. Frankfurt am Main: Fischer Athenäum Taschenbücher, 1974.

Heller, Ágnes. "Von der Armut am Geiste: A Dialogue by the Young Lukács." *The Philosophical Forum*, III, 3–4 (Spring–Summer 1972), pp. 360–70.

Hermann, István. *Lukács György gondolatvilága*. Budapest: Magvetö Kiadó, 1974.

Hoefnagels, Harry. *Frankfurter Soziologie. Einführung in das soziologische Denken der Frankfurter Schule*. Essen: Verlag der Scharioth'schen Buchhandlung, 1972.

Holborn Hajo. "Der deutsche Idealismus in sozialgeschichlicher Beleuchtung." *Historische Zeitschrift*, *174*, 2 (Oct. 1952), pp. 359–384.

The Holy Bible. King James Version. New York: A Meridian Book, n.d.

Homans, George C. "Social Behavior as Exchange," *American Journal of Sociology*, *LXII*, (May 1958), pp. 597–606.

Honigsheim, Paul. *On Max Weber.* New York: The Free Press, 1968.

Horkheimer, Max. *Aus der Pubertät. Novellen und Tagebuchblätter.* München: Kösel Verlag, 1974.

———. "Bemerkungen zur philosophischen Anthropologie." *ZfS*, *IV*, 1 (1935), pp. 1–25.

———. *Critical Theory.* New York: Herder and Herder, 1972.

———. *Critique of Instrumental Reason.* New York: The Seabury Press, 1974.

———. *Eclipse of Reason.* New York: Oxford University Press, 1947.

———. "Ein neuer Ideologiebegriff? *Grünberg Archiv.*, *XV* (1930), pp. 33–56.

———. "Die gegenwärtige Lage der Sozialphilosophie und die Aufgaben eines Instituts für Sozialforschung." In *Frankfurter Universitätsreden*, Frankfurt am Main, 1931, pp. 3–16.

———. *Gesellschaft im Übergang. Aufsätze, Reden und Vorträge 1942–1970.* Werner Brede (Ed.). Frankfurt am Main: Athenäum–Fischer Taschenbuch Verlag, 1972.

———. "Die Juden und Europa", *ZfS*, *VIII*, 1/2 (1939), pp. 115–137.

———. *Kritik der instrumentellen Vernunft*, Frankfurt am Main: Fischer Verlag, 1967.

———. *Kritische Theorie*, 2 Vols. Alfred Schmidt (Ed.). Frankfurt am Main: S. Fischer Verlag, 1968.

———. "Materialismus und Metaphysik." *ZfS*, *II*, 1 (1933), pp. 1–33.

———. "Materialismus und Moral." *ZfS*, *II*, 2 (1933), pp. 162–197.

———. "Nachbemerkung", *ZfS*, *IV*, 2 (1935), pp. 307–8.

———. "On the Concept of Freedom." *Diogenes* (Paris), No. 53 (1966), pp. 73–81.

———. *Die Sehnsucht nach dem ganz Anderen.* Hamburg: Furche Verlag, 1971.

———. "Philosophie und kritische Theorie." *ZfS*, *VI*, 3 (1937).

———. "Die Soziologie der Gegenwart (Sprachanalyse von Karl Kraus)." In Karl Kraus Archives, Vienna.

——. *Survey of the Social Sciences in Western Germany.* Washington, D. C. Library of Congress, 1952.

——. "Traditionelle und kritische theorie." *ZfS*, VI, 2 (1937), pp. 245–292.

——. *Verwaltete Welt?* Zürich: Die Arche, 1970.

——. Vorwort." *ZfS*, I (1932).

——. (Ed.). *Studien über Authorität und Familie.* Paris: Alcan, 1936.

——. and Theodor W. Adorno, *Dialektik der Aufklärung.* Amsterdam: Querido Verlag, N. V., 1947.

——. and Theodor W. Adorno, *Sociologica II.* Frankfurt am Main, Europäische Verlagsanstalt, 1962.

Horowitz, Irving Louis (Ed.). *Sociological Self-Images.* Beverly Hills, Calif.: Sage Publications, 1969.

Hughes, H. Stuart. *The Sea Change. The Migration of Social Thought, 1930–1965.* New York: Harper & Row, 1975.

Huster, Ernst-Ulrich et al. *Determination der westdeutschen Restauration 1945–1949.* Frankfurt am Main: Suhrkamp Verlag, 1972.

Institut für Sozialforschung. *Soziologische Exkurse.* Frankfurt am Main: Europäische Verlagsanstalt, 1956.

Jablinski, Manfred. *Theodor W. Adorno. "Kritische Theorie" als Literatur- und Kunstkritik.* Bonn: Bouvier Verlag, 1976.

Jaccard, Pierre. "Kunst und Religion. Das Verbot bildlicher Darstellungen im alten Judentum und im Islam." *KZfSS*, 21, 3 (Sept. 1969), pp. 453–462.

Jaeggi, Urs. *Kapital und Arbeit in der Bundesrepublik.* Frankfurt am Main: Fischer Taschenbuch Verlag, 1973.

James, William. *The Varieties of Religious Experience.* New York, 1902.

Janouch, Gustav. *Conversations with Kafka.* New York: A New Directions Book, 1971.

Jaspers, Karl. "Heidelberger Erinnerungen." *Heidelberger Jahrbücher,* V (1961), pp. 1–10.

Jay, Martin Evan. *The Dialectical Imagination. A History of the Frankfurt School and the Institute of Social Research 1923–1950.* Boston: Little, Brown, 1973.

Jimenez, Marc. *Adorno: art, idéologie et théorie de l'art.* Paris: Union générale d'éditions, 1973.

Johnson, Harry M. *Sociology: A Systematic Introduction.* New York: Harcourt, Brace & World, 1960.

Kafka, Franz. *Briefe 1902–1924.* New York: Schocken Verlag, 1958.

——. *Tagebücher 1910–1923.* New York: Schocken Books, 1949.

Kaiser, Gerhard. *Benjamin. Adorno. Zwei Studien.* Frankfurt am Main: Fischer Athenäum Taschenbücher, 1974.

Kant, Immanuel. *Werke,* Vol. VI. Berlin: Akademieausgabe, 1914.

Katz, Jacob. *Emancipation and Assimilation. Studies in Modern Jewish History.* Westmead, Farnborough, Hants, England: Gregg International Publishers Ltd., 1972.

Kedrov, B. M. "Marx and the Unity of Science—Natural and Social." *Soviet Studies in Philosophy,* VII, 2 (Fall 1968), pp. 3–14.

Kirscht, J. P. and R. C. Dillehay, *Dimensions of Authoritarianism: A Review of Research and Theory.* Lexington, Ky., University of Kentucky Press, 1967.

Kiss, Gabor. *Marxismus als Soziologie.* Reinbek bei Hamburg: Rowohlt, 1971.

Knütter, Hans-Helmuth. *Die Juden und die deutsche Linke in der Weimarer Republik 1918–1933.* Düsseldorf: Droste Verlag, 1971.

Koch, Thilo (Ed.). *Porträts deutsch–jüdischer Geistesgeschichte.* Köln: Verlag M. du Mont Schauberg, 1961.

Koch, Traugott et al. *Negative Dialektik und die Idee der Versöhnung. Eine Kontroverse über Theodor W. Adorno.* Stuttgart-Berlin: W. Kohlhammer Verlag; Urban-Taschenbücher, Bd. 850, 1973.

König, René "Die Situation der emigrierten deutschen Soziologen in Europa," *KZfSS,* XI, 1 (1959), pp. 113–131.

————. (Ed.). *Soziologie.* Frankfurt am Main: Fischer Verlag, 1967.

Kohn, Caroline. *Karl Kraus.* Stuttgart: J. B. Metzlersche Verlagsbuchhandlung, 1966.

Korsch, Karl. *Karl Marx.* New York: Wiley, 1938.

————. Marxismus und Philosophie. Leipzig: C. L. Hirschfeld Verlag, 1923.

————. "Über die amerikanische Wissenschaft." *Alternative* (Berlin), No. 41 (April 1965), pp. 76–77.

Kovács, András. "Kritikai társadalomtudomány és kriticista filozófia között. Max Horkheimer kritikai elmeletéről." *Magyar Filozofiai Szemle,* 18, 4–5 (1974), pp. 617–642.

Kraft, Werner. "Ludwig Wittgenstein und Karl Kraus." *Die neue Rundschau,* 72, 4 (1961), pp. 812–844.

Krahl, Hans-Jürgen. *Konstitution und Klassenkampf.* Frankfurt am Main: Verlag Neue Kritik KG, 1971.

Kühnl, Reinhard. "Problems of a Theory of German Fascism." *New German Critique,* 4 (Winter 1975), pp. 26–50.

Künzli, Arnold. *Aufklärung und Dialektik Politische Philosophie von Hobbes bis Adorno.* Freiburg: Verlag Rombach, 1971.

Kuhn, Thomas S. "The History of Science." In *International Encyclopedia of the Social Sciences*, Vol. 14, David L. Sills (Ed.), New York: Macmillan, 1968, pp. 74–83.

———. *The Structure of Scientific Revolutions.* Chicago: The University of Chicago Press, 1962.

Kurucz, Jenö. *Struktur und Funktion der Intelligenz während der Weimarer Republik.* Köln: Grote, 1967.

Kutzbach, Karl August (Ed.). *Paul Ernst und Georg Lukács. Dokumente einer Freundschaft.* Emsdetten, Westf.: Verlag Lechte, 1974.

Lamm, Hans. "Karl Marx und das Judentum." In *Karl Marx 1918–1968. Neue Studien zu Person und Lehre.* Mainz: v. Hasse & Koehler Verlag, 1968, pp. 11–66.

Landmann, Michael. *Entfremdende Vernunft.* Stuttgart: Ernst Klett Verlag, 1975.

———. *Das Israelpseudos der Pseudolinken.* Berlin: Colloquium Verlag, 1971.

———. "Melancholie der Erfüllung," In *Anklage gegen die Vernunft.* Stuttgart: Ernst Klett Verlag, 1976, pp. 208–230.

———. *Philosophical Anthropology.* Philadelphia, Pa.: The Westminster Press, 1974.

Lange, Oskar. *Totality. Development and Dialectics in the Light of Cybernetics.* Washington D. C.: U.S. Joint Publication Research Service, 1962.

Laqueur, Walter. *Weimar. A Cultural History 1918–1933.* London: Weidenfeld and Nicolson, 1974.

Laue, Max von. *History of Physics.* New York: Academic Press 1950.

Lazarsfeld, Paul. *Qualitative Analysis. Historical and Critical Essays.* Boston: Allyn & Bacon, 1972.

Lefebvre, Henri. *The Sociology of Karl Marx.* New York: Vintage Books, 1969.

Leiss, William. *The Domination of Nature.* New York: George Braziller, 1972.

Lenin, V. I., *Materialism and Empirio-Criticism.* Moscow: Foreign Languages Publishing House, 1952.

———. *Selected Works*, 12 vols. New York: International Publishers, 1929.

————. "What the 'Friends of the People' are and How they Fight the Social Democrats." *Collected Works.* Vol. 1. London: Lawrence & Wishart, 1960.

Lenk, Kurt. *Marx in der Wissenssoziologie.* Neuwied-Berlin: Hermann Luchterhand Verlag; Soziologische Texte, Bd. 78, 1972.

Lenzer, Gertrud (Ed.). *Auguste Comte and Positivism. The Essential Writings.* New York: Harper Torchbooks, 1975.

Leon, Abram. *The Jewish Question. A Marxist Interpretation.* New York: Pathfinder Press, 1970.

Lepenies, Wolf. *Melancholie und Gesellschaft.* Frankfurt am Main: Suhrkamp Verlag, 1972.

Lichtheim, George. *From Marx to Hegel.* New York: The Seabury Press, 1974.

Lichtheim, George. "Socialism and the Jews." *Dissent* (July–Aug. 1968), pp. 314–342.

Liebeschütz, Hans. *Von Georg Simmel zu Franz Rosenzweig.* Tübingen: J. C. B. Mohr (Paul Siebeck), 1970.

Lilienfeld, Robert. "Reflections on Karl Kraus." *The Nation*, Nos. 17 and 18 (23 and 30 April 1973), pp. 534–537 and 568–572.

Lipset, Seymour Martin. *Political Man.* Garden City, N. Y.: Anchor Books, 1963.

Löwith, Karl. *Meaning in History.* Chicago: The University of Chicago Press, 1962.

Ludz, Peter C., *The Changing Party Elite in East Germany.* Cambridge, Mass.: The MIT Press, 1972.

————. "Zur Frage nach den Bedingungen der Möglichkeit einer kritischen Gesellschaftstheorie." *Archiv für Rechts—und Sozialphilosophie*, XLIX, 4 (1963), pp. 409–432.

Lukács, Georg. "Alte Kultur und neue Kultur." *Kommunismus*, I, 43 (1920), pp. 1538–1549.

————. *Geschichte und Klassenbewusstsein.* Berlin: Der Malik Verlag, 1923.

————. *Soul and Form.* Anna Bostock (Transl.). Cambridge, Mass.: The MIT Press, 1974.

————. "Tactics and Ethics." in *Political Writings 1919–1929.* Rodney Livingstone (Ed.), Michael McColgan (Transl.), London: NLB, 1972.

————. *Die Theorie des Romans.* Neuwied am Rhein: Luchterhand Verlag, 1963.

————. *Die Zerstörung der Vernunft.* Berlin (East): Aufbau Verlag, 1954.

Lukács, György. "A bolsevizmus mint erkölcsi probléma." *Szabadgondolat* (Budapest), (Dec. 1918), pp. 228–232.

——. *Esztétikai kultura (Aesthetic Culture).* Budapest: Athenaeum Rt., 1913.

——. *A marxista filozofia feladatai az új demokráciában (The Tasks of Marxist Philosophy in the New Democracy).* Budapest: Székesfövárosi irodalmi intézet, n.d.

——. *A polgári filozófia válsága (The Crisis of Bourgeois Philosophy).* Budapest: Hungária, 1947.

Lynd, Robert. *Knowledge for What? The Place of Social Science in American Culture.* Princetown, N. J.: Princeton University Press, 1939.

Madge, John. *The Origins of Scientific Sociology.* New York: The Free Press, 1962.

Mamelet, Albert. *Le relativisme philosophique chez Georg Simmel.* Paris: Alcan, 1914.

Mannheim, Karl. "German Sociology: 1918–1933." In *Essays on Sociology and Social Psychology.* Paul Kecskeméti (Ed.). London: Routledge & Kegan Paul, 1953.

——. *Ideology and Utopia.* New York: Harcourt, Brace & World; Harvest Books, n.d.

Marcus Tar, Judith. *Thomas Mann und Georg Lukács.* Unpublished diss. for the German Dept. of the University of Kansas, 1976.

Marcuse, Herbert. *An Essay on Liberation.* Boston Beacon Press, 1969.

——. *Versuch über die Befreiung.* Frankfurt am Main: Suhrkamp Verlag, 1969.

——. "Zur Kritik des Hedonismus." *ZfS*, VI (1937), pp. 55–89.

Marramao, Giacomo. "Zum Verhältnis von politischer Ökonomie und kritischer Theorie." *Ästhetik und Kommunikation* 11 (April 1973), pp. 79–93.

Marti, Jean. "La psychoanalyse en Russie 1909–1930." *Critique* (Paris), *XXII*, 346 (March 1976), pp. 199–236.

Marx, Karl. *Capital*, Vol. I. New York: International Publishers, 1970.

——. *A Contribution to the Critique of Political Economy.* New York: International Publishers, 1970.

——. *Early Writings.* T. B. Bottomore, (Transl. and Ed.). New York: McGraw-Hill, 1964.

——. *The Economic & Philosophic Manuscripts of 1844.* Dirk J. Struik (Ed.). New York: International Publishers, 1964.

———. *Grundrisse. Introduction to the Critique of Political Economy.* London: Pelican Books, 1973.

Marx, Karl. *Mathematische Manuskripte.* Wolfgang Endemann (Ed.). Kronberg, Taunus: Scriptor Verlag GmbH., 1974.

———. and Frederick Engels. *The Communist Manifesto,* New York: International Publishers, 1948.

———. and Frederick Engels. *The German Ideology.* New York: International Publishers, 1970.

Marx-Engels-Gesamtausgabe (MEGA), Pt. 3, Vol. 3. Berlin, 1931–1932.

Marx Karl and Engels, Friedrich. *Werke.* Institut für Marxismus-Leninismus beim ZK der SED (Ed.) Berlin (East): Dietz, 1956–1968.

Mason, Stephen F. *A History of the Sciences.* New York: Collier Books, 1962.

Massing, Otwin. *Adorno und die Folgen. Über das 'hermetische Prinzip' der Kritischen Theorie.* Neuwied-Berlin: Hermann Luchterhand Verlag GmbH, 1970.

Maus, Heinz. "Der achte Deutsche Soziologentag." *Die Umschau. Internationale Revue, II,* 1 (Jan. 1947), pp. 72–92.

———. "Bericht über die Soziologie in Deutschland 1933 bis 1945." *KZfSS, XI,* 1 (1959), pp. 72–92.

Mayer, Gustav. "Der Jude in Karl Marx." *Neue Jüdische Monatshefte, II* (April 25 1918), pp. 327–331.

Mayer, Hans. *Der Repräsentant und der Märtyrer.* Frankfurt am Main: Suhrkamp Verlag, 1971.

———. *Der Aussenseiter.* Frankfurt am Main: Suhrkamp Verlag, 1975.

McLeish, John. *Soviet Psychology. History, Theory, Content.* London: Methuen & Co. Ltd., 1975.

Mehring, Franz. *Gesammelte Schriften und Aufsätze,* Vol. 6: Zur Geschichte der Philosophie. Berlin: Soziologische Verlagsanstalt, 1929–33.

Merton, Robert K., *On Theoretical Sociology.* New York: The Free Press, 1967.

Mészáros, István (Ed.). *Aspects of History and Class Consciousness.* London: Routledge & Kegan Paul, 1971.

Mészáros, István. *Lukács' Concept of Dialectic.* London: The Merlin Press, 1972.

Mills, C. Wright. *Power, Politics and People.* New York: Ballantine, 1963.

———. *The Sociological Imagination.* New York: Grove Press, 1961.

Misrahi, Robert. *Marx et la question juive.* Paris: Gallimard, 1972.

Mohrman, Walter. *Antisemitismus. Ideologie und Geschichte im Kaiserreich und in der Weimarer Republik.* Berlin (East): VEB Deutscher Verlag der Wissenschaften, 1972.

Mommsen, Wolfgang J. *Max Weber und die deutsche Politik, 1890–1920,* 2nd ed., Tübingen J. C. B. Mohr (Paul Siebeck), 1974.

————. Max Weber: Gesellschaft, Politik und Geschichte. Frankfurt am Main: Suhrkamp Verlag, 1974.

Moore, Barrington Jr. *Social Origins of Dictatorship and Democracy.* Boston: Beacon Press, 1966.

Morris, Charles W. *Logical Positivism, Pragmatism and Scientific Empiricism.* Paris: Hermann et Cie. Editeurs, 1937.

Mosse, George L. *Germans & Jews.* New York: Grosset & Dunlap, 1970.

Mosse, George L. *The Crisis of German Ideology.* New York: Grosset & Dunlap, 1964.

Müller-Strömsdörfer, Ilse. "Die helfende Kraft bestimmter Negation." *Philosophische Rundschau,* 8 (1960), pp. 81–105.

Nagel, Ernest. "On the Statement 'The Whole is More than the Sum of Its Parts.' " In *The Language of Social Research.* Paul F. Lazarsfeld and Morris Rosenberg (Eds.). New York: The Free Press, 1955.

————. "Methodological Issues in Psychoanalytic Theory." *Psychoanalysis, Scientific Method and Philosophy.* Sidney Hook (Ed.). New York: New York University Press, 1959.

Needham, Joseph. *Science and Civilization in China,* Vol. 2. London: Cambridge University Press, 1956.

Nettl, J. P. "Ideas, Intellectuals, and Structure of Dissent." In *On Intellectuals,* Philipp Rieff (Ed.). New York: Doubleday 1969, pp. 53–124.

Neumann, Franz. *Behemoth. The Structure and Practice of National Socialism 1933–1944.* New York: Harper & Row, 1963.

Nietzsche, Friedrich. *The Genealogy of Morals.* New York: Doubleday; A Doubleday anchor Book, 1956.

Nisbet, Robert. *Sociology as an Art Form.* New York: Oxford Press, 1976.

Noack, Hermann. *Die Philosophie Westeuropas im 20. Jahrhundert.* 2. vermehrte Auflage. Stuttgart-Basel: 1976.

Novack, George (Ed.). *Existentialism versus Marxism, Conflicting Views on Humanism.* New York: A Delta Book, 1966.

O'Connor, James. *The Fiscal Crisis of the State.* New York: St. Martin's Press, 1973.

Pachter, Henry M. *The Fall and Rise of Europe. A Political, Social and*

Cultural History of the Twentieth Century. New York: Praeger Publishers, 1975.

Palmier, Jean-Michel (Ed.) "La Traversee du siecle d'Ernst Bloch. Voyage à 'Blochingen.' " *Les Nouvelles Litteraires* (April 29, 1976), pp. 8–9 and (May 6, 1976), pp. 8–9.

Parkinson, G. H. R. (Ed.), *Georg Lukács. The Man, His Work and His Ideas.* London: Weidenfeld and Nicolson, 1970.

Parsons, Talcott. *Societies. Evolutionary and Comparative Perspectives.* Englewood Cliffs, N. J.; Prentice Hall, 1966.

———. *Social Structure and Personality.* New York: Macmillan, 1970.

———. *The System of Modern Societies.* Englewood Cliffs, N. J.; Prentice Hall, 1971.

Perlini, Tito. *Che Cosa Ha 'Veramente' Detto. Adorno.* Roma: Casa Editrice Astrolabio, 1971.

Peter, Klaus. *Idealismus als Kritik, Friedrich Schlegels Philosophie der unvollendeten Welt.* Stuttgart: Verlag W. Kohlhammer, 1973.

Piaget, Jean. *Introduction a l'épistémologie génétique.* Vol. 3. Paris: Presses Universitaires de France, 1950.

———. *Logique et Connaissance Scientifique.* Paris: Editions Gallimard, 1967.

———. *Main Trends in Psychology.* New York: Harper & Row; Harper Torchbooks, 1973.

———. *The Place of the Sciences of Man in the System of Sciences.* New York: Harper & Row: Harper Torchbooks, 1974.

———. *Sagesse et illusions de la philosophie.* Paris: Presses Universitaires de France, 1968.

Piven, Frances Fox and A., Cloward. *Regulating the Poor.* New York: Random House, 1971.

Planck, Max. *Physikalische Abhandlungen und Vorträge,* Vol. 3. Braunschweig: Friedrich and Sohn, Vieweg, 1958, (Transl.).

Platos's The Republic. B. Jowett, (Transl.). New York: Random House; The Modern Library Series, n.d.

Plekhanov, G. V. *Materialismus Militans.* Moscow, Progress Publishers, 1973.

Plessner, Helmuth. "Adornos Negative Dialektik. Ihr Thema mit Variationen." *Kantstudien,* 61, 4 (1970), pp. 507–519.

Pollock, Friedrich, *Stadien des Kapitalismus.* Helmut Dubiel (Ed.). München: C. H. Beck, 1975.

Popper, Karl. "Reason or Revolution." *European Journal of Sociology,* XI (1970), pp. 252–262.

Post, Werner. *Kritische Theorie und metaphysischer Pessimismus. Zum Spätwerk Max Horkheimers.* München: Kösel Verlag, 1971.

Puder, Martin. "Die Frankfurter Schule und die neue Linke," *Neue Deutsche Hefte*, 18, 1 (1971), pp. 113–122.

———. "Adorno heute." *Neue Deutsche Hefte.* 23, 1 (1976), pp. 3–21.

Quotations from Chairman Mao Tse-Tung, Peking: Foreign Languages Press, 1966.

Ramm, Thilo. "Die künftige Gesellschaftsordnung nach der Theorie von Marx and Engels." In *Marxismusstudien II.* Iring Fetscher (Ed.). Tübingen: J. C. B. Mohr (Paul Siebeck), 1957.

Regius, Heinrich (Max Horkheimer's pseudonym). *Dämmerung. Notizen in Deutschland.* Zürich: Verlag Oprecht & Helbling, 1934.

Rehm, Walter. *Griechentum und Goethezeit.* Bern: Francke Verlag, 1952.

Reich, Wilhelm. "On Marx and Freud." *Studies on the Left, 6*, 4 (1966), pp. 5–57.

Reiprich. Kurt. *Die philosophisch—naturwissenschaftliche Arbeiten von Karl Marx und Friedrich Engels.* Berlin (*East*): Dietz Verlag, 1969.

Riemer, Svend. "Die Emigration der deutschen Soziologen nach den USA." *KZfSS, XI* 1 (1959), pp. 100–112.

Riesman, David. "Some Observations on Social Science Research." *Antioch Review, 1* (1951), pp. 259–278.

Ritsert, Jürgen, and Claus Rolshausen. *Der Konservatismus der kritischen Theorie.* Frankfurt am Main: Europäische Verlagsanstalt, 1971

Röttges, Heinz. *Nietzsche und die Dialektik der Aufklärung.* Berlin: Walter de Gruyter, 1972.

Rohrmoser, Günther. *Das Elend der kritischen Theorie. Theodor W. Adorno, Herbert Marcuse, Jürgen Habermas*, 3rd ed., Freiburg: Verlag Rombach; Rombach Hochschul Paperback, 1973.

Rosenberg, Arthur. *Entstehung und Geschichte der Weimarer Republik.* Frankfurt am Main: Suhrkamp Verlag, 1955.

Rosenfeld, Leon. "Strife about Complementarity." *Science Progress.* XLI, 163 (1953), pp. 393–410.

Rosenzweig, Franz. *The Star of Redemption.* Boston: Beacon Press, 1972.

Rosmarin, Trude Weiss. *Religion of Reason. Hermann Cohen's System of Religious Philosophy.* New York: Bloch Publishing Co., 1936.

Rubel, Maximilien. *Karl Marx. Essai de biographie intellectuelle.* Paris: Riviere, 1957.

Rudy, Zvi. *Soziologie des jüdischen Volkes.* Reinbek bei Hamburg: Rowohlt Verlag, 1965.

Rücker, Silvie. "Totalität als ethisches und ästhetisches Problem." *Text + Kritik,* 39/40 (Okt. 1973), pp. 52–64.

Rusconi, G. E. *La Teoria Critica della Societa.* Bologna: Il Mulino, 1970.

Sallech, David L. "Critical Theory and Critical Sociology: the Second Synthesis." *Social Inquiry,* 43 2 (Spring 1973) pp. 131–140.

Sandkühler, Hans Jörg (Ed.). *Marxistische Erkenntnistheorie. Texte zu ihrem Forschungsstand in den sozialistischen Ländern.* Stuttgart-Bad Cannstatt: Friedrich Frommann Verlag, Günther Holzbog KG 1973.

―――. *Marxistische Wissenschaftstheorie. Studien zur Einführung in ihren Forschungsbereich.* Frankfurt am Main: Fischer Athenäum, 1975.

Sanford, R. Nevitt. "The Approach to the Authoritarian Personality." *Psychology of Personality. Six Modern Approaches* . J. L. McCary (Ed.). New York: Logos, 1956, pp. pp. 253–319.

Sarcevic, Abdulah. "Theodor W. Adorno (1903–1969). Die Unwahrheit der modernen Gesellschaft zwischen Revolution und Kritik." *Praxis,* 6, 1–2 (1970), pp. 184–214.

Sauer, Wolfgang. "National Socialism: Totalitarianism or Fascism?" *American Historical Review,* LXXIII, 2 (1967), pp. 404–424.

Scheible, Hartmut. "Von der bestimmten zur abstrakten Negation. Max Horkheimer und die Antinomien der kritischen Theorie." *Neue Rundschau,* 87, 1 (1976), pp. 86–111.

―――. "Wie Adorno zu lesen sei. Zur Rezeption der ästhetischen Theorie." *Frankfurter Rundschau* (1 July, 1972).

Schelsky, Helmut. *Ortsbestimmung der deutschen Soziologie.* Düsseldorf-Köln Deiderich Verlag, 1959.

Scheuch, Erwin K. "Produziert die Soziologie Revolutionäre?" *Der Volkswirt* (Frankfurt am Main), 18 (May 3, 1968), pp. 29–30.

Schiller, Friedrich. *On the Aesthetic Education of Man.* New York: Frederick Ungar, 1965.

Schmidt, Alfred. *Die kritische Theorie als Geschichtsphilosophie.* München: Carl Hanser Verlag, 1976. ·

―――. *Zur Idee der Kritischen Theorie.* Frankfurt am Main: München: Carl Hanser Verlag, 1974.

———. and G. E. Rusconi, *La Scuola di Francoforte*. Bari: De Donato, 1973.

Schneider, Michael. *Neurosis and Civilization. A Marxist/Freudian Synthesis*. New York: The Seabury Press, 1975.

Scholem, Gershom. *Walter Benjamin—Die Geschichte einer Freundschaft*. Frankfurt am Main: Suhrkamp Verlag, 1975.

Schröter, Klaus. *Thomas Mann. In Selbstzeugnissen und Bilddokumenten*. Reinbek bei Hamburg: Rowohlt Taschenbuch Verlag GmbH.; 1964.

Schroyer, Trent. *The Critique of Domination*. New York: George Braziller, 1973.

Schulz, Klaus-Peter. *Kurt Tucholsky. In Selbstzeugnissen und Bilddokumenten*. Reinbek bei Hamburg: Rowohlt Taschenbuch Verlag GmbH., 1959.

Schumpeter, Joseph A., *Capitalism, Socialism and Democracy*, 3rd ed. New York: Harper Torchbooks, 1962.

Schweicher, Reinhard. "Max Horkheimers Konzeption einer kritischen Theorie der Gesellschaft." *Protokolle, 2* (1973), pp. 26–47.

Sears, R. R., *Survey of Objective Studies of Psychoanalytic Concepts*. New York: Social Science Research Council, 1943.

Shapiro, Jeremy. "The Critical Theory of Frankfurt." *TLS* (Oct. 4 1974), pp. 1094–1095.

Shils, Edward. "Tradition, Ecology and Institution in the History of Sociology." *Daedelus*, 99 (Fall 1970).

Siebert, Rufold. "Horkheimer's Sociology of Religion." *Telos*, No. 30 (Winter 1976–77), pp. 127–144.

Silbermann, Alfons. "Theodor W. Adornos kunstsoziologischer Vermächtnis." *KZfSS*, 4 (1969), pp. 712–717.

Silberner, Edmund. "Was Marx an Anti-Semite?" *Historica Judaica, XI* (1949), pp. 3–52.

Simmel, Georg. "The Stranger." in *The Sociology of Georg Simmel*. Kurt H. Wolff, (Ed.). New York: The Free Press, 1950.

———. *Schopenhauer und Nietzsche*. Leipzig: Verlag Duncker & Humblot, 1907.

Simon-Schaefer, Roland. "Karl Marx—Dialektiker oder Positivist?" *Beiträge zur Theoriediskussion II*, Georg Lühr (Ed.), Berlin: Vlg J. H. W. Dietz Nachf. GmbH., 1974, pp. 207–229.

Skuhra, Anselm. *Max Horkheimer. Eine Einführung in sein Denken.*

Stuttgart–Berlin: Verlag W. Kohlhammer; Urban Taschenbücher, Reihe 80, 1974.

Slater, Phil. *Origin and Significance of the Frankfurt School. A Marxist Perspective.* London: Routledge & Kegan Paul, 1976.

Sonnemann, Ulrich. "Hegel und Freud." *Psyche*, 24, 3 (1970), pp. 208–218.

Speier, Hans. "The Social Conditions of the Intellectual in Exile." *Social Order and the Risks of War: Papers in Political Sociology.* New York: 1952.

Sperber, Manés. "Churban oder Die unfassbare Gewissheit." In *Die Kontroverse: Hannah Arendt, Eichmann und die Juden.* München: Nymphenburger Verlagsbuchhandlung GmbH., 1964.

Stammer, Otto (Ed.). *Max Weber und die Soziologie heute.* Tübingen: J. C. B. Mohr (Paul Siebeck), 1965.

Stegmüller, Wolfgang. *Main Currents in Contemporary German, British and American Philosophy.* Bloomington: Indiana Univ. Press, 1970.

Stern, Laurent. "Georg Lukács. An Intellectual Portrait." *Dissent*, V, (Spring 1958), pp. 162–173.

Stern, Selma. *The Court Jew.* Ralph Weiman (Transl.). Philadelphia: The Jewish Publication Society of America, 5710–1950.

Steiner, George. *Language and Silence.* New York: Atheneum, 1972.

Stölzl, Christoph. *Kafkas böses Böhmen. Zur Sozialgeschichte eines Prager Juden.* München: Edition Text + kritik, 1975.

Strauss, Heinrich. "On Jews and German Art. The Problem of Max Liebermann." *LBI Yearbook*, 2 (1957), pp. 255–269.

Struik, Dirk J. "Marx and Mathematics." *Science and Society.* XII, 1 (Winter 1948), pp. 181–196.

Sumner, William G. *Folkways.* Boston: Ginn & Company, 1906.

Swingewood, Alan. *Marx and Modern Social Theory.* New York: Wiley, 1975.

Szczepanski, Kan. *Socjologia Rozwoj Problematyki i Metod.* Warsaw: PWN, 1969.

Tar, Zoltán. "The Career of 'Critical Theory'." *The Nation*, (5 Nov. 1973), pp. 473–475.

Theunissen, Michael. *Gesellschaft und Geschichte.* Berlin: Walter de Gruyter & Co., 1969.

Therborn, Göran. *Critica e revoluzione. La Scuola di Francoforte.* Bari: Laterza, 1972.

———. *Science, Class and Society.* London: NLB 1976.

————. "The Frankfurt School." *New Left Review*, 63 (Sept.–Oct. 1970), pp. 65–96.

Tomberg, Friedrich. "Utopie und Negation. Zum ontologischen Hintergrund der Kunsttheorie Theodor W. Adornos." *Das Argument*. 5, 26 (1963), pp. 36–48.

Trotsky, Leon. *The Revolution Betrayed. What is the Soviet Union and Where is it Going?* New York: Pathfinder Press, 1972.

————. *The Russian Revolution*. Garden City, N.Y.: Doubleday, 1959.

Ulmen, G. L. *The Science of Society. Toward an Understanding of the Life and Work of Karl August Wittfogel*. The Hague: Mouton, 1977.

Vacatello, Marzio. *Th. W. Adorno: il rinvio della prassi*. Firenze: La Nuova Italia, 1972.

Vagts, Alfred. "Die Familie Marc und der Durchbruch zur Malerei." *Bulletin des Leo Baeck Instituts*, 9, 33 (1966), pp. 85–96.

Vajda, Mihály. "Karl Korsch's 'Marxism and Philosophy.' " in *The Unknown Dimension. European Marxism Since Lenin*. Dick Howard and Karl E. Klare (Eds.). New York: Basic Books, 1972.

van den Berghe, Pierre. "Dialectics and Functionalism: Toward a Theoretical Synthesis." *American Sociological Review*, *XXVIII*, 5 (Oct. 1963), pp. 695–705.

Veblen, Thorstein. "The Intellectual Pre-eminence of Jews in Modern Europe." In *Thorstein Veblen. Selections from his work*. Bernard Rosenberg (Ed.). New York: Thomas Y. Cromwell., 1963.

Viereck, Peter. *Metapolitics. The Roots of the Nazi Mind*. New York: Capricorn Books, 1965.

Vucinich, Alexander, "Marx and Parsons in Soviet Sociology," *The Russian Review*, 33, 1 (Jan. 1974), pp. 1–19.

————. *Social Thought in Tsarist Russia. The Quest for a General Science of Society, 1861–1917*. Chicago: The University of Chicago Press, 1976.

Weber, Marianne. *Max Weber. A Biography*. Harry Zohn (Transl. and Ed.). New York: Wiley, 1975.

Weber, Max. *Economy and Society*, 3 vols. Günther Roth and Claus Wittich (Eds.). New York: Bedminster Press, 1968.

————. *Gesammelte Aufsätze zur Soziologie und Sozialpolitik*. Tübingen: Verlag von J. C. B. Mohr (Paul Siebeck), 1924.

————. *The Methodology of the Social Sciences*. E. A. Shils and H. A. Finch (Transl. and Ed.). New York: The Free Press, 1949.

———. *The Protestant Ethic and the Spirit of Capitalism.* New York: Scribner's, 1958.

Weinberg, Elizabeth Ann. *The Development of Sociology in the Soviet Union.* London: Routledge & Kegan Paul, 1974.

Wellmer, Albrecht. *Critical Theory of Society.* New York: The Seabury Press, 1974.

Werckmeister, O. K. "Das Kunstwerk als Negation. Zur Kunsttheorie Theodor W. Adornos." *Die Neue Rundschau, 73,* 1 (1962), pp. 111–130.

———. *Ende der Ästhetik. Essays über Adorno, Bloch; Das gelbe Unterseeboot und der eindimensionale Mensch.* Frankfurt am Main: S. Fischer, 1971.

Westarp, M. V. Graf. "Kritische Theorie in der Sackgasse. Weg und Werke von Max Horkheimer." *Merkur, 24,* 5 (1970), pp. 477–484.

Wippermann, Wolfgang. *Faschismustheorien. Zum Stand der gegenwärtigen Diskussion.* Darmstadt: Wissenschaftliche Buchgesellschaft, 1972.

Wistrich, Robert S. *Revolutionary Jews. From Marx to Trotsky.* London: Harrap, 1976.

Witschel, Günther. *Die Wertvorstellungen der Kritischen Theorie.* Bonn: Bouvier Verlag, 1975.

Wittgenstein, Ludwig. *Tractatus Logico–Philosophicus.* London: Routledge & Kegan Paul, 1961.

Wolff, R. P., B. Moore, Jr., and H. Marcuse, *A Critique of Pure Tolerance.* Boston: Beacon Press, 1965.

Zima, Pierre V. *L'école de Francfort. Dialectique de la particularité.* Paris: Editions Universitaires, 1974.

———. "Le Philosophe exile." *Les Lettres Nouvelles,* (Dec. 1972–Jan. 1973), pp. 76–97.

Zohn, Harry. *Karl Kraus.* New York: Twayne Publishers, 1971.

Zwerenz, Gerhard. *Kopf und Bauch. Geschichte eines Arbeiters der unter die Intellektuellen gefallen ist.* Frankfurt am Main: S. Fischer, 1971.

AUTHOR INDEX

Author Index

SUBJECT INDEX

Alienation, and language, 59–60
Anti-Semitism, inquiry into,
    104–105
Art, unity of science and, 170–172
    versus science, 153–155
Authoritarian Personality, The
    Freud's influence on, 104
    genesis of, 102–103
    method of study, 105–109

Critical Theory, biographical and
    existential matrix of, 17–21
    and epistemology, 37–39
    evaluation of, 202–203
    fascism, theory of, 115–116
    confrontation with, 74–84
    genesis of, 28–35
    Marxian social theory, 42–43
    and Marxism, 39–41
    pessimism of, 51–55, 174–181
    in postwar decades, 132–134,
        174–178
    shift in emphasis, 102–103

Dialectic of Enlightenment, 205–206
    anti-semitism, 83–84
    genesis of, 79–81
    pessimism of, 80–81
    terror and civilization, 83
Domination, 165–166
    critique of, 87–92
    enlightenment and, 89–90
    language and, 91–92

Eclipse of Reason, genesis of, 84
    subjective and objective reason,
        84–87
Elitism, of Critical Theory, 179–180

Empirical sociology, 152, 202
    Adorno on, 153–155, 171–172
    see also Sociology
Epistemology, 37–39, 148
    Marxian, 42–43
Essence, *see* Theory of Society
Ethics, 175, 177, 204
    primacy of, 39
    and violence, 44–48
Exile, 172–174
    impact of, 116–120
    Existentialism, 204–206
    Lukács on, 204

Fascism, 179
    and Critical Theory, 115–116
    confrontation with, 74–84
    Lukács on, 115
    definition of, 75
    Horkheimer on, 75–79

Institute for Social Research,
    background, 16–17
    Bloch on, 206
    Horkheimer's initial program,
        26–28
Intellectuals, 206–207
    and exile, 116–118, 172–173
    role of, 35–37

Jews, 182–183
    emancipation of, 78
    European, and language, 59–60
Judaic influence, on Adorno,
        188–189
    on Horkheimer, 55–60
Judaic thought, and Frankfurt
        School, 181

241

Subject Index